1/05

THE PUEBLOAN SOCIETY OF CHACO CANYON

Titles in the Series
Greenwood Guides to Historic Events of the Medieval World

THE PUEBLOAN SOCIETY OF CHACO CANYON

Paul F. Reed

Greenwood Guides to Historic Events of the Medieval World
Jane Chance, Series Editor

GREENWOOD PRESS
Westport, Connecticut • London

Library of Congress Cataloging-in-Publication Data

Reed, Paul F.
    The Puebloan society of Chaco Canyon / Paul F. Reed.
      p. cm.—(Greenwood guides to historic events of the medieval world)
    Includes bibliographical references and index.
    ISBN 0–313–32720–3 (alk. paper)
    1. Pueblo Indians—New Mexico—Chaco Culture National Historical Park—
History.   2. Pueblo Indians—New Mexico—Chaco Culture National Historical
Park—Antiquities.   3. Chaco Culture National Historical Park (N.M.)—
History.   4. Chaco Culture National Historical Park (N.M.)—Antiquities.
I. Title. II. Series.
E99.P9R28   2004
978.9'82004974—dc22   2004042530

British Library Cataloguing in Publication Data is available.

Library of Congress Catalog Card Number: 2004042530
ISBN: 0–313–32720–3

First published in 2004

Greenwood Press, 88 Post Road West, Westport, CT 06881
An imprint of Greenwood Publishing Group, Inc.
www.greenwood.com

Printed in the United States of America

The paper used in this book complies with the
Permanent Paper Standard issued by the National
Information Standards Organization (Z39.48–1984).

10 9 8 7 6 5 4 3 2 1

In memory of my father, James Bennett Reed Sr. (1926–82)

CONTENTS

Photo essay follows Chapter 8

SERIES FOREWORD

The Middle Ages are no longer considered the "Dark Ages" (as Petrarch termed them), sandwiched between the two enlightened periods of classical antiquity and the Renaissance. Often defined as a historical period lasting, roughly, from 500 to 1500 C.E., the Middle Ages span an enormous amount of time (if we consider the way other time periods have been constructed by historians) as well as an astonishing range of countries and regions very different from one another. That is, we call the "Middle" Ages the period beginning with the fall of the Roman Empire as a result of raids by northern European tribes of "barbarians" in the late antiquity of the fifth and sixth centuries and continuing until the advent of the so-called Italian and English renaissances, or rebirths of classical learning, in the fifteenth and sixteenth centuries. How this age could be termed either "Middle" or "Dark" is a mystery to those who study it. Certainly it is no longer understood as embracing merely the classical inheritance in the west or excluding eastern Europe, the Middle East, Asia, or even, as I would argue, North and Central America.

Whatever the arbitrary, archaic, and hegemonic limitations of these temporal parameters—the old-fashioned approach to them was that they were mainly not classical antiquity, and therefore not important—the Middle Ages represent a time when certain events occurred that have continued to affect modern cultures and that also, inevitably, catalyzed other medieval events. Among other important events, the Middle Ages saw the birth of Muhammad (c. 570–632) and his foundation of Islam in the seventh century as a rejection of Christianity which led to the imperial conflict between East and West in the eleventh and twelfth centuries. In western Europe in the Middle Ages the foundations for modern nationalism and modern law were laid and the concept of romantic love arose in the Middle Ages, this latter event partly one of the indirect consequences of the Crusades. With the shaping of national identity came the need to defend boundaries against invasion; so the castle emerged as a military outpost—whether in northern Africa, during the Crusades, or in Wales, in the eleventh century, to defend William of Normandy's newly acquired provinces—to satisfy that need. From Asia the invasions of Genghis Khan changed the literal and cultural shape of eastern and southern Europe.

In addition to triggering the development of the concept of chivalry and the knight, the Crusades influenced the European concepts of the lyric, music, and musical instruments; introduced to Europe an appetite for spices like cinnamon, coriander, and saffron and for dried fruits like prunes and figs as well as a desire for fabrics such as silk; and brought Aristotle to the European university through Arabic and then Latin translations. As a result of study of the "new" Aristotle, science and philosophy dramatically changed direction—and their emphasis on this material world helped to undermine the power of the Catholic Church as a monolithic institution in the thirteenth century.

By the twelfth century, with the centralization of the one (Catholic) Church, came a new architecture for the cathedral—the Gothic—to replace the older Romanesque architecture and thereby to manifest the Church's role in the community in a material way as well as in spiritual and political ways. Also from the cathedral as an institution and its need to dramatize the symbolic events of the liturgy came medieval drama—the mystery and the morality play, from which modern drama derives in large part. Out of the cathedral and its schools to train new priests (formerly handled by monasteries) emerged the medieval institution of the university. Around the same time, the community known as a town rose up in eastern and western Europe as a consequence of trade and the necessity for a new economic center to accompany the development of a bourgeoisie, or middle class. Because of the town's existence, the need for an itinerant mendicancy that could preach the teachings of the Church and beg for alms in urban centers sprang up.

Elsewhere in the world, in North America the eleventh-century settlement of Chaco Canyon by the Pueblo peoples created a social model like no other, one centered on ritual and ceremony in which the "priests" were key, but one that lasted barely two hundred years before it collapsed and its central structures were abandoned.

In addition to their influence on the development of central features of modern culture, the Middle Ages have long fascinated the modern age because of parallels that exist between the two periods. In both, terrible wars devastated whole nations and peoples; in both, incurable diseases plagued cities and killed large percentages of the world's population. In both periods, dramatic social and cultural changes took place as a result of these events: marginalized and overtaxed groups in societies rebelled against imperious governments; trade and a burgeoning middle class came to the fore; outside the privacy of the family, women began to have a greater role in Western societies and their cultures.

How different cultures of that age grappled with such historical change is the subject of the Greenwood Guides to Historic Events of the Medieval World. This series features individual volumes that illuminate key events in medieval world history. In some cases, an "event" occurred during a relatively limited time period. The troubadour lyric as a phenomenon, for example, flowered and died in the courts of Aquitaine in the twelfth century, as did the courtly romance in northern Europe a few decades later. The Hundred Years War between France and England generally took place during a precise time period, from the fourteenth to mid-fifteenth centuries.

In other cases, the event may have lasted for centuries before it played itself out: the medieval Gothic cathedral, for example, may have been first built in the twelfth century at Saint-Denis in Paris (c. 1140), but cathedrals, often of a slightly different style of Gothic architecture, were still being built in the fifteenth century all over Europe and, again, as the symbolic representation of a bishop's seat, or chair, are still being built today. And the medieval city, whatever its incarnation in the early Middle Ages, basically blossomed between the eleventh and thirteenth centuries as a result of social, economic, and cultural changes. Events—beyond a single dramatic historically limited happening—took longer to affect societies in the Middle Ages because of the lack of political and social centralization, the primarily agricultural and rural nature of most countries, difficulties in communication, and the distances between important cultural centers.

Each volume includes necessary tools for understanding such key events in the Middle Ages. Because of the postmodern critique of authority that modern societies underwent at the end of the twentieth century, students and scholars as well as general readers have come to mistrust the commentary and expertise of any one individual scholar or commentator and to identify the text as an arbiter of "history." For this reason, each book in the series can be described as a "library in a book." The intent of the series is to provide a quick, in-depth examination and current perspectives on the event to stimulate critical thinking as well as ready-reference materials, including primary documents and biographies of key individuals, for additional research.

Specifically, in addition to a narrative historical overview that places the specific event within the larger context of a contemporary perspective, five to seven developmental chapters explore related focused aspects of the event. In addition, each volume begins with a brief chronology and ends with a conclusion that discusses the consequences and impact of the event. There are also brief biographies of twelve to twenty key individuals (or places or buildings, in the book on the cathedral); primary documents from the period (for example, letters, chronicles, memoirs, diaries, and other writings) that illustrate states of mind or the turn of events at the time, whether historical, literary, scientific, or philosophical; illustrations (maps, diagrams, manuscript illuminations, portraits); a glossary of terms; and an annotated bibliography of important books, articles, films, and CD-ROMs available for additional research. An index concludes each volume.

No particular theoretical approach or historical perspective characterizes the series; authors developed their topics as they chose, generally taking into account the latest thinking on any particular event. The editors selected final topics from a list provided by an advisory board of high school teachers and public and school librarians. On the basis of nominations of scholars made by distinguished writers, the series editor also tapped internationally known scholars, both those with lifelong expertise and others with fresh new perspectives on a topic, to author the twelve books in the series. Finally, the series editor selected distinguished medievalists, art historians, and archaeologists to complete an advisory board: Gwinn Vivian, retired professor of archaeology at the University of Arizona Museum; Sharon Kinoshita, associate professor of French literature, world literature, and cultural studies at the University of California–Santa Cruz; Nancy Wu, associate museum educator at the Metropolitan Museum of Art, The Cloisters, New York City; and Christopher A. Snyder, chair of the Department of History and Politics at Marymount University.

In addition to examining the event and its effects on the specific cultures involved through an array of documents and an overview, each volume provides a new approach to understanding these twelve events. Treated in the series are: the Black Death; the Crusades; Eleanor of Aquitaine, courtly love, and the troubadours; Genghis Khan and Mongol rule; Joan of Arc and the Hundred Years War; Magna Carta; the medieval castle, from the eleventh to the sixteenth centuries; the medieval cathedral; the medieval city, especially in the thirteenth century; medieval science and technology; Muhammad and the rise of Islam; and the Puebloan society of Chaco Canyon.

The Black Death, by Joseph Byrne, isolates the event of the epidemic of bubonic plague in 1347–52 as having had a signal impact on medieval Europe. It was, however, only the first of many related such episodes involving variations of pneumonic and septicemic plague that recurred over 350 years. Taking a twofold approach to the Black Death, Byrne investigates both the modern research on bubonic plague, its origins and spread, and also medieval documentation and illustration in diaries, artistic works, and scientific and religious accounts. The demographic, economic, and political effects of the Black Death are traced in one chapter, the social and psychological patterns of life in another, and cultural expressions in art and ritual in a third. Finally, Byrne investigates why bubonic plague disappeared and why we continue to be fascinated by it. Documents included provide a variety of medieval accounts—Byzantine, Arabic, French, German, English, and Italian—several of which are translated for the first time.

The Crusades, by Helen Nicholson, presents a balanced account of various crusades, or military campaigns, invented by Catholic or "Latin" Christians during the Middle Ages against those they perceived as threats to their faith. Such expeditions included the Crusades to the Holy Land between 1095 and 1291, expeditions to the Iberian Peninsula, the "crusade" to northeastern Europe, the Albigensian Crusades and the Hussite crusades—both against the heretics—and the crusades against the Ottoman Turks (in the Balkans). Although Muslim rulers included the concept of jihâd (a conflict fought for God against evil or his enemies) in their wars in the early centuries of Islam, it had become less important in the late tenth century. It was not until the middle decades of the twelfth century that jihâd was revived in the wars with the Latin Christian Crusaders. Most of the Crusades did not result in victory for the Latin Christians, although Nicholson concedes they slowed the advance of Islam. After Jerusalem was destroyed in 1291, Muslim rulers did permit Christian pilgrims to travel to holy sites. In the Iberian Peninsula, Christian rulers replaced Muslim rulers, but Muslims, Jews, and dissident Christians were compelled to convert to Catholicism. In northeastern Europe, the Teutonic Order's campaigns allowed German colonization that later encouraged twentieth-century German claims to land and led to two world wars. The Albigensian Crusade wiped out thirteenth-century aristocratic families in southern France who held to the Cathar heresy, but the Hussite crusades in the 1420s failed to eliminate the Hussite heresy. As a result of the wars, however, many positive changes occurred: Arab learning founded on Greek scholarship entered western Europe through the acquisition of an extensive library in Toledo, Spain, in 1085; works of western European literature were inspired by the holy wars; trade was encouraged and with it the demand for certain products; and a more favorable image of Muslim men and women was fostered by the crusaders' contact with the Middle East. Nicholson also notes that America may have been discovered because Christopher Columbus avoided a route that had been closed by Muslim conquests and that the Reformation may have been advanced because Martin Luther protested against the crusader indulgence in his Ninety-five Theses (1517).

Eleanor of Aquitaine, Courtly Love, and the Troubadours, by ffiona Swabey, singles out the twelfth century as the age of the individual, in which a queen like Eleanor of Aquitaine could influence the development of a new social and artistic culture. The wife of King Louis VII of France and later the wife of his enemy Henry of Anjou, who became king of England, she patronized some of the troubadours, whose vernacular lyrics celebrated the personal expression of emotion and a passionate declaration of service to women. Love, marriage, and the pursuit of women were also the subject of the new romance literature, which flourished in northern Europe and was the inspiration behind concepts of courtly love. However, as Swabey points out, historians in the past have misjudged Eleanor, whose independent spirit fueled their misogynist attitudes. Similarly, Eleanor's divorce and subsequent stormy marriage have colored ideas about medieval "love courts" and courtly love, interpretations of which have now been challenged by scholars. The twelfth century is set in context, with commentaries on feudalism, the tenets of Christianity, and the position of women, as well as summaries of the cultural and philosophical background, the cathedral schools and universities, the influence of Islam, the revival of classical learning, vernacular literature, and Gothic architecture. Swabey provides two biographical chapters on Eleanor and two on the emergence of the troubadours and the origin of courtly love through verse romances. Within this latter subject Swabey also details the story of Abelard and Heloise, the treatise of Andreas Capellanus (André the Chaplain) on courtly love, and Arthurian legend as a subject of courtly love.

Genghis Khan and Mongol Rule, by George Lane, identifies the rise to power of Genghis Khan and his unification of the Mongol tribes in the thirteenth century as a kind of globalization with political, cultural, economic, mercantile, and spiritual effects akin to those of modern globalization. Normally viewed as synonymous with barbarian destruction, the rise to power of Genghis Khan and the Mongol hordes is here understood as a more positive event that initiated two centuries of regeneration and creativity. Lane discusses the nature of the society of the Eurasian steppes in the twelfth and thirteenth centuries into which Genghis Khan was born; his success at reshaping the relationship between the northern pastoral and nomadic society with the southern urban, agriculturalist society; and his unification of all the Turco-Mongol tribes in 1206 before his move to conquer Tanquit Xixia, the Chin of northern China, and the lands of Islam. Conquered thereafter were the Caucasus, the Ukraine, the Crimea, Russia, Siberia, Central Asia, Afghanistan, Pakistan, and Kashmir. After his death his sons and grandsons continued, conquering Korea, Persia, Armenia, Mesopotamia, Azerbaijan, and eastern Europe—chiefly Kiev, Poland, Moravia, Silesia, and Hungary—until 1259, the end of the Mongol Empire as a unified whole. Mongol rule created a golden age in the succeeding split of the Empire into two, the Yuan dynasty of greater China and the Il-Khanate dynasty of greater Iran. Lane adds biographies of important political figures, famous names such as Marco Polo, and artists and scientists. Documents derive from universal histories, chronicles, local histories and travel accounts, official government documents, and poetry, in French, Armenian, Georgian, Chinese, Persian, Arabic, Chaghatai Turkish, Russian, and Latin.

Joan of Arc and the Hundred Years War, by Deborah Fraioli, presents the Hundred Years War between France and England in the fourteenth and fifteenth centuries within contexts whose importance has sometimes been blurred or ignored in past studies. An episode of apparently only moderate significance, a feudal lord's seizure of his vassal's land for harboring his mortal enemy, sparked the Hundred Years War, yet on the face of it the event should not have led inevitably to war. But the lord was the king of France and the vassal the king of England, who resented losing his claim to the French throne to his Valois cousin. The land in dispute, extending roughly from Bordeaux to the Pyrenees mountains, was crucial coastline for the economic interests of both kingdoms. The series of skirmishes, pitched battles, truces, stalemates, and diplomatic wrangling that resulted from the confiscation of English Aquitaine by the French form the narrative of this Anglo-French conflict, which was in fact not given the name Hundred Years War until the nineteenth century.

Fraioli emphasizes how dismissing women's inheritance and succession rights came at the high price of unleashing discontent in their male heirs, including Edward III, Robert of Artois, and Charles of Navarre. Fraioli also demonstrates the centrality of side issues, such as Flemish involvement in the war, the peasants' revolts that resulted from the costs of the war, and Joan of Arc's unusually clear understanding of French "sacred kingship." Among the primary sources provided are letters from key players such as Edward III, Etienne Marcel, and Joan of Arc; a supply list for towns about to be besieged; and a contemporary poem by the celebrated scholar and court poet Christine de Pizan in praise of Joan of Arc.

Magna Carta, by Katherine Drew, is a detailed study of the importance of the Magna Carta in comprehending England's legal and constitutional history. Providing a model for the rights of citizens found in the United States Declaration of Independence and Constitution's first ten amendments, the Magna Carta has had a role in the legal and parliamentary history of all modern states bearing some colonial or government connection with the British Empire. Constructed at a time when modern nations began to appear, in the early thirteenth century, the Magna Carta (signed in 1215) presented a formula for balancing the liberties of the people with the power of modern governmental institutions. This unique English document influenced the growth of a form of law (the English common law) and provided a vehicle for the evolution of representative (parliamentary) government. Drew demonstrates how the Magna Carta came to be—the roles of the Church, the English towns, barons, common law, and the parliament in its making—as well as how myths concerning its provisions were established. Also provided are biographies of Thomas Becket, Charlemagne, Frederick II, Henry II and his sons, Innocent III, and many other key figures, and primary documents—among them, the Magna Cartas of 1215 and 1225, and the Coronation Oath of Henry I.

Medieval Castles, by Marilyn Stokstad, traces the historical, political, and social function of the castle from the late eleventh century to the sixteenth by means of a typology of castles. This typology ranges from the early "motte and bailey"—military fortification, and government and economic center—to the palace as an expression of the castle owners' needs and purposes. An introduction defines the various contexts—military, political, economic, and social—in which the castle appeared in the Middle Ages. A concluding interpretive essay suggests the impact of the castle and its symbolic role as an idealized construct lasting until the modern day.

Medieval Cathedrals, by William Clark, examines one of the chief contributions of the Middle Ages, at least from an elitist perspective—that is, the religious architecture found in the cathedral ("chair" of the bishop) or great church, studied in terms of its architecture, sculpture, and stained glass. Clark begins with a brief contextual history of the concept of the bishop and his role within the church hierarchy, the growth of the church in the early Christian era and its affiliation with the bishop (deriving from that of the bishop of Rome), and the social history of cathedrals. Because of economic and political conflicts among the three authorities who held power in medieval towns—the king, the bishop, and the cathedral clergy—cathedral construction and maintenance always remained a vexed issue, even though the owners—the cathedral clergy—usually held the civic responsibility for the cathedral. In an interpretive essay, Clark then focuses on Reims Cathedral in France, because both it and the bishop's palace survive, as well as on contemporary information about surrounding buildings. Clark also supplies a historical overview on the social, political, and religious history of the cathedral in the Middle Ages: an essay on patrons, builders, and artists; aspects of cathedral construction (which was not always successful); and then a chapter on Romanesque and Gothic cathedrals and a "gazetteer" of twenty-five important examples.

The Medieval City, by Norman J. G. Pounds, documents the origin of the medieval city in the flight from the dangers or difficulties found in the country, whether economic, physically threatening, or cultural. Identifying the attraction of the city in its *urbanitas*, its "urbanity," or the way of living in a city, Pounds discusses first its origins in prehistoric and classical Greek urban revolutions. During the Middle Ages, the city grew primarily between the eleventh and thirteenth centuries, remaining essentially the same until the Industrial Revolution. Pounds provides chapters on the medieval city's planning, in terms of streets and structures; life in the medieval city; the roles of the Church and the city government in its operation; the development of crafts and trade in the city; and the issues of urban health, wealth, and welfare. Concluding with the role of the city in history, Pounds suggests that the value of the city depended upon its balance of social classes, its need for trade and profit to satisfy personal desires through the accumulation of wealth and its consequent economic power, its political power as a representative body within the kingdom, and its social role in the rise of literacy and education and in nationalism. Indeed, the concept of a middle class, a bourgeoisie, derives from the city—from the *bourg*, or "borough." According to Pounds, the rise of modern civilization would not have taken place without the growth of the city in the Middle Ages and its concomitant artistic and cultural contribution.

Medieval Science and Technology, by Elspeth Whitney, examines science and technology from the early Middle Ages to 1500 within the context of the classical learning that so influenced it. She looks at institutional history, both early and late, and what was taught in the medieval schools and, later, the universities (both of which were overseen by the Catholic Church). Her discussion of Aristotelian natural philosophy illustrates its impact on the medieval scientific worldview. She presents chapters on the exact sciences, meaning mathematics, astronomy, cosmology, astrology, statics, kinematics, dynamics, and optics; the biological and earth sciences, meaning chemistry and alchemy, medicine, zoology, botany, geology and meteorology, and geography; and technology. In an interpretive conclusion, Whitney demonstrates the impact of medieval science on the preconditions and structure that permitted the emergence of the modern world. Most especially, technology transformed an agricultural society into a more commercial and engine-driven society: waterpower and inventions like the blast furnace and horizontal loom turned iron working and cloth making into manufacturing operations. The invention of the mechanical clock helped to organize human activities through timetables rather than through experiential perception and thus facilitated the advent of modern life. Also influential in the establishment of a middle class were the inventions of the musket and pistol and the printing press. Technology, according to Whitney, helped advance the habits of mechanization and precise methodology. Her biographies introduce major medieval Latin and Arabic and classical natural philosophers and scientists. Extracts from various kinds of scientific treatises allow a window into the medieval concept of knowledge.

The Puebloan Society of Chaco Canyon, by Paul Reed, is unlike other volumes in this series, whose historic events boast a long-established historical record. Reed's study offers instead an original reconstruction of the Puebloan Indian society of Chaco, in what is now New Mexico, but originally extending into Colorado, Utah, and Arizona. He is primarily interested in its leaders, ritual and craft specialists, and commoners during the time of its chief flourishing, in the eleventh and twelfth centuries, as understood from archaeological data alone. To this new material he adds biographies of key Euro-American archaeologists and other individuals from the nineteenth and twentieth centuries who have made important discoveries about Chaco Canyon. Also provided are documents of archaeological description and narrative from early explorers' journals and archaeological reports, narratives, and monographs. In his overview chapters, Reed discusses the cultural and environmental setting of Chaco Canyon; its history (in terms of exploration and research); the Puebloan society and how it emerged chronologically; the Chaco society and how it appeared in 1100 c.e.; the "Outliers," or outlying communities of Chaco; Chaco as a ritual center of the eleventh-century Pueblo world; and, finally, what is and is not known about Chaco society. Reed concludes that ritual and ceremony played an important role in Chacoan society and that ritual specialists, or priests, conducted ceremonies, maintained ritual artifacts, and charted the ritual calendar. Its social organization matches no known social pattern or type: it was complicated, multiethnic, centered around ritual and ceremony, and without any overtly hierarchical political system. The Chacoans were ancestors to the later Pueblo people, part of a society that rose, fell, and evolved within a very short time period.

The Rise of Islam, by Matthew Gordon, introduces the early history of the Islamic world, beginning in the late sixth century with the career of the Prophet Muhammad (c. 570–c. 632) on the Arabian Peninsula. From Muhammad's birth in an environment of religious plurality—Christianity, Judaism, and Zoroastrianism, along with paganism, were joined by Islam—to the collapse of the Islamic empire in the early tenth century, Gordon traces the history of the Islamic community. The book covers topics that include the life of the Prophet and divine revelation (the Qur'an) to the formation of the Islamic state, urbanization in the Islamic Near East, and the extraordinary culture of Islamic letters and scholarship. In addition to a historical overview, Gordon examines the Caliphate and early Islamic Empire, urban society and economy, and the emergence, under the Abbasid Caliphs, of a "world religious tradition" up to the year 925 C.E.

As editor of this series I am grateful to have had the help of Benjamin Burford, an undergraduate Century Scholar at Rice University assigned to me in 2002–2004 for this project; Gina Weaver, a third-year graduate student in English; and Cynthia Duffy, a second-year graduate student in English, who assisted me in target-reading select chapters from some of these books in an attempt to define an audience. For this purpose I would also like to thank Gale Stokes, former dean of humanities at Rice University, for the 2003 summer research grant and portions of the 2003–2004 annual research grant from Rice University that served that end.

This series, in its mixture of traditional and new approaches to medieval history and cultures, will ensure opportunities for dialogue in the classroom in its offerings of twelve different "libraries in books." It should also propel discussion among graduate students and scholars by means of the gentle insistence throughout on the text as primal. Most especially, it invites response and further study. Given its mixture of East and West, North and South, the series symbolizes the necessity for global understanding, both of the Middle Ages and in the postmodern age.

Jane Chance, Series Editor
Houston, Texas
February 19, 2004

PREFACE

Unlike most of the other contributors to this series (the Greenwood Guides to Historic Events of the Medieval World), my work here does not benefit from a well-documented historic record. The ensuing discussion of Puebloan society in Chaco Canyon, as part of a larger series discussing a variety of worldwide medieval events and derived largely from archaeological data, was difficult to envision and challenging to write.

Puebloan leaders, ritual and craft specialists, and common folk of eleventh- and twelfth-century Chaco Canyon did not leave behind written accounts of their lives. Attempting to document these lives and understanding the events and processes that led to the emergence of Chacoan society constitute a painstaking (and often frustrating) archaeological undertaking. Quite frankly, we will probably never know or understand the full richness of Chacoan history. Thus, the reader should not pick up this book expecting a historical tale comparable, for example, to Joseph Byrne's *The Black Death*, written for this series. Nevertheless, what I hope to achieve with this work, and to convey to the reader, is some sense of the magnificence of ancient Chaco and, perhaps, its place in the larger context of medieval period history.

Writing about the rise of the remarkable Puebloan society of Chaco Canyon while striving for the perspective of a historian describing a well-documented historical event is challenging, to say the very least. My approach will undoubtedly fail to satisfy both archaeologists and historians, because I have endeavored to walk the jagged line between the two. Archaeologists may be uncomfortable with the extent to which I render knowledge (data) of the Chacoans as "history." Historians may find the doubt generated by archaeological research, as illustrated by qualifiers such as "probably," "perhaps," "undoubtedly," and even "maybe," unworthy of historical description and writing. Further, some of what we "know" about Chaco is still subject to debate. Archaeologists, like other social scientists, are known for debating and disagreeing ad nauseam. Nevertheless, I believe that both archaeologists and historians would benefit from seeing the others' perspectives more often. Beyond this, one goal of the Greenwood Medieval World series is to render historical events understandable and "real" to students and laypeople. This goal, then, was paramount in my mind as I crafted this work.

My primary goals in this volume are to describe and explain the development of the Puebloan society in Chaco Canyon (Chacoan society, in short) from the tenth through twelfth centuries. Authors in this series were asked to augment their treatment of historical events with biographies and selected excerpts from historical documents, diaries, and other firsthand accounts of direct relevance to the medieval topic at hand. As an archaeologist used to dealing with a very limited repertoire of historical documents, this requirement provided me with a special challenge.

My solution is to offer excerpts from historical documents relating to the discovery, exploration, and excavation of Chaco Canyon by Euro-Americans in the late nineteenth and early twentieth centuries. In lieu of biographies of the Puebloan people who "made Chaco happen," I instead furnish profiles of archaeologists and other individuals who pioneered exploration and research in Chaco Canyon and outlying communities.

ACKNOWLEDGMENTS

No undertaking of this type is a solitary project. I had help from a number of people and institutions. The Center for Desert Archaeology and Salmon Ruins provided workspace for this project. The library at Salmon Ruins is an amazing resource to have close at hand, and I am very grateful to have had ready access to it.

Joyce Raab of the National Park Service's Chaco Archive at Zimmerman Library, University of New Mexico, provided access to rare and not-so-rare documents and reports. Dabney Ford graciously opened the library at Chaco Canyon National Park for research. Joan Mathien and Tom Windes helped clarify different aspects of Chacoan archaeology. Rodney Ross of the National Anthropological Archives tracked down negatives for the Richard Kern drawings reproduced in this volume. Aztec Ruins National Monument and Salmon Ruins Museum provided access to historic photographs included in the photo essay in the middle of this volume. Adriel Heisey, ultralight pilot and photographer extraordinaire, provided the aerial views of the Chacoan ruins presented in the photo essay. I thank Doug Dykeman for helping me solve a last-minute photograph problem.

Lynne Bluestein with the University of New Mexico Press expedited permission for an extended quote from Edgar Hewett's 1936 Chaco book that appears herein in the Primary Documents section. Similarly, John Montgomery with Eastern New Mexico University's Department of Anthropology and Applied Archaeology provided permission to quote Cynthia Irwin-Williams's 1972 essay on Salmon Ruins.

The greatest challenge in any writing is getting one's point across in an understandable and effective manner. In this task, colleagues and friends who read earlier drafts of this work aided me. Gwinn Vivian, dean of Chaco archaeologists, reviewed the manuscript for Greenwood Press and provided much helpful commentary. Steadman Upham, friend and mentor, provided critical input and helped focus my approach to this work. I also thank the following individuals for insightful comments: Tristan K. Regnaudot, Larry Baker, Nancy Sweet Espinosa, Susan Reed, Jean Karcher, and Lori Stephens Reed.

In addition to being a critical reader, Lori has been one of my biggest supporters for many years. My sons, Kevin and Sean, have been through this before, and could be considered veterans of the "Dad is gone, doing research" syndrome. Nevertheless, they were troopers, and I owe them my thanks.

To anyone I may have overlooked for help rendered, I offer thanks. With all the wonderful help I have received, I alone am responsible for the descriptions and interpretations herein.

CHRONOLOGY

c. 10,000–6000
B.C.E.

Paleoindian people begin sporadic use of Chaco Canyon and surrounding areas for hunting large game animals and gathering plants.

6000–5500
B.C.E.

Transition from Paleoindian to Archaic period lifestyle, with greater focus on broad use of plants and animals for subsistence.

c. 600 B.C.E.

First use of Chaco Canyon by Basketmaker II–era peoples, who practiced corn horticulture and continued to rely on hunting and gathering.

C.E. 500s

First sedentary villages established in Chaco Canyon by Puebloan people (classified by archaeologists as the Basketmaker III period).

700–750

Construction of first above-ground masonry (pueblo) structures in Chaco Canyon.

850–75

Initial construction (as dated by tree rings) begins at Pueblo Bonito. Pueblo Bonito is to become the largest and most impressive great house in Chaco Canyon and the American Southwest.

920s–1020

Construction continues at Pueblo Bonito and a few other Chacoan great houses.

1020–50	A big construction effort ensues in Chaco Canyon, with Pueblo Alto, Hungo Pavi, Pueblo del Arroyo, Pueblo Bonito, and Chetro Ketl, among others, constructed or greatly expanded.
1050–75	The Great North Road is built and the attention of Chacoans begins to shift to the North.
1090–1105	Salmon Pueblo, a three-story, 250-room great house on the San Juan River north of Chaco, is laid out in the form of a giant E and constructed.
1100	The Puebloan Society of Chaco Canyon reaches its peak in population, organizational complexity, and geographic extent.
1105–15	Construction begins at the Western Pueblo of Aztec Ruins, a 400-room structure, on the Animas River north of Salmon Pueblo. By 1125 C.E., Aztec is the largest community outside of Chaco Canyon.
1115–25	Chacoans leave Salmon Pueblo and journey to settle at the Aztec Community. Salmon Pueblo is remade as a San Juan–style pueblo.
1125–50	The ancient Aztec Community, with three great houses, a great kiva, two or three triwall structures, and a host of other dwellings, assumes a primary but short-lived role as the Chacoan center in the North.
1128	Last tree-ring date from a Chaco Canyon great house in the twelfth century.
1130	A prolonged drought begins across the ancient Puebloan region, lasting until 1190–1200. Settlement across the region is disrupted. The Chaco System begins to collapse.
1150	Effective end of Chacoan society.

1150–1300	Reduced occupation and habitation at Chaco Canyon.
1200s	Post-Chacoan societies emerge across the greater San Juan Basin with descendant links to Chacoan society but local and largely autonomous social, political, ritual, and economic institutions.
1280s	A catastrophic fire sweeps much of Salmon Pueblo, causing the abandonment of the great house.
1280s–90s	Fire destroys much of Aztec Ruins, leading to its abandonment.
1300–1325	Abandonment of most of the greater San Juan Basin by the Puebloans. Relocation of groups to the Rio Grande, Zuni-Acoma, and Hopi areas.
1300s–1800s	Sporadic, unrecorded visits to great houses in Chaco Canyon by Pueblo people.
1540–1800s	Sporadic, undocumented visits to Chaco Canyon by Spanish explorers and colonists.
1776	Spanish cartographer Bernado de Miera y Pacheco produces the first known map that applies the name "Mesa de Chaca" to the Chaco Canyon area.
1823	Spanish officer José Antonio Vizcarra makes the first documented trip through Chaco Canyon and observes the ruined great houses.
1849	Lt. James Simpson explores Chaco Canyon and its ruins, completing the first documentation of the sites.
1874	Members of the Wheeler Survey visit Aztec and Salmon ruins. Timothy O'Sullivan takes photographs of "Pueblo San Juan," the site that would come to be known as Salmon Ruin.

1877   Photographer William Henry Jackson visits Chaco Canyon and documents the great houses, discovering several new sites.

1878   Anthropologist Lewis Henry Morgan visits Aztec Ruins.

1888   Victor Mendeleff travels to Chaco Canyon and takes the first successful photographs of the great houses.

1896–1900   The Hyde Exploring Expedition conducts excavations at Pueblo Bonito, and other sites, under the direction of George Pepper and Richard Wetherill.

1906   The Antiquities Act is passed, protecting Chaco and other sites on public lands from unauthorized excavations.

1907   Chaco Canyon National Monument is designated, providing additional protection for the Chacoan sites.

1916–21   Earl Morris directs excavations at the West Ruin of Aztec.

1921–27   Neil Judd leads National Geographic Society–sponsored excavations at Pueblo Bonito and Pueblo del Arroyo.

1929   Edgar Hewett initiates two decades of archaeological work in Chaco Canyon, under the auspices of the School of American Research and the University of New Mexico.

1941   On January 22, Threatening Rock falls from the cliff behind Pueblo Bonito, crushing sixty rooms in the pueblo.

1947   Flood damage reveals an amazing cache of ritual artifacts in Chetro Ketl.

1971	The Chaco Project, a multiyear joint undertaking of the National Park Service and the University of New Mexico, is initiated.
1970	Cynthia Irwin-Williams and her colleagues begin the large-scale excavation of ruins of Salmon Pueblo.
1999–2002	The Chaco World Conferences and Synthesis are held, with the goal of producing an integrated and comprehensive series of publications on Chaco Canyon and the outliers.

CHAPTER 1

SETTING THE STAGE

To veteran travelers of the American Southwest, the name Chaco Canyon invokes an inaccessible, vast land of tremendous vistas and huge, empty stone houses. Today, the Canyon appears as a barren land, and most visitors are struck by its apparent inhospitable nature. Yet almost 1,000 years ago, Chaco Canyon was the hub of a flourishing Pueblo Indian society, with twelve multistory great houses built of stone and wood, a dozen great kivas (large, subterranean ceremonial structures), and hundreds of smaller habitation sites, "pueblos," along the intermittent drainage known today as Chaco Wash. This society peaked in the year 1100 C.E., when more than 150 Chacoan towns or "outliers," in addition to the twelve great houses in Chaco Canyon, and perhaps 30,000 people across the greater San Juan Basin of the southwestern United States were affiliated with Chaco (Figure 1.1). This land mass, which extends across portions of the four modern states of New Mexico, Arizona, Utah, and Colorado, is roughly equal in size to the country of Portugal.

Chacoan society endured for more than 200 years, evolving and changing in the period from 950 to about 1150 C.E. The peak of Chacoan society can be more narrowly dated from 1020 to 1130 C.E. Undoubtedly, many leaders came and went during these hundred years. But we have no written records to name these leaders. Unlike the history of other continents, in the Americas, the near absence of written aboriginal languages means that written chronologies (excepting Aztec and Mayan codices) of the events, processes, and lives of people do not exist. This simple fact makes reconstruction and understanding of America's pre-European past very challenging.

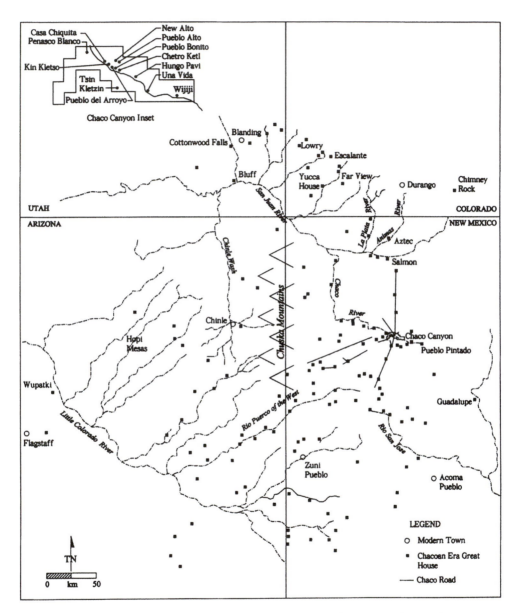

Figure 1.1. Map showing distribution of Chaco Era great houses in the southwestern United States.

In place of written documents and records, archaeologists study the material remains of past peoples—their houses, their trash, and the remaining pieces of their tools, clothing, pottery, and foodstuffs. Archaeologists refer to these material remains as the archaeological record—the physical remnants that have survived decades, centuries, or millennia. These material remains, then, constitute the "texts," the "documents," and the "narratives" that archaeologists "read" to understand the past.

We can discuss this another way and shed more light on the differences between the research historians and archaeologists undertake. Historians and archaeologists approach their studies from very different beginning points. At the risk of oversimplifying things, historians work predominantly with specific documents, accounts, letters, and diaries—the particularistic "paperwork" of daily and yearly life. Archaeologists, by contrast, work with the detritus, the reduced debris of everyday life, accumulated over a number of years, decades, centuries, or even millennia. Historical archaeologists, archaeologists who study the material remains of periods for which written documents are available, are sometimes blessed with documents to add to the archaeological data studied. Archaeologists studying ancient America, however, never have original "paperwork" to complement their research.

In part because of these constraints, and given the availability of particularistic historical data, historians primarily concern themselves first with questions of "how" things happened. Lacking these data, and typically studying sites and processes over a larger spatial and temporal arena, American archaeologists of the last thirty years have focused more on the "why" questions that address more general concerns beyond the specific history of a single village or tribe. Put another way, historians primarily concern themselves with describing events in detail. Archaeologists are more likely to describe phenomena (events and activities) as a beginning point and then move on to explaining processes.

Although it may come as a surprise to some readers, archaeologists only know part of the Chacoan story. Much remains unknown, and some of it is unknowable. We cannot reconstruct the ceremonial practices of the Chacoans. Archaeologists can begin with what is known about the modern Pueblo Indians and project backward. This methodology was the dominant paradigm in American archaeology for decades—the so-called cultural-historical approach. But this endeavor is fraught with much uncertainty, and the number-one nemesis of archaeologists, and of most social scientists and historians, inevitably comes into play—*equifinality*. In laymen's terms, equifinality means that for any given single outcome, multiple explanations are possible. This can be true even at the end of a lengthy research project; sometimes there is simply no valid scientific basis upon which to choose one interpretation over another. Such a situation holds with much of Chacoan archaeology and reconstructions of Chacoan society. Of course, this does not mean that archaeologists do not make choices and offer one interpretation over another. They do, and they debate these interpretations. Eventually, consensus, or near-consensus, emerges. Chacoan archaeology, however, is not at this point of consensus, nor does it seem that this will happen anytime soon.

Nonetheless, the last few years have seen a collective effort to produce an integrated and, perhaps, consensus understanding of Chaco Canyon and the Chacoan world. The Chaco World Conferences were held between 1999 and 2002 in different locations across the greater American Southwest and covered five primary topical areas: society and polity, economy and ecology, architecture, organization of production, and Chaco world (relating to the outlying great houses associated with Chaco). Proceedings of some of these conferences have been published (see the Annotated Bibliography), and results are incorporated here, as appropriate. Final conclusions of the multiyear Chaco Synthesis, however, await publication in 2005.

In this book, I invite the reader to take a journey back in time, to visit the Puebloan Society of Chaco Canyon more than 900 years ago, at 1100 c.e. Chapter 2 sets the stage for the emergence of Chacoan society by discussing the cultural and environmental setting of Chaco Canyon, first at a general level, then more specifically. In Chapter 3, we are introduced to the contemporary Pueblo peoples, the ancestors and inheritors of the Chacoan legacy. Chapter 3 lays out the "history" of Chaco Canyon. In this case, history is a narrative relating more than 150 years of exploration, discovery, mapping, recording, excavation, photography, and reconstruction in Chaco. Chapter 3 introduces most of the central "characters" critical to our literary expedition through Chaco's ancient and more recent history. Chapter 4 tracks the earlier developments of ancestral groups in Chaco Canyon, and across the northern Southwest, that led to the Chacoan society and helps set the stage for Chapter 5. Chapter 5, then, takes us into the heart of Chacoan society, with a "frozen-in-time" look at developments, activities, traits, and characteristics of the society in 1100 c.e. Chapter 6 greatly expands our focus, both geographically and conceptually, by touring the Chacoan outliers—the Chaco-like sites and actual Chaco colonial sites that lie outside Chaco Canyon. As we shall see, much of the discussion/debate/argument in Chacoan archaeology centers on the interpretation of these outliers. Chapter 7 delves into the ritual nature of Chaco Canyon—the part of our story that simultaneously entices (because of the power of ritual) and yet frustrates (because we know so few of the specifics of Chacoan ritual) archaeologists and laypeople alike. In Chapter 8, I recap what we know about Chaco—in some ways, the easy part of the chapter. Then I discuss what is not known about Chaco—another frustrating aspect of this study.

Biographies of twelve people important in Chaco's recent history comprise the Biographies portion of this volume. The individuals profiled include Florence Hawley Ellis, Alden Hayes, Edgar Hewett, Cynthia Irwin-Williams, William Henry Jackson, Neil Judd, Robert Lister, Earl Morris, George Pepper, Lt. James Simpson, Gordon Vivian, and Richard Wetherill. Although only twelve are profiled here, by no means are these the only important contributors to Chacoan research and history.

An extensive Primary Documents section relating to the history of exploration and research on Chaco Canyon and the outliers follows the Biographies. These documents date from 1844 to 1990 and consist primarily of excerpts from early explorers' journals and accounts and archaeological reports, narratives, and monographs. Several documents illustrate the importance of Chaco Canyon to the contemporary Pueblo people. More than any other part of this book, these documents help transport us back in time, to give us a taste of Chaco's history.

A Glossary of terms follows the Primary Documents section. Finally, an Annotated Bibliography with suggestions for additional reading and films/videos for viewing effectively closes this volume.

CHAPTER 2

THE CULTURAL AND ENVIRONMENTAL SETTING OF CHACO CANYON

As a prelude to our discussion of the people of Chaco Canyon and the unprecedented Pueblo Indian society they constructed, we need some background information on the environment. Chaco Canyon is a shallow but wide canyon that runs about twenty miles east to west and is about one-half mile across at its widest point. The canyon occupies the middle portion of the Chaco River, which begins miles to the east in the highlands along the Continental Divide and empties into the San Juan River a few miles east of Shiprock, New Mexico.

Climatically, Chaco is a land of extremes. Daytime summer temperatures can easily exceed 100 degrees, while nighttime lows during the winter commonly drop many digits below zero. On average, Chaco Canyon receives around 8.5 inches of precipitation during the year, including summer thunderstorms and winter snow. Especially critical to subsistence-level farmers like the Puebloans, who depended largely on a trio of crops (corn, beans, and squash), was the length of the growing season. Good, warm years allowed up to 140 days for corn to mature, while colder years sometimes shortened the summer-autumn growing season to as little as 90 days. Droughts lasting several years or even decades were common, and these climatic shifts certainly put a lot of stress on the Chacoans. Nevertheless, it would be a mistake to embrace one popular view of the Puebloans as impoverished farmers barely eking out an existence. Quite to the contrary, Puebloans in Chaco Canyon (and elsewhere) routinely produced agricultural surpluses that allowed them to develop an incredibly rich social and ceremonial life.

Chacoan people, like all of the sedentary inhabitants of the Southwest, depended on three primary agricultural crops for subsistence: corn, beans, and squash (including several varieties of squash, pumpkins, and gourds). This basic diet was supplemented with a variety of natural plant foods including so-called weedy plants like pigweed and goosefoot, other seed plants, piñon nuts, and cactus pods and pads. Protein was provided by a couple of varieties of beans and of course meat from numerous animals, predominantly deer, elk, antelope, rabbit, turkey, and small animals and rodents.

Before delving into the specifics of the Puebloan society of Chaco Canyon, we need to put the Chacoans into context—to understand their place in the world and in North America. Native North and South Americans produced some of the most remarkable societies that have existed on planet Earth.

PRE-HISPANIC NATIVE AMERICA

When explorer Christopher Columbus landed on the island of Hispaniola, in the Caribbean Sea in 1492, he "discovered" an entirely New World—one that was previously unknown to Europeans and other Old World residents. Columbus, of course, was unaware that native North America, as it would come to be called, was home to at least 5 million and perhaps as many as 10 million people. These people were organized into more than 200 ethnolinguistic groups or tribes. Among the more well known of these tribes are the Iroquois, Cherokee, Shawnee, Sioux or Lakota, Arapahoe, Tlingit, Nez Perce, Chumash, and the southwestern American Indians groups, including the Apache, Navajo, Tohono O'odham, Yavapai, and the Pueblos, to name only a few. Our interest here is with the Pueblo people of Arizona and New Mexico.

THE MODERN PUEBLO PEOPLE

The myth of the disappearing "Anasazi" or early Pueblo people, induced by the many spectacular, abandoned sites (like those in Chaco Canyon), has deep roots in the history of the Southwest and is very persistent and hard to dispel. Yet the notion that early Puebloans mysteriously vanished is nothing but fiction. Sites were abandoned, at several different periods in time, and the central Puebloan region was

Table 2.1
Contemporary Pueblo Villages

Pueblo Village	Language Group
Nambe	Tewa
Pojoaque	Tewa
San Ildefonso	Tewa
San Juan	Tewa
Santa Clara	Tewa
Tesuque	Tewa
Jemez	Towa
Picuris	Northern Tiwa
Taos	Northern Tiwa
Isleta	Southern Tiwa
Sandia	Southern Tiwa
Cochiti	Eastern Keresan
San Felipe	Eastern Keresan
Santa Ana	Eastern Keresan
Santo Domingo	Eastern Keresan
Zia	Eastern Keresan
Acoma	Western Keresan
Laguna	Western Keresan
Zuni	Zuni
Hopi villages	Hopi

depopulated permanently around 1300 C.E. But these folks did not vanish; instead, they migrated to new homes to the east, south, and west, joining their brethren at Tano, Tewa, Tiwa, Towa, Hopi, Zuni, and Keresan pueblos (Table 2.1).

Today the Pueblo people live across New Mexico and into Arizona, stretched out from Taos on the northeast to Isleta on the south and Hopi in the far west. The lands occupied today are much reduced from the ancient past, when Pueblo dwellings reached south of Socorro, New Mexico, and reached far to the north into the modern states of Utah and Colorado.

Culturally, the Pueblos are divided by anthropologists into Western and Eastern groups, with the primary differences relating to social organization and kinship. Hopis, on the west, are organized in matrilineal (kinship affiliation organized through the mother's side) clans. The six Tewa-speaking Eastern Pueblos, on the east, are organized into bilateral extended families. For these villages, dual organizations called moieties separate the villages into two parts (winter and summer moieties). Descent is mostly patrilineal (through the father's side) but can vary. Ceremonial societies, or sodalities, are another important social grouping in the west. Ceremonial Katsina societies are present in both Western and Eastern Pueblos (except for Taos) but seem to be more integral to village life in the west. The Keresan Pueblos in between exhibit different combinations of these social and kinship patterns: matrilineal clans are present, as are patrilineal moieties linked to kiva membership.

PUEBLOAN VIEWS OF CHACO CANYON

Chaco Canyon is very important to the Pueblo people of today. Links to the past figure prominently in their origin stories and in other ceremonial stories of villages and individual clans. Many current Pueblo villages are located on lands that hold abandoned towns and villages of the recent and more remote past. This is true for many of the Hopi villages, Zuni and its ancestral pueblo sites, Tewa villages, Jemez Pueblo, the Eastern Keresan villages of Cochiti, Zia, and Santo Domingo, at a minimum, and the Western Keresan town of Acoma Pueblo.

Ancestral linkages to Chaco are less clear because of separation both in time—Chaco was completely abandoned by 1300 c.e.—and space— Chaco is not geographically close to any modern Pueblo town (although Acoma is the closest modern Pueblo). Despite the temporal and spatial separation of Chaco from most Pueblos, almost every group maintains a tradition of affiliation with Chaco. That is, most believe that they have ancestral links to Chaco. Certainly, archaeological evidence supports the notion that the people of Chaco migrated and contributed, over time, to many of the modern Pueblos.

Specific stories that refer to Chaco in a recognizable manner are not apparent in the oral history of most Pueblos. But at least two Pueblo groups identify a place important in their oral traditions that probably refers to Chaco: the Hopi and many of the Keresan-speaking Pueblos.

A portion of the Acoma Pueblo origin story is printed, in brief, in the Primary Documents part of this book, and these traditions are high-lighted here.

Keresan tradition describes a place north of the modern villages known as White House, which may refer to Pueblo Bonito. White House was a place where wandering ancestors stopped and lived for a period of time. Acoma tradition, regarding the Katsina initiation, indicates that the initiation ceremony goes back in time and place to White House, where the real Katsinas lived and where the original Katsina society was organized.[1]

Hopi oral history contains many stories about the mythological mi-grations of the Hopi clans. Hopi stories refer to places that have been identified in the physical world as the Rio Grande, Canyon de Chelly, and the Little Colorado areas. These areas are described as stopping points along the path of the migrations. In most of the literature on Hopi origins, ceremonialism, and migrations, however, no specific ref-erence to or association with Chaco Canyon is made.[2] One writer, Frank Waters, refers to Chaco Canyon as a crossroads of the Hopi clans.[3] Chaco is described as being on the migration route of the Flute Clan, which still uses the heads of macaws (parrots) and feathers in ceremo-nies, and the Snake Clan, which uses seashells. Anthropologists have been unable to confirm many of Waters's stories with other knowledge-able Hopi individuals. We should, therefore, be skeptical about the details of the stories in Waters's narrative. Nevertheless, a Hopi con-nection to Chaco Canyon seems clear.

Most of the anthropological work at Zuni Pueblo, completed between 1870 and about 1960, does not mention Chaco Canyon by name. Ma-tilda Coxe Stevenson (1904) undertook ethnographic work at Zuni for several years.[4] She described the mythological migration of the Wood fraternity (also known as the Sword Swallowers society) from a place to the west (Hän'ᵗ lipĭnkĭa). Stevenson did not suggest that the Zuni iden-tified this place as Chaco Canyon, given its location west and not east of Zuni. Nevertheless, archaeologist Frank H. H. Roberts related a sim-ilar story told by a Zuni consultant (Tsa'wehle) that describes the mi-gration of the Zuni Winter People, led by the Sword Swallowers.[5] On their trip to the north, the Winter People stopped in Chaco Canyon and built the great towns, before proceeding further north to the San Juan River.

Another story was related by Zuni historian Andrew Napatcha. Napatcha visited Chaco with author Kendrick Frazier in the early 1980s and identified Chaco Canyon as an important place in Zuni tradition.[6] In brief, Chaco Canyon was identified as a stop on the migration route of the Zuni Sword Swallowers, just prior to settling at Zuni. Napatcha believed that other groups at Zuni were also from Chaco and that many Zuni ceremonial and political traditions had their roots in Chacoan society.

This brief overview of Puebloan views of Chaco Canyon shows that several groups have mythological and ceremonial connections to sites in the Canyon. Attributing Chaco's legacy to any single modern group, therefore, is not just politically incorrect but historically inaccurate. I would venture to say that descendants of Chaco Canyon's pueblos are probably found in almost every Pueblo village and that the social and ceremonial legacy of Chaco is part of pan-Pueblo tradition.

NAVAJOS AND CHACO CANYON

Based on archaeological research, Navajo or Diné Indian groups first came into the American Southwest in the fifteenth century. By this time, the Puebloans had abandoned much of their former territory, including the greater San Juan Basin and all of the sites formerly associated with the Chacoan world. Navajos, like their Apache cousins, are Athapaskan language speakers and, upon entry into the Southwest, were culturally and linguistically distinct from the Puebloan occupants they encountered. Through interaction and marriage beginning in the 1500s, the Navajo adopted many aspects of culture and religion from the Pueblos, and the ruins of Chaco Canyon and other prominent sites were incorporated into Navajo cosmology. Chaco Canyon was occupied and used by Navajo folks by the early 1700s, perhaps earlier. Although they are culturally and linguistically distinct from the original occupants, Chaco Canyon is nonetheless a very important place for the Navajo. Stories and songs about the great houses in Chaco Canyon and Chacoan outliers play a significant role in Navajo oral history and ceremonialism. Prominent among the stories is the tale of a prominent chief or leader known as the Great Gambler who ruled Chaco from his home at Pueblo Alto.[7]

As far as we can determine, the original version of the Great Gambler story was told to William Henry Jackson by Jemez Pueblo ex-governor Hosta, who was guiding Jackson's group through Chaco Canyon in 1877. To quote Jackson:

> I endeavored to obtain some information from Hosta as to its [Pueblo Alto's] name among the Navajos or Pueblos. At first he professed entire ignorance of its existence, and said that none of his people or any of the Navajos knew anything of it. A day or two afterwards, however, while on the way home, he modified this statement by saying that there was a tradition among his pueblo, of one pueblo among the others that was above them all, not only in position but in strength and influence, and was called *El Capitan* (the captain) or *El Jugador* (the gambler). He explains the latter name by saying that among his people the gambler was regarded as a type of a superior people. Whether or not this explanation was gotten up for the occasion, to explain something he knew nothing of, and yet did not wish to confess his ignorance, a manner in which most of these traditions are gotten up, it is impossible for me to determine; but as a compromise I have called the ruin Pueblo Alto.[8]

Alden Hayes pointed out that Hosta did not invent the name for the site but was only repeating a translation of the Navajo name for the site.[9] Most of the names Hosta provided for sites, to Simpson in 1849 and to Jackson in 1877, were derived from Spanish names for the ruined great houses. Jackson was essentially carrying on in this tradition when he named the site Pueblo Alto, or Tall Town. It is unclear whether the Great Gambler story originated with Navajos in Chaco Canyon or was derived from a much older Pueblo story about Chaco Canyon.

SUMMARY

In summary, Chaco Canyon is a place of great importance to the modern Pueblo people. It is located roughly in the middle of the current distribution of Pueblo villages that fan out across New Mexico and into Arizona. Contemporary Pueblo peoples are the clear descendants of the ancient inhabitants of Chaco Canyon. But because of the passage of many centuries, it is difficult to track direct linkages between modern Pueblo villages and the ancient, ruined Chacoan great houses. Navajo people came into the American Southwest after the florescence of

Chaco Canyon had passed and after the Pueblo people had abandoned most of the greater San Juan region. Navajos today have significant ceremonial associations with Chaco Canyon and its amazing pueblos, but archaeological data indicate that they are not directly descended from its ancient inhabitants.

NOTES

1. Katsina societies are one of several ceremonial groups among the Hopi, Zuni, and Western Keresan Pueblos. These societies have deep roots and probably originated in Chaco Canyon and other ancestral settings. Matthew W. Stirling, *Origin Myth of Acoma and Other Records*, Smithsonian Institution Bureau of American Ethnology Bulletin no. 135 (Washington, DC: Government Printing Office, 1942), p. 108.

2. Edmund Nequatewa, *Truth of a Hopi: Stories Relating to the Origin Myth and Clan Histories of the Hopi*, edited by M. F. Colton (Flagstaff, AZ: Northland Press, 1967).

3. Frank Waters, *The Book of the Hopi* (New York: Viking Press, 1963), p. 42.

4. Matilda Coxe Stevenson, *The Zuni Indians: Their Mythology, Esoteric Fraternities, and Ceremonies*, Twenty-third Annual Report of the Bureau of American Ethnology (Washington, DC: Smithsonian Institution, 1904).

5. Frank H. H. Roberts, *The Ruins at Kiatuthlanna, Eastern Arizona*, Bureau of American Ethnology Bulletin no. 100 (Washington, DC: Smithsonian Institution, 1931), p. 8.

6. Kendrick Frazier, *People of Chaco* (New York: Crown Publishers, 1999), pp. 210–212.

7. The primary reference for the Navajo version of the Great Gambler story is Gretchen Chapin, "A Navajo Myth from Chaco Canyon," *New Mexico Anthropologist* 4, no. 4 (1940): 63–67. Other references include: Lloyd M. Pierson, "A History of Chaco Canyon National Monument" (Chaco Canyon: Manuscript on file, Chaco Culture National Historic Park, 1956); and Alden C. Hayes, "A Survey of Chaco Canyon Archaeology," in *Archaeological Surveys of Chaco Canyon, New Mexico*, by Alden C. Hayes, David M. Brugge, and W. James Judge (Albuquerque: University of New Mexico Press, 1981), pp. 6–7.

8. William Henry Jackson, "Report on the Ancient Ruins Examined in 1875 and 1877," in *Tenth Annual Report of the United States Geological and Geographical Survey of the Territories*, by F. V. Hayden (Washington, DC: Government Printing Office, 1878), p. 447.

9. Hayes, "A Survey of Chaco Canyon Archaeology," p. 7.

CHAPTER 3

Chaco's History:
Exploration and Research at Chaco Canyon in Historical Context

CHACO CANYON IN THE NINETEENTH CENTURY

The "discovery" of the spectacular great houses of Chaco Canyon is hard to pinpoint precisely. To begin, the notion of discovery is very Euro-centric and insulting to many Native Americans. Even after the aban-donment of dwellings in Chaco by 1300 C.E., we can infer that Puebloans and other indigenous people continued to visit the great houses on pilgrimages and simply to reconnect with the past. Abundant references to Chaco exist in the ceremonial and origin stories, and oral histories of the modern Puebloans, particularly Keresan groups. Thus, it is fair to say that Chaco Canyon never passed out of the memory or experience of Puebloan people.

As to Chaco's "rediscovery" by Euro-Americans, visits by Spanish explorers and other travelers (from the early C.E. 1600s on) undoubtedly occurred, but because of the destruction of Spanish records during the Pueblo Revolt of 1680, little or no documentation has survived into the present. More surprising, perhaps, and unexplained is the absence of written descriptions of the Chacoan ruins from about 1700 through the early 1800s. Historical records indicate that the Spanish launched nu-merous punitive expeditions against Navajo and Apache Indians in areas east of Santa Fe and the Rio Grande. Some of the routes described passed through the Chaco country, and the name *Chaco* or *Chaca* was first applied to the Canyon and surrounding lands at this time, in the eighteenth century. Although it is unlikely he ever visited the Canyon, Spanish cartographer Bernado de Miera y Pacheco identified the general area around Chaco, and particularly to the south, as Mesa de Chaca on his 1776 map.[1]

The earliest documented trip through Chaco Canyon was made by a Spanish military officer named José Antonio Vizcarra, who was pursuing Navajo Indians accused of raiding settlements in 1823. Vizcarra's pursuit took his company down Chaco Wash, and he observed and recorded several large Pueblo ruins in the Canyon.[2] Additional accounts, mostly made by Spanish military expeditions, mentioned the ruins over the next several decades, but it was not until 1849 that the first comprehensive descriptions and maps of the Chaco Canyon towns were made.

At the end of the Mexican War in 1848, the United States was in possession of millions of acres of new southwestern lands. With the new lands came problems with the Native American inhabitants, and a military expedition was launched into the Navajo country in 1849.[3] Under the command of Col. John Washington, military governor of New Mexico, the expedition also included Lt. James Simpson and two brothers, Richard and Edward Kern, both accomplished artists. As the company passed through Chaco Canyon, headed west toward the Chuska Mountains and Navajo country, Simpson was interested in exploring the ruins and obtained permission to make a side trip to do so. A man of considerable diligence, Simpson set about a detailed recording of the ruined great houses, while Richard Kern prepared the first known drawings of sites in the Canyon. So accurate were his descriptions and drawings that they stood the test of time and were not surpassed (in detail or quality) for nearly 100 years. The group's Mexican guide Carravahal, from San Ysidro, New Mexico, identified most of the largest ruins by name. Simpson applied these names to the sites, and they are still with us today. Pueblo Pintado (painted town), the first ruin encountered, lies several miles to the east of the main group. The other ruins have predominantly Spanish-language names: Pueblo Bonito ("beautiful town"), Chetro Ketl (interpreted by the Mexican guide Carravahal as "rain town"), Pueblo del Arroyo ("arroyo" or "canyon town"), Una Vida ("one life"), and Peñasco Blanco ("white bluff"). But two have Native American names: Hungo Pavi (thought to be a Hopi place name, a mispronunciation of the Hopi village of Shungopovi, or a corruption of a Spanish term meaning "hooked nose") and Wijiji (a variant of a Navajo word that means "black greasewood").[4]

Francisco Hosta, governor of Jemez Pueblo and the Indian guide for the group, told Simpson that Montezuma and his Aztec people had built the ruins in Chaco, on a northern sojourn, before heading south to construct the urban center at Tenochitlan, Mexico. Following Hosta, Simpson speculated that the ruins were built by the Aztecs or another Mesoamerican kingdom and so initiated a period of many years of ill-informed understanding of the origins of the Chacoan great houses.

Simpson's journal and the drawings of Richard Kern made the spectacular structures of Chaco Canyon known to only a few people, and the "secret" of Chaco remained hidden for several decades. The 1870s, though, saw renewed interest in Chaco Canyon. Photographer William Henry Jackson and William Henry Holmes together made a trip in 1877, as part of the U.S. Geologic and Geographic Survey of the Territories (also known as the Hayden Survey). Jackson was aware of the spectacular ruins and intended to produce the first photographs of the outstanding remains. The Hayden Survey hired the same Jemez Indian guide, Hosta, who had led Simpson through Chaco. Jackson spent most of a week studying the ruins and exposing photographic plates. Unfortunately, Jackson was experimenting with a new technique, and none of his photographs of Chacoan houses came out; all failed to develop properly. It was decades before Jackson was able to duplicate some of his shots and produce photographs of Chaco. Even without his much desired photographic record of the amazing Chacoan ruins, Jackson's trip and subsequent narrative of Chaco truly opened the floodgates and moved Chaco and its ruins into a new period. Most important, perhaps, was Jackson's determination that the ruins were not built by the Aztecs or another vanished tribe but were the ancestral homes of the modern Pueblo people of New Mexico and Arizona.[5]

Other visits occurred during the last quarter century of the 1800s, but few left a lasting legacy. One important visit was made by Victor Mindeleff, who briefly studied architecture in Chaco in 1887 and 1888. Mindeleff went on to produce the groundbreaking *A Study of Pueblo Architecture in Cibola and Tusayan*, which became the definitive study of Pueblo architecture for more than half a century.[6] Perhaps of greatest significance is the set of photographs made by Mindeleff, the first successful images of the spectacular ruins in the Canyon.

Of special interest here, Scott Morris, father of archaeologist Earl Morris, was drawn to Pueblo Bonito in 1893 by stories of the site. He dug the first trench through the trash mounds in front of Pueblo Bonito, hoping to find burials with rich accompanying artifacts. Morris was disappointed, finding no burials and only a few artifacts.[7] His son Earl, however, was infected with the archaeological bug at an early age and would spend his life pursuing the past.

In 1897, Warren K. Moorehead, curator in the Department of Archaeology, Phillips Academy, came to Chaco Canyon. Like most curators of the time, Moorehead's chief mission was to find and procure collections for his museum. In just three weeks of undocumented excavations at Pueblo Bonito, Moorehead had amassed a collection of more than 2,000 artifacts of stone, ceramic, bone, and perishable materials for the Phillips Academy Museum.[8]

In 1896, sponsored archaeological work was initiated at Chaco Canyon. The American Museum of Natural History sponsored the Hyde Exploring Expedition in its excavations at Pueblo Bonito, with field supervision by George Pepper and explorer–cowboy Richard Wetherill as field foreman. Professor Frederic W. Putnam, curator at the Museum, provided academic oversight and credibility for the project. Primary goals of the expedition included securing specimens for the Museum and understanding the history of Pueblo Bonito. Specimen collection was the primary modus operandi for museums during this period of American archaeology. Unfortunately, these collections frequently came at the expense of scientific work and documentation, and the secondary goal of research was often neglected. This seems to have been the case with the Hyde Expedition's work at Pueblo Bonito. In addition to excavations in the Pueblo Bonito trash mounds and room blocks, the trash middens of many smaller sites up and down the Canyon were explored, and many burials and associated grave artifacts were collected. In short order, the younger, inexperienced but more educated Pepper and Wetherill (older, a seasoned cowboy and explorer but with little formal education) developed a rivalry that would endure throughout the project. Both men, along with Professor Putnam, were very interested in furthering their own success and fortunes, alongside the larger goals of the expedition.[9]

In all, about 190 rooms and kivas were excavated at Pueblo Bonito. Pepper and Wetherill's approach to excavation involved digging a room out, removing the artifacts and samples, taking limited notes, and then moving on to the next room, while backfilling rooms already excavated. This approach did not allow the architecture (and other attributes) to be studied comprehensively and led to mixing of deposits from adjacent rooms—a huge problem for archaeologists trying to understand the sequence of occupation in a room and pueblo. Another troubling aspect of the work at Pueblo Bonito was the tendency for occasional artifacts to "disappear" from the floors of rooms during excavation and "reappear" for sale to Wetherill, in his capacity as trading post operator. Trading operations were expanded during the course of the Hyde Expedition's work at Pueblo Bonito, and more than a dozen posts were in operation by the early 1900s. Once Navajo workers and other local folk became aware of the money to be made selling antiquities to traders, looting and vandalism accelerated at Chaco Canyon and other locales. Thus, the trading activities of the Hydes and Wetherill, and other traders across the San Juan Basin, served to encourage indiscriminate looting of Puebloan sites for profit.

Some amazing ceremonial artifacts were found, including a carved frog made of jet with inlaid turquoise eyes and an inlaid turquoise necklace, a jet buckle with inlaid turquoise decoration, painted wooden sticks, perhaps *pahos* or prayer sticks, several carved wooden flutes, hundreds of crooked sticks, several deer bone scrapers with inlaid turquoise and jet decoration, the skeletal remains of more than thirty macaws or parrots, several carved turquoise bird effigies, and abundant turquoise pendants and raw material. Room 28 at Pueblo Bonito contained a huge cache of pottery including more than 100 of the famous Chaco cylindrical vessels, numerous other ceramic vessels, and coiled baskets. Pepper suggested that the ritual items were linked to a macaw or parrot clan at Pueblo Bonito.[10] (Neil Judd later reached the same conclusion, after several years of work at Bonito, funded by National Geographic.)

Work by the Hyde Expedition was stopped in late 1900, largely through the efforts of Edgar Hewett. Hewett filed complaints with the General Land Office about the Hyde Expedition's work at Pueblo Bonito and elsewhere in the Canyon, contending that it was nothing more than looting. The General Land Office sent out investigator Samuel J. Holsinger in the spring of 1901, to examine the work of the Hyde Expedition and Wetherill's 1900 homestead claim. Holsinger spent four weeks at Chaco and produced a report that went well beyond just an investigation of the Hyde Expedition.[11] He described most of the major ruins in the Canyon, compared his findings to those of W. H. Jackson, speculated about water use and other environmental factors, and even wrote a reconstruction of Pueblo life at Chaco. Holsinger's findings suggested that Wetherill's homestead claim had less to do with farming and ranching and was more related to controlling access to Pueblo Bonito, Chetro Ketl, and Pueblo del Arroyo. Further, most of Wetherill's activities were judged to be trading related and not within the realm of homesteading. Wetherill's claim was suspended in 1902. Although he found little to criticize regarding the Hyde Expedition's work, Holsinger nevertheless recommended that the ruins in Chaco be protected as a national park. On the basis of Holsinger's report, the temporary suspension of the Hyde Expedition work in Chaco Canyon was made permanent in 1902.[12]

The primary charges leveled against the Hyde-sponsored excavators by Hewett were inadequate record keeping and documentation and pillaging of the site to acquire specimens. Given that such collecting was standard at the time, it is interesting that the Hyde Expedition was singled out. As archaeologist Gwinn Vivian has pointed out, the failure of the Hyde Expedition to collect and preserve hundreds of wooden beams from collapsed roofs in Pueblo Bonito is perhaps the greatest loss to archaeology and science.[13] In the late 1920s, the science of dendrochronology (dating wood samples by counting and correlating tree rings) was in development and would revolutionize understanding of the dating of sites in the Southwest. Politics clearly played a role, and Hewett had his own ideas about how best to undertake archaeological work in Chaco. It seems clear that additional work by the Hyde Expedition would not have added substantively to knowledge of Chaco Canyon and its inhabitants. Much of Pepper's published works on Pueblo Bonito focused on artifacts of presumed ritual or ceremonial importance. In the early twentieth century, techniques for dating archaeological sites like Pueblo Bonito had not yet been developed. Thus, Pepper was unable to locate the site in time and could only infer that it predated the historic Pueblo villages of the Southwest. Further, the archaeological methods and theoretical frameworks necessary to understand a complex and large site like Pueblo Bonito were still in their infancy. In short, the end of the Hyde Expedition's work was beneficial because more of Pueblo Bonito was preserved for the subsequent research that would begin to address important questions.[14]

EARLY-TWENTIETH-CENTURY RESEARCH AT CHACO

A few years later, in 1906, the Antiquities Act was passed by the U.S. Congress and signed into law by President Theodore Roosevelt. The act limited excavations at sites to professional archaeologists and required permits for excavation and collection of artifacts. On the heels of passage of the Antiquities Act of 1906, Chaco Canyon National Monument was created in 1907. This new status provided greater protection, at least on paper, for the fragile sites within the boundary of the new monument. In actuality, the new monument was managed and protected for years through the efforts of only a single custodian. In 1916, the National Park Service was created, and greater attention was paid to managing and protecting the irreplaceable treasures of Chaco Canyon.

Archaeologists with the American Museum of Natural History briefly revisited Chaco Canyon in 1916. Nels Nelson had undertaken the first stratigraphic excavations in the American Southwest, paying close attention to soil and sediments as a guide to a site's relative antiquity. With the support of the Museum and accompanied by Earl Morris, Nelson brought this approach to Pueblo Bonito. He excavated in the same mound that both Scott Morris and Wetherill had trenched. Like the two men who proceeded him, Nelson was disappointed by the lack of artifacts and his inability to track a ceramic sequence in the supposed trash midden. He concluded that the mound had been used mainly as a depository for leftover and exhausted architectural materials. As an aside, the Pueblo Bonito "trash" mounds have puzzled almost every archaeologist who has studied Chaco over the last 100 years. These mounds, which were initially assumed to represent the routine trash-dumping areas associated with many pueblo sites, were found to contain very little trash (in the form of discarded and broken ceramics and stone tools and bone debris from meals). Furthermore, many pueblo trash mounds were used as burial grounds, but the Chacoan mounds, upon excavation, did not reveal burials. The most plausible explanation, recently proposed by archaeologist Stephen Lekson, suggests that the mounds are earthen architecture that were specifically constructed in front of Pueblo Bonito and other great houses. According to this view, earthen mounds were built in front of great houses as part of an intentional, constructed sacred landscape.[15]

Neil Judd directed the most extensive work to date in Chaco Canyon, beginning in 1921 and continuing through 1927. Like Wetherill and Pepper, Judd concentrated on the Chaco crown jewel—Pueblo Bonito. National Geographic Society sponsored this work, and 138 rooms and twenty-four kivas (two were great kivas) were excavated during seven field seasons of work. Judd's assistant, Karl Ruppert, worked at Pueblo del Arroyo, a smaller but still large great house located quite close to Pueblo Bonito, for three years. Ruppert's crews cleared about half of the 290 rooms at Pueblo del Arroyo. The National Museum of the Smithsonian Institution was the designated repository for the artifacts derived from Judd's work, and the work was conducted under a permit issued by the Department of the Interior. With the passage of more than fifteen years between the earlier work at Pueblo Bonito and Judd's effort, archaeological method and theory had "caught up" to a great extent. Tree-ring dating (dendrochronology) was developed in the 1910s and 1920s by the astronomer A. E. Douglass and provided a basis for ordering southwestern sites, using dated wood samples, on a relative scale. Stratigraphic excavations that paid heed to the deposition of distinct soil and sediment horizons, and thus provided an accurate means of relatively dating archaeological structures and sites, was pioneered by archaeologist Nels Nelson through work in the Galisteo Basin (south of Santa Fe, New Mexico) and at Chaco. In 1927, the first Pecos Conference was convened at Pecos Pueblo by A. V. Kidder. One result of the conference was a chronology of sites in the Anasazi-Pueblo sequence. The Chacoan sites were placed into the Pueblo III or Great Pueblo period—the apogee of prehistoric Puebloan achievements. Although the tree-ring chronology was not connected to the Christian calendar until years later, thus becoming an absolute dated chronology, the relative ordering that emerged demonstrated relationships among the Chaco Canyon sites.[16]

Pepper and the Hyde Expedition's earlier work was finally published in 1920, and this allowed Judd to avoid rooms that had been previously excavated and backfilled. Unlike Pepper, Judd focused on clearing rooms completely of the sediments and debris that had accumulated over the centuries. Using mules to pull mine cars along narrow-gauge railroad tracks, Judd and his crews were able to remove tons of debris in an efficient manner. Earl Morris used the same technique a few years earlier at Aztec, and it was probably at Morris's suggestion that Judd implemented this methodology.[17] Judd's approach resulted in a series of well-excavated and -exposed rooms that could be studied more completely. Beyond this, Judd also took steps to protect the pueblo. Although the work did not meet later stabilization standards, Judd's crews repaired rooms as they became exposed, replacing stone and mortar and digging drainage outlets in many rooms to minimize water damage. The National Geographic work contributed to the known sequence of Puebloan and Chacoan sites. Through careful excavation and documentation, the complicated and lengthy history of Pueblo Bonito began to emerge, with multiple use and reuse of rooms, kivas, and great kivas added at various points in time and frequent relocation of the primary trash middens or disposal areas at the site. Lasting contributions of Judd and the National Geographic work include a ceramic chronology derived from excavations in the main trash midden to the south of the site (and from throughout the rest of the site) developed by archaeologist Frank H. H. Roberts. Judd studied masonry in Pueblo Bonito and created a typology of four distinct wall-facing or veneer patterns that, with some modification, is still in use today.[18] Drawing on all his work and prior work, Judd hypothesized that the original group of occupants of Pueblo Bonito, the Old Bonitians, were replaced by newcomers from the San Juan area, the New Bonitians, who greatly expanded the site and developed most of the characteristics that we associate today with Chaco and Chacoan great houses.

Sponsored by the School of American Research and Royal Ontario Museum, Edgar Hewett initiated work in Chaco in 1920, with excavations at the second largest site, Chetro Ketl.[19] The second season, in 1921, focused on the great kiva in the east plaza. After only two seasons, work was stopped because of a perceived conflict with the National Geographic Society–sponsored work at Pueblo Bonito.

In 1929, after years of waiting, Edgar Hewett again initiated research in Chaco Canyon, after the National Geographic excavations by Judd and his associates ended. With Pueblo Bonito intensively excavated twice by the late 1920s, Hewett chose to focus his attention on Chetro Ketl. He initiated a joint field endeavor with his School of American Research, teaming up with the University of New Mexico (where he was chair of the newly created anthropology department). Thus began two decades of work at Chetro Ketl and a number of smaller sites in the Canyon.[20] Among the students trained during Hewett's time in Chaco were many prominent southwestern archaeologists of the mid-twentieth century: Florence Hawley Ellis, Paul Reiter, Gordon Vivian, Bertha Dutton, Frank Hibben, Anna Shepard, Donald Brand, and Stanley Stubbs, among others.[21] Unfortunately, much of the work initiated by Hewett was never published or publication was delayed for years. Chetro Ketl, for example, was not published until 1983, through the efforts of the Chaco Project and archaeologist Steve Lekson.

The joint School of American Research–University of New Mexico project completed more work than any previous effort in Chaco and trained hundreds of students in the essentials of southwestern archaeological field techniques. One of the programs to emerge from this time involved the stabilization and protection of the standing walls and other fragile parts of the Chacoan great houses and smaller sites. Some such work was done by Judd, as Pueblo Bonito was excavated. With Hewett's leadership, a comprehensive and systematic stabilization program was initiated, headed by Gordon Vivian. Hewett taught his students to excavate with great care, leaving as much original structure standing intact as possible. He further instructed them to repair walls with the least possible intrusion and change to the original fabric. Hewett championed the concept that the sites should be stabilized as ruins and not as "ghastly restorations."[22] Under Hewett's program, and the succeeding National Park Service effort, thousands of walls at hundreds of sites were shored up, fixed, or had faulty masonry and mortar replaced. This work laid the groundwork for much of the stabilization that is still being undertaken today in Chaco Canyon and across the Southwest. Further, Vivian recruited local Navajo men to form the core of his stabilization crew. This tradition lives on today, with much of the current National Park Service stabilization work drawing on skilled Navajos. Such a pattern also holds for the stabilization work undertaken through Salmon Ruins.

In 1941, a calamitous event occurred in Chaco Canyon. A massive slab of sandstone weighing thousands of tons completely separated from the sandstone bluff above Pueblo Bonito and crashed into the site. "Threatening Rock" was identified as a threat to the site by the first Euro-Americans to come through Chaco. Indeed, the giant sandstone boulder was a threat to the Chacoans, who tried to keep it from falling using large pine timbers placed under it to support its weight and through construction of a retaining wall with rock and dirt fill in front of and at the base of the rock. The Chacoans' efforts succeeded, and the rock was stabilized for perhaps 1,000 years. It became clear in the

1930s, however, that the rock was moving outward at an increasing rate. Threatening Rock was monitored and various solutions debated. But very little was done. On January 22, 1941, the rock fell and destroyed some sixty rooms of Pueblo Bonito below it. The sheer weight of the rubble precluded easy cleanup. Park Service archaeologists decided to leave most of the debris where it fell and integrate the story of Threatening Rock and its fall into the interpretation of the Pueblo.[23]

One of the more significant finds in Chaco Canyon came during a torrential rainstorm in 1947. First-story rooms along the north side of Chetro Ketl were flooded and began to collapse. To relieve the pressure, Gordon Vivian excavated an upper floor of Room 93 and found an amazing cache of 200 ritual artifacts. Most of these artifacts were made of carved and painted wood and were in an excellent state of preservation.[24] Most of the artifacts were zoomorphic (animal depictions) including birds and serpents. Some human forms were present, as well. Various pieces of wooden forms were identified including slats, discs, and triangular and rectangular forms. Because of similarity with altars and ritual items at Hopi, Zuni, and other Pueblo villages, the archaeologists initially thought that the objects in Room 93 represented an intact altar that was crushed when the roof of the room collapsed. Gordon Vivian died before completing a report on the objects. That task was completed by his son Gwinn Vivian, who, with his colleagues, concluded that Room 93 was a storage area for ritual objects and did not represent an intact altar.

Although some projects were undertaken and various studies completed, the period between about 1950 and 1970 may have been the least active in Chaco's history. Gwinn Vivian completed his dissertation on Chaco in 1970, focusing specifically on prehistoric social organization and society in Chaco Canyon.[25] Although prior work had addressed aspects of social organization, Vivian's work was the first to attempt a comprehensive explanation for the rise of Chacoan society and social organization and to relate it to other factors (for example, the use of an extensive system of canals and other facilities to collect and channel runoff from rainfall on the north side of Chaco). Vivian continued research at Chaco for more than thirty years and has probably made the greatest single contribution to our understanding of ancient Chacoan society.

LATE-TWENTIETH-CENTURY RESEARCH IN CHACO CANYON

The Chaco Project, a joint undertaking of the National Park Service and the University of New Mexico, under the direction of archaeologists James Judge and Robert Lister, was initiated in 1971. Excavation focused in several areas: (1) great house studies, through excavation of Pueblo Alto; (2) small house or unit pueblo studies, with work at a number of smaller Pueblo II and III sites; (3) other sites, such as Basketmaker III habitation, field houses, and shrines. Survey of much of Chaco Culture National Historical Park (the official name of Chaco after a 1980 congressional "upgrade" from National Monument status) was also an important part of the Chaco Project. Thousands of sites were recorded during the Chaco survey, reflecting a chronology from Paleoindian (c. 10,000 B.C.E.) scatters of surface artifacts to twentieth-century Navajo camps with multiple hogans (traditional Navajo structures).

The excavation of Pueblo Alto is probably the most significant accomplishment of the Chaco Project.[26] Pueblo Alto is the only great house in Chaco Canyon that has been excavated in the last fifty years. Thus, its significance lies in the wealth of remains (ceramics, chipped stone, animal bone, tools, ornaments, and other artifacts) that were recovered with modern excavation techniques that pinpointed their locations and contexts. As the history detailed above shows, most of the large Chacoan sites were excavated long ago, before archaeologists fully understood the importance of recovering artifacts in their contexts and the need to map the contents of rooms by stratigraphic level. Much of the work at Pueblo Bonito, in particular, essentially amounted to laborers shoveling rooms out in haste, without much concern for any but the most obvious artifacts and room features (e.g., fire pits, mealing bins, storage pits).

Somewhat ironically, perhaps, is the fact that along with being the most carefully excavated great house in the Canyon, Pueblo Alto is also atypical. The site is medium sized for a Chacoan great house, with about 130 rooms. But with only a single, massive story with twelve-foot-high ceilings, the site is unique in Chaco Canyon and across the Chacoan world. Further, as a result of intensive research, the site has been interpreted as a gateway community, which apparently served a largely ritual function related to periodic ceremonies held in the Canyon.

The last ten years represents a time of renewed interest in Chaco Canyon and in new research directions. This research has been divided between sites in the Canyon itself and the outliers. New work at outliers has resulted in a different view of the Chaco System. New researchers appear less willing to invoke a central Chacoan system to explain the construction and use of the outlying sites.[27] Work at the Bluff great house, for example, over the last few years has revealed a very "local" character to its architecture.[28] In contrast, Bluff has copper bells imported from Mesoamerica and other artifacts that undoubtedly came through the Chaco exchange network. Thus, Bluff may best be seen as a local phenomenon built by local leaders who wanted a Chaco-like great house but who did not have direct access to Chacoan expertise in construction and design. But the presence of exotic artifacts indicates participation in the Chaco exchange network and may suggest that Bluff was as equal a participant in the economic portion of the Chaco world as were outlier sites actually built by the Chacoans (Chimney Rock or Guadalupe, for example).

The Chaco World Conferences and Synthesis, initiated in 1999, is intended to produce an integrated and, perhaps, consensus view of Chaco Canyon and the outliers. Even if this goal is achieved, however, by no means will the final word on Chaco be written. Research continues to this day, and views of Chaco will continue to evolve.

SUMMARY

Scientific exploration and research at Chaco Canyon spans more than 150 years. The earliest work in the middle and late nineteenth century focused primarily on documentation of the spectacular great houses and collection of representative artifacts. Around the turn of the nineteenth century, focused archaeological excavations were begun, and what would eventually become millions of artifacts were collected from Chacoan sites. Research eventually "caught up" in Chaco Canyon, and the focus shifted in the early and middle twentieth century to describing and understanding the Chacoan sites. Throughout this history, the uniqueness of Chaco in the greater Pueblo world was clear to most researchers. In the latter part of the twentieth century, the focus shifted again, to not only describing and documenting the Chaco Phenomenon or System but also to understanding its origin and evolution. The most recent work on Chaco Canyon and Chacoan society has produced appreciation of its complexity—not necessarily in terms of "status" in evolutionary terms (i.e., was Chaco a tribe or a chiefdom?). Rather, archaeologists and researchers have come to understand the diversity of Chacoan society and appreciate its complicated nature.

NOTES

1. David M. Brugge, *A History of the Chaco Navajos*, Reports of the Chaco Center no. 4 (Albuquerque: National Park Service, 1980).

2. Ibid., p. 12.

3. Frank McNitt, *Navaho Expedition* (Norman: University of Oklahoma Press, 1964).

4. Lt. James H. Simpson, *Journal of a Military Reconnaissance from Santa Fe, New Mexico to the Navaho Country, Made with the Troops under Command of Lt. Col. John M. Washington in 1849* (Washington, DC: Report of the Secretary of War, 31st Cong., 1st sess., Senate Executive Document 64, 1850), pp. 56–139.

5. William Henry Jackson, "Report on the Ancient Ruins Examined in 1875 and 1877," in *Tenth Annual Report of the United States Geological and Geographical Survey of the Territories*, by F. V. Hayden (Washington, DC: Government Printing Office, 1878).

6. Victor Mindeleff, *A Study of Pueblo Architecture: Tusayan and Cibola* (Washington, DC: Smithsonian Institution Press, 1989). Originally published in *Eighth Annual Report of the Bureau of Ethnology 1886–1887* (Washington, DC, 1891).

7. Florence C. Lister and Robert H. Lister, *Earl Morris and Southwestern Archaeology* (Albuquerque: University of New Mexico Press, 1968).

8. Warren K. Moorehead, *A Narrative of Exploration in New Mexico, Arizona, Indiana, Etc.*, Phillips Academy Department of Anthropology Bulletin III (Andover, MA: Andover Press, 1906).

9. Robert H. Lister and Florence C. Lister, *Chaco Canyon: Archaeology and Archaeologists* (Albuquerque: University of New Mexico Press, 1981).

10. George Pepper, *Pueblo Bonito* (New York: Anthropological Papers of the American Museum of Natural History, vol. 27, 1920; reprint, Albuquerque: University of New Mexico Press, 1996).

11. S. J. Holsinger, "Report on Prehistoric Ruins of Chaco Canyon, New Mexico" (manuscript on file, Chaco Culture National Historic Park, 1901).

12. Lister and Lister, *Chaco Canyon: Archaeology and Archaeologists*, p. 56.

13. R. Gwinn Vivian, *The Chacoan Prehistory of the San Juan Basin* (San Diego: Academic Press, 1990), pp. 45–46.

14. Lister and Lister, *Chaco Canyon: Archaeology and Archaeologists*, p. 62.

15. John R. Stein and Stephen H. Lekson, "Anasazi Ritual Landscapes," in *Anasazi Regional Organization and the Chaco System*, edited by D. E. Doyel (Albuquerque: Maxwell Museum of Anthropology, Anthropological Papers no. 5, 2001), pp. 87–100.

16. Lister and Lister, *Chaco Canyon: Archaeology and Archaeologists*, pp. 65–90, passim.

17. Ibid., p. 70.

18. Neil M. Judd, *The Architecture of Pueblo Bonito*, Smithsonian Miscellaneous Collections, vol. 147, no. 1 (Washington, DC: Smithsonian Institution, 1964); Stephen H. Lekson, *Great Pueblo Architecture of Chaco Canyon, New Mexico* (Albuquerque: University of New Mexico Press, 1986).

19. Vivian, *The Chacoan Prehistory of the San Juan Basin*, p. 52.

20. Edgar L. Hewett, *The Chaco Canyon and Its Monuments* (Albuquerque: University of New Mexico Press and the School of American Research Press, 1936).

21. Lister and Lister, *Chaco Canyon: Archaeology and Archaeologists*, p. 95.

22. Hewett, *The Chaco Canyon and Its Monuments*, p. 215.

23. Lloyd M. Pierson, "A History of Chaco Canyon National Monument" (Chaco Canyon: Manuscript on file, Chaco Culture National Historic Park, 1956).

24. R. Gwinn Vivian, Dulce N. Dodgen, and Gayle H. Hartmann, *Wooden Ritual Artifacts from Chaco Canyon, New Mexico*, Anthropological Papers of the University of Arizona no. 32 (Tucson: University of Arizona Press, 1978), p. 1.

25. R. Gwinn Vivian, "Aspects of Prehistoric Society in Chaco Canyon, New Mexico" (Ph.D. diss., Department of Anthropology, University of Arizona, 1970).

26. Francis Joan Mathien and Thomas C. Windes, eds., *Investigations at the Pueblo Alto Complex, Chaco Canyon*, Publications in Archaeology 18F, Chaco Canyon Studies (Santa Fe, NM: National Park Service, 1987).

27. Many of the essays in the following volume discuss Chacoan outliers from a fresh perspective. John Kantner and Nancy M. Mahoney, eds., *Great House Communities across the Chacoan Landscape*, Anthropological Papers of the University of Arizona no. 64 (Tucson: University of Arizona Press, 2000).

28. Joseph Peter Jalbert and Catherine Cameron, "Chacoan and Local Influences in Three Great House Communities in the Northern San Juan Region," in *Great House Communities across the Chacoan Landscape*, edited by John Kantner and Nancy M. Mahoney, Anthropological Papers of the University of Arizona no. 64 (Tucson: University of Arizona Press, 2000), pp. 79–99.

CHAPTER 4

THE EMERGENCE OF CHACOAN SOCIETY:
A CHRONOLOGICAL VIEW

With good background information for Chaco Canyon in place and an introduction to contemporary Pueblo peoples, we proceed to a discussion of the emergence of Chaco. First, we explore the underpinnings, the roots of Chacoan society, and then take a chronological journey through Chaco Canyon.

THE ROOTS OF CHACOAN SOCIETY

The roots of Chacoan society extend thousands of years before 950 C.E., as the timeline shows. Puebloans evolved culturally through this long period of time, setting the stage for the Chaco florescence. The beginnings of the Pueblo lifeway occurred around 600 B.C.E., during the time period archaeologists call the Basketmaker II period (dated between 600 B.C.E. and 500 C.E.). These people had evolved from a hunting-and-gathering lifestyle that had dominated in the American Southwest for thousands of years during the Archaic time period. By 600 B.C.E, some groups had begun to experiment with and depend on cultivated corn for a substantial portion of their diet. Early Pueblo groups continued to use natural plant foods and resources and to hunt various game animals to provide protein. This adaptation continued across the northern Southwest for more than a thousand years, with some changes, but nothing dramatic (from our long-term perspective). By 500 C.E., however, fundamental changes had occurred, and the Puebloans had added fired pottery to their tool repertoire, along with cultivation and consumption of beans, another critical addition. These two cultural developments, along with other changes, had a profound effect on Basketmaker II groups, leading to greater sedentism (more time living in the same location) and significant population growth. This period is identified by archaeologists as the Basketmaker III period (500–750 C.E.).

By the Basketmaker III period, many of the distinctive aspects of Puebloan society were in place. These characteristics included: (1) the production and use of plain culinary (cooking) and decorated pottery; (2) construction and use of pit houses, large storage cists, and late in the period, surface rooms; (3) a full commitment to and dependence on the agricultural production of corn, beans, squash, and other crops; and (4) the emergence of varying degrees of economic and sociopolitical differentiation.[1] These basic building blocks, then, laid the foundation of Anasazi-Pueblo culture that continued to evolve through time.

The ensuing Pueblo I period (750–900 C.E.) continued and amplified these trends. Above-ground "pueblo" construction became widespread across the region, although subterranean pit house structures and kivas (undoubtedly the loci of some ceremonial practices) were used. Population was concentrated during this period in various locales across the San Juan Basin, including Chaco Canyon and the Dolores Region (north of Mesa Verde National Park). The first truly large villages, with several hundred inhabitants, were built during this period, in the middle C.E. 800s. Such structures were different from the later Chaco great houses because they grew through accretion and were not planned in advance but certainly reflected the organizational principles that came to fruition during the Chaco Era.

By 850 C.E., Chaco Canyon was home to perhaps 500 to 750 people. Chacoan families lived mostly in small villages or pueblos (apartmentlike dwellings of four to eight rooms per family) occupied by single families or small groups of related families. Although trade in pottery, marine shell, turquoise, obsidian, and a variety of other, rare minerals was commonplace, most families were largely self-reliant. At this time, we see groups of Puebloans spread across the San Juan Basin, in many of the same locales that would later see tremendous growth as Chacoan communities expanded.

In the late 800s, construction began at three of the great houses in

Table 4.1
Chaco Canyon Great Houses

Name	Size	Great Kivas
Pueblo Bonito	650 rooms	3
Chetro Ketl	580 rooms	2
Pueblo del Arroyo	290 rooms	0
Penasco Blanco	220 rooms	4
Wijiji	190 rooms	0
Una Vida	160 rooms	1
Tsin Kletzin	155 rooms	0
Hungo Pavi	150 rooms	1
Kin Kletso	140 rooms	0
Pueblo Alto	130 rooms	0
Casa Chiquito	80 rooms	0
New Alto	50 rooms	0

Chaco: Pueblo Bonito, Penasco Blanco, and Una Vida. These sites were positioned along the Canyon at points where tributary drainages entered Chaco Wash. As archaeologist Gwinn Vivian has pointed out, these sites were built in the best locales for practicing runoff agriculture.[2] By 1050 c.e., these original three great houses had been dramatically expanded and joined by six others. At 1100, three other great houses were built, for a total of twelve in the Canyon. Table 4.1 summarizes information about the eleventh- and early-twelfth-century Chacoan great houses.

RECONSTRUCTED CLIMATE AT CHACO

Before looking closely at the emergence of Chaco as the Puebloan center in the eleventh century, we first need to assess climatic trends. If we look at reconstructed climate in Chaco over several hundred years, what do we see? Figure 4.1 shows 200 years of Palmer Drought Severity Index (PDSI) values reconstructed using the detailed record of tree growth derived from sampling of structural wood at Chaco Canyon.[3] The PDSI measures overall available moisture and is cumulative, mean-

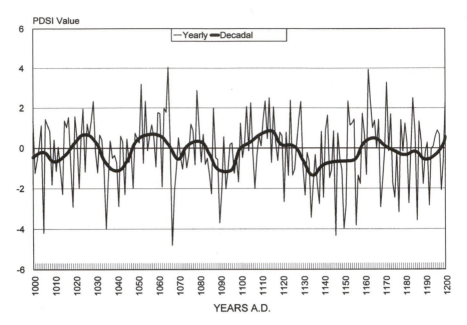

Figure 4.1. Reconstructed Palmer Drought Severity Index values for Chaco Canyon, 1000–1200 C.E.

ing that the effects of a number of preceding bad years, or good years, will be reflected in the value for any given year. A departure from the 0 index value of 2 in either direction is considered significant enough to impact human response to the climatic conditions.[4] According to archaeologist Jeff Dean, however, the positive index values are not as reliable an indication of favorable conditions as negative ones are of poor conditions. For the purposes of this study, then, and to focus on the impact of drought conditions on the prehistoric inhabitants of the area, a drought is considered to be a negative value of 1 or more that lasts for at least ten years. Yearly data were averaged to produce ten-year running averages (i.e., the values from 1015 to 1024 were averaged to produce a single value plotted at 1020). I chose to plot decadal means because human populations rarely respond to changes at a yearly or even multiyear level.[5] In other words, climatic changes of longer duration are necessary to impact human behavior. Thus, a severe drought occurring in a single year (with a PDSI value of negative 5 or 6) is unlikely to have a lasting effect on human behavior unless it is preceded or followed by other drought years.

Looking first at yearly PDSI values, we see a great deal of fluctuation between 1000 and 1200 C.E. Decadal running averages smooth out some of this variation and provide a good climatic pattern with which to compare human activity in Chaco. The 1000s started out below average and did not have good conditions for farmers until 1020 C.E. Then a drought occurred from 1030 to 1050, followed by predominantly good conditions until 1080. At 1080, a twenty-year drought began. By 1100, the climate was favorable again, lasting until 1130 C.E. At this time, a long drought lasting until about 1060 ensued. With a short ten years of good climate between 1057 and 1067, the climate again was unfavorable until 1095.

At this fairly broad level of analysis, we can see that the climate of Chaco Canyon, as measured by the PDSI 10-year running averages, was highly variable over 300 years. Until the long drought that began around 1130 C.E., conditions in Chaco followed a fairly regular pattern of 10 to 15 years of good climate, followed by 10 to 15 years of poor climate. The surge in construction that began around 1020 C.E. coincided with a good period, but a drought followed, from 1030 to 1050 C.E.

One conclusion that emerges after examining the climatic record is that the rise of Chacoan society occurred during a 300-year period of highly variable climate. At a finer scale, the 1020 to 1080 C.E. period of greatest Chacoan construction in the Canyon, and expansion in the larger Chacoan world, coincided with periods of good and bad climate. A good climate, then, does appear to have contributed to the rise of Chaco. In contrast, the drought that began around 1130 C.E. and lasted until 1160, with a short respite, and then continued until almost 1200, was undoubtedly devastating to the Chacoan agricultural economy. Whereas the climatic fluctuations produced serious effects on the Chacoan lifeway, it is perhaps more remarkable that through much of the uncertain times the Chacoans adapted and life continued.

CHACO COALESCES AND EMERGES, 1050–1100 C.E.

With a basic understanding of the roots of Chacoan society and a look at climate in Chaco, let us proceed to a short exploration of critical changes in the mid-eleventh century and beyond that led to the unique and short-lived Chacoan society. The outstanding potential of Chaco Canyon's north side for runoff agriculture on a large scale and above-average rainfall for several decades seem to have been the most important factors that initially allowed Chaco to flourish.[6] These circumstances came about after 975 c.e., and the three initial Chacoan great houses (Pueblo Bonito, Penasco Blanco, and Una Vida) experienced substantial growth. Most Chacoan archaeologists agree that the period between 1000 and 1050 c.e. was critical to the emergence of Chaco Canyon as a regional ritual center.[7] Many archaeologists relate the rise of Chaco to favorable climatic conditions. Clearly, during many of these years, a wet and warm climate allowed for expanded agricultural production. Surplus production, in turn, allowed more people to be supported in the Canyon and led to increased construction of great houses, small houses, and other features such as roads and shrines.

By 1060 c.e., the cluster of structures in what has been termed "downtown" Chaco—the immediate vicinity of Pueblo Bonito—was laid out and largely constructed. Within about a square kilometer were four great houses—Pueblo Bonito, Chetro Ketl, Pueblo del Arroyo, and Pueblo Alto, along with numerous small house pueblos, and the stand-alone great kiva at Casa Rinconada. Development of the North Road occurred after 1050 c.e., and all of the northern outliers postdate 1075 c.e.

With downtown Chaco fully constructed, work also proceeded at other great houses. By 1070 c.e., Chacoan great houses at Hungo Pavi, Una Vida, Wijiji, Penasco Blanco, and Tsin Kletzin were largely complete and occupied. It was during this time, the interval roughly from 1050 to 1080 c.e., that the rituality (Chacoan society organized through ritual and ceremony) in Chaco emerged.[8] Chaco ritual was, by this time, "proven," and the appeal of the Chacoan approach rapidly expanded. As a result, more and more people came into Chaco, some to try to settle and others to participate in periodic ceremonies. After 1100 c.e., the last three Chaco Canyon great houses were finished—Kin Kletso, Casa Chiquito, and New Alto—and Chaco reached its final, constructed form.

By 1090 c.e., northern Chacoan outliers at Chimney Rock, Salmon, Wallace, Lowry, and Morris site 41 (and several other sites) were built and occupied. The East and West Pueblos at Aztec were built between 1105 and 1125 c.e., This northern shift of focus, of people, and perhaps, of ceremonial importance was complete by 1110–25 c.e., when Aztec emerged as the largest Chacoan complex.

What happened in Chaco, then, between 1100 and 1130 c.e.? Archaeologist Jim Judge suggests that Chaco's preeminence began to fade in the C.E. 1090s, as a result of declining agricultural returns because of the drought that occurred between 1080 and 1100 C.E. The shift to the north, then, follows this "period of doubt" in Chaco, when the society probably did not appear functional to the population because of declining harvests.[9] Judge suggests that the populace lost confidence in the Chacoan leadership and that the system began to unravel.

An important question to raise at this juncture relates to the identity of the colonists that journeyed first to Salmon (in the late 1080s), then to Aztec (in the early 1100s). Was this northern movement initiated by the Chacoan leadership (presumably based in Pueblo Bonito)? Or were the emigrants a disaffected group in the Canyon whose lands were marginalized by the drought? The consensus of Chacoan researchers seems to lie with the first scenario—that the leadership in Chaco became convinced of the need to migrate. Salmon Pueblo, then, was the first attempt to establish a foothold in the San Juan region. Salmon, however, was not the final destination. Construction at the West Pueblo of Aztec began only fifteen years (at 1105 C.E.) after the founding of Salmon. Aztec's East Pueblo was constructed in the late 1110s and early 1120s. I suggest that the Chacoans who founded Salmon stayed only about a generation, until 1115–20 C.E., before heading north to Aztec, to concentrate effort on the East Pueblo.[10] I would further propose that the Chacoans at Salmon found the San Juan River overly difficult to use for irrigation because of its large size and the devastating flooding that occurred. The Aztec pueblos were built on the Animas River, which by contrast, was about one-third as big as the San Juan and undoubtedly more amenable to the water management techniques that the Chacoans had used in Chaco Canyon.

POST-1130 C.E. CHACOAN SOCIETY

By 1130 C.E., a region-wide drought was under way. Although the ancient Puebloans had no way of knowing how long the drought would last, this was nevertheless the second drought to occur within a few decades and perhaps was viewed by the Chacoan masses as a failure of the rituality. By 1150 C.E., the drought continued unabated and by this time had probably completely disrupted the Chaco System. We can infer disruption because no new construction was initiated in Chaco Canyon or in any of the outliers after 1130 c.e. The volume of imported items, particularly pottery, dropped significantly in sites that were occupied into this period.

In 1130 c.e., Chaco Canyon was bursting at its seams. Twelve great houses and numerous smaller sites were occupied, and it is likely that all types of resources (water, wood for fires, agricultural fields, native plants used for food and medicine, and game animals) in the Canyon and in nearby areas were being used at their maximum level. With so many great houses to manage, high resident population levels at small house sites, as well as the periodic gatherings of great numbers of people, the Chacoan leadership was probably stressed. In the face of these growing challenges, the 1130 c.e. drought probably proved to be the proverbial straw that broke the camel's back. Thus, the drought is best viewed not as the sole cause of the Chacoan collapse but as a major contributing factor.

Although the data are less than conclusive, some of the great houses in Chaco, and across the region (Salmon Pueblo, for example) show signs of occupation through the middle 1100s. It seems clear that some of the population "held on" in the face of the environmental conditions. By the late c.e. 1180s, the drought was ending across much of the region. In the north, Salmon and Aztec Pueblos both experienced growth and a significant increase in population by the early 1200s. Some Chaco Canyon great houses were used well into the 1200s as well.

THE c.e. 1200s AFTER CHACO

By 1200 c.e., I suspect that the Chaco System was a fading memory for the ancient Puebloans. Certainly, the great houses in Chaco Canyon still projected monumentality and were still the focus of pilgrimages. Further, archaeological data show sites in the Canyon, including most of the great houses, were occupied and served as residences. But, to use a modern metaphor, the magic was gone.

With the late-eleventh-century movement to the north, the founding of Salmon and Aztec Pueblos, and the construction of a huge complex of great houses and ritual structures at Aztec, we can ask the question: Was Aztec the successor to Pueblo Bonito? Did Chacoan society endure through the twelfth century and reemerge after 1200 c.e.? Steve Lekson has suggested that Aztec was the descendant capital of the Chacoan world in the 1200s.[11] Lekson based his argument on the presence of Chacoan architecture at Aztec and the huge complex that included three great houses, great kivas, and at least two triwall structures. The Aztec Community is quite impressive, even today in ruins. Aztec may have been built by the Chacoan leadership as the new Chaco capital in the north. If so, then Aztec "presided" over the Chacoan world for perhaps two or three decades, until Chacoan society collapsed by 1150 C.E.

To answer the first question, yes, Aztec endured through the C.E. 1100s. And by the early 1200s, the data indicate that Aztec was "booming" once again. But, in my opinion, Aztec cannot be considered the Chacoan capital of the C.E. 1200s for one simple reason: Chacoan society, as most archaeologists have defined and as we have explored in this volume, was gone by 1150 C.E. The C.E. 1200s across the northern Pueblo world represented a return to mostly local concerns, after at least 150 years of Chacoan organization and structure. Pueblos occupied through the 1200s (Salmon, for example) reveal a much more local orientation—ceramics were not traded as far and wide. Architecture returned to a pre-Chacoan state with river cobbles, blocky sandstone, and other local materials widely used. Patterns of animal use also showed a more local orientation. Use of domestic turkeys soared, and big game such as deer, antelope, and elk were much less common than in Chacoan times. In short, Chacoan society, as it had existed in the eleventh and twelfth centuries, was gone by 1200 C.E.

NOTES

1. Paul F. Reed, ed., *Foundations of Anasazi Culture: The Basketmaker–Pueblo Transition* (Salt Lake City: University of Utah Press, 2000).

2. R. Gwinn Vivian, *The Chacoan Prehistory of the San Juan Basin* (San Diego: Academic Press, 1990).

3. PDSI data were provided by Jeff Dean, of the Laboratory of Tree-ring Research at the University of Arizona, as a result of years of research on the Southwest Paleoclimatic Project.

4. Jeffrey S. Dean, "A Model of Anasazi Behavioral Adaptation," in *The Anasazi in a Changing Environment*, edited by G. J. Gumerman (Cambridge: Cambridge University Press, 1988), pp. 25–44.

5. Ibid.

6. W. James Judge, "A Trial Timeline for Chacoan Society and Polity" (draft manuscript prepared for Chaco Capstone Conference, Albuquerque, NM, October 2002); R. Gwinn Vivian, Carla Van West, and Jeffrey S. Dean, "Chaco Ecology and Economy: Final Draft Synthesis" (draft manuscript prepared for Chaco Capstone Conference, Albuquerque, NM, October 2002).

7. Judge, "A Trial Timeline," pp. 4–10, passim.

8. Ibid.

9. Ibid., p. 11.

10. Paul F. Reed, "Salmon Ruins: From Cynthia Irwin-Williams's Vision to a Central Place in the Totah," *Archaeology Southwest* 16, no. 2 (2002): 7–9.

11. Stephen H. Lekson, *The Chaco Meridian: Centers of Political Power in the Ancient Southwest* (Walnut Creek, CA: Alta Mira Press, 1999).

CHAPTER 5

CHACOAN SOCIETY AT 1100 C.E.: A STATIC VIEW

With a good understanding of the chronology of Chacoan society in mind, let us turn to a description of its primary characteristics—a static or synchronic view. What are the characteristics that made the Puebloan Society at Chaco unique? How did the Chacoan great houses appear, and of what materials were they constructed? How did the Chacoans make a living? Or, as archaeologists refer to it, what were their patterns of subsistence? What craft industries did the Chacoans pursue? How did roads and stairways figure in the Chaco world? What was the size and nature of the human population of Chaco? How were the Chacoans organized socially?

CHACOAN GREAT HOUSES

Let us begin with the great houses—the monumental markers of "medieval" Chacoan presence. Chacoan great houses are distinct from the majority of Puebloan structures of earlier and later periods for several reasons. First, great houses were constructed symmetrically and massively, with a specific type of architecture described as core-veneer. The massive walls (up to a meter thick) consisted of a rubble, dirt, or masonry core with inner and outer veneers of carefully selected, shaped sandstone slabs. Part of the need for such massive walls was to support upper stories that rose as high as four stories at sites such as Pueblo Bonito and Chetro Ketl. But even single-story sites like Pueblo Alto were constructed using the massive core-veneer technique. Clearly, core-veneer was more than just a construction technique and probably had intrinsic importance to the Chacoans. Tied to the core-veneer technique were a number of distinct types or styles of masonry facing patterns. Neil Judd initially identified these types in the 1920s and created a typology of four types. In the 1980s, Steve Lekson expanded Judd's typology and assigned dates to the styles.[1] Beyond massive core-veneer construction and distinctive masonry types, Chacoan great houses were also characterized by kivas (round ceremonial rooms) built directly into the pueblo (described as "blocked-in" kivas), some of which were built at the second- and third-story levels. The many rooms built within Chacoan structures were also huge by Pueblo standards, up to twelve feet square, with ceilings sometimes over ten feet high.

Certainly, the effort required to raise the Chacoan great houses was massive. More than 200,000 trees (mostly varieties of pine, fir, and spruce, with some juniper) were used to build roofs and support walls in the twelve primary Chaco Canyon great houses. Fine sandstone slabs and blocks were quarried at sites in the Canyon, and from areas beyond, when the best sources were exhausted. These efforts and the imposing size and height of these structures, and other factors, support the idea that the great houses were landscape monuments (in addition to having other functions). As monuments, the great houses were intended to impress and awe local residents, as well as outsiders.

Thus, Chacoan great houses were massive, tall structures and were analogous to (although smaller than) the medieval castles spread across Europe in the eleventh and twelfth centuries. They were visible across the landscape for miles, and beyond Chaco Canyon, great houses were often built on hills, ridges, and other high points to increase their visibility. Pueblo Pintado, for example, is visible today for several miles when approaching from the north. The analogy can be carried beyond appearance, as well, because like medieval castles, Chacoan great houses were the economic and social centers of the eleventh- and twelfth-century Puebloan landscape.

SUBSISTENCE PRACTICES—MAKING A LIVING IN CHACO

Chacoan subsistence, like that of all ancient Pueblo groups, depended on the production of three primary crops: corn, beans, and squash (including various types, as well as pumpkins and gourds). We can easily envision the fertile plain of the Canyon floor at 1075 c.e. covered with these crops, with corn particularly dominant and visible, as far as the eye could see. The Chacoans were, first and foremost, subsistence farmers, and this agricultural basis underlay every aspect of Chacoan society. As modern Pueblo people do today, we can infer that the Chacoans tried to produce a significant agricultural surplus—one that went well beyond their yearly needs—and that these surpluses were what allowed the monumental construction to occur. We can suggest that crop surpluses "funded" monumental construction of Chacoan great houses, great kivas, roads, and agricultural support facilities in several ways. First, surplus food was probably used to feed and thus compensate workers who undertook construction activities. Second, food surpluses were traded for more durable goods such as finished pottery, stone tools, basketry, woven items such as clothing and pouches, digging sticks, and bows and arrows. These items could then be offered as "payment" for work completed. Aside from situations that may have led to direct compensation for labor, more indirect means were probably also operating. For example, we can infer that as some Chacoan leaders had success with agricultural pursuits, they were able to attract additional people to live in or near great houses. Thus, the overall pool of people available for a variety of tasks relating to construction, farming, or craft production would have increased and contributed to the rise of these leaders.

Beyond agricultural pursuits, the Chacoan undertook a number of other subsistence activities in the course of living their lives. Hunting a variety of game animals, including deer, antelope, elk, and rabbits, was very important, providing sources of much needed protein. Bears, mountain lions, and smaller predators and birds were hunted to provide hides, claws, and other body parts for rituals. A great variety of natural plants were gathered, some for food like pigweed and wild mustard, others for ritual or medicinal purposes (including sage, Mormon tea, and wild tobacco).

TURQUOISE INDUSTRY IN CHACO

Common hallmarks of complex societies include sophisticated systems of economy and trade. In certain respects, Chaco follows this pattern. Craft specialization, wherein part- or full-time specialists produce certain products for a society (such as leather goods, jewelry, pottery, or woven textiles), typically characterizes the economy in such societies. In Chaco, the production of turquoise pendants and beads was widespread, occurring prior to the main florescence of Chaco in the eleventh century. The importance of turquoise was clear early in Chaco's history. George Pepper's work for the American Museum of Natural History at Pueblo Bonito revealed more than 56,000 pieces of worked turquoise (mostly pendants and beads) from a single room.[2] Turquoise worked in Chaco was traded far and wide, perhaps even traveling as far south as Mayan sites in the Yucatan. Archaeologists have identified numerous turquoise sources in the Southwest, and at least some of the Chacoan turquoise was derived from the Cerillos mine, near Santa Fe.

Archaeological work at several small house sites in the East Community at Chaco has revealed evidence of a widespread turquoise industry.[3] Turquoise production occurred at many small house sites, and at great houses, and does not appear to have been restricted or limited. In contrast to widespread production, consumption of turquoise was very restricted. Almost one-quarter of the beads from Chaco were recovered from only two burials in Rooms 32 and 33 at Pueblo Bonito.[4] Clearly, consumption and use of turquoise items were restricted—turquoise did not circulate freely among all members of Chacoan society. The burial rooms with the tremendous amounts of turquoise were nearby rooms holding ritual artifacts, including some turquoise items. Thus, it seems reasonable to conclude that turquoise artifacts played an important role in Chacoan ritual.

CHACO'S MESOAMERICAN (MEXICAN) CONNECTION

Chacoan archaeologists and researchers have long thought that a connection existed between Chaco and the advanced societies located to the south in Mesoamerica.[5] Items such as copper bells and exotic macaws (parrots) indicate trade with areas to the south. Even today, few southwestern archaeologists would deny that some level of contact, trade, or exchange occurred between these areas. The major point of contention and debate, however, centers on the extent and nature of contact between Mesoamerican societies and Chaco Canyon. Some archaeologists believe that Mesoamerican traders (*pochteca* or *trocadores*) were frequent visitors in Chaco Canyon and exerted considerable influence on Chacoan affairs.[6]

Others have proposed more radical scenarios for Mesoamerican involvement in Chacoan society, with archaeologist Christy Turner suggesting that a group of Mesoamericans terrorized the Southwest, using Chaco as their base of operations.[7] Such views assume that the Toltecs or other Mesoamericans were responsible for the rise of Chacoan society. Most archaeologists would agree that little or no evidence supports the hypothesis that Chaco arose as a result of direct outside influence.

More moderate views of Mesoamerican-Chaco interaction suggest that goods like copper bells and macaws were exchanged, perhaps directly or through intermediaries. Beyond this, it is possible that actually Mesoamerican, perhaps Toltec, traders visited Chaco Canyon from time to time. But the presence of these individuals is not believed to have dramatically affected the course of events at Chaco Canyon.

PRODUCTION OF POTTERY AND STONE TOOLS

The production and use of ceramic (pottery) containers and stone tools follows the general trends seen in other areas of Chacoan economics. That is, early (875–1000 C.E.) patterns are similar to other Puebloan areas around Chaco, with a few exceptions. The Chuska Valley, which lies seventy-five kilometers (about forty-seven miles) west of Chaco Canyon, is an early and a persistently important area for the Chacoans. A valuable stone tool resource, Narbona Pass chert, derives from the Chuska Mountains. This material comprises a high percentage of the stone raw materials used at Chacoan sites and was either directly obtained by Chacoans or traded into the Canyon. Other raw materials, including obsidian from the Jemez Mountains east of Chaco, were also used for stone tool production.[8]

Chuska Valley pottery was highly valued by the Chacoans, and high percentages of it were imported into the Canyon after 1020 C.E.; more than 50 percent of the utilitarian (cooking) pottery at the great house site of Pueblo Alto was of Chuskan origin.[9] Chuskan pottery was traded far and wide in the Pueblo Southwest, especially during the Chaco Era. In addition to the imported Chuskan pottery, the Chacoan themselves made some pottery in the Canyon. Although distinct kiln facilities have not been found in great numbers, pottery-quality clay and the sand favored by Chacoan potters are still present in sediments at Chaco. It is likely that a good percentage of the ceramic containers used and broken at sites in the Canyon was produced in the local area.

CHACOAN ROAD NETWORK

One of the more compelling aspects of the Chacoan world is the network of roads that were constructed between about 1050 and 1100 C.E. Perhaps 400 miles of roads have been detected using aerial photography, and many segments have been "ground-truthed"—confirmed by a field inspection. Typically, the roadways are very wide, up to nine meters (about thirty feet) across, and run arrow-straight across huge expanses of flat land, climbing up steep mesas and descending directly into canyons. Roads were not built to follow topographic features or use natural contours, suggesting that easy or fast transportation of goods was not their primary function. Roads are associated with several of the great houses in Chaco Canyon, including Pueblo Alto, Penasco Blanco, and Pueblo Pintado to the east.

Road segments are also associated with many of the outliers. Aztec Ruins, for example, has evidence of at least two road segments that emanate from its great houses. Other great houses were probably built as part of a road-related landscape. Halfway House, for example, is a small Chacoan great house that lies along the Great North Road (which runs north from Pueblo Alto for a distance of more than fifty kilometers (about thirty-one miles) toward the San Juan River). Pierre's Ruin lies a few miles north along the same ancient thoroughfare.

A compelling component of the roadway system is the network of numerous stairways, ramps, and other supportive features. Within Chaco Canyon, several stairways were cut into the sandstone flanks of the mesa walls. Most notable is the Jackson Stairway, on the south side of the Canyon, east of Pueblo Bonito. William Henry Jackson was the first Euro-American to document this dramatic, beautiful, and highly functional construction that bears his name. The stairway was painstakingly carved into the rock by a skilled and patient stoneworker. Other such steps and carved passageways are known from the earliest Basketmaker times and throughout the Pueblo cultural sequence. Thus, they are not unique to the Chacoans. But their extensive use in a road network is uniquely Chacoan.

Initial interpretations of the roads envisioned their use strictly as present and how many of these are great houses. Undoubtedly, some undiscovered sites, large and small, still exist. But given the extent of archaeological survey completed, it is unlikely that any additional great houses will be found in Chaco Canyon. Thus, we have a good understanding of sites in the Canyon that were part of Chacoan society. We have good counts for great houses, great kivas, small houses, and the total number of rooms and kivas in use during the peak of Chacoan culture. At least eighteen great houses exist in the greater Chaco Canyon area, what has been called the Chaco Core.

With eighteen great houses, numerous great kivas, and dozens of smaller pueblos going full throttle by 1050 C.E., Chaco was home to thousands of people. Exact estimates of Chaco provoke some of the most spirited debate among southwestern archaeologists. Estimates vary from below 1,000 (which seems unreasonably low) to over 10,000. (Early archaeologists counted rooms in all the great houses and small pueblos and applied a standard number of three persons per room to get these superhigh estimates). Most Chacoan archaeologists would probably agree that the number of people living in Chaco Canyon at 1075 C.E., what archaeologists term a *momentary population*, was between 1,500 and 4,000. Some recent studies have tried to minimize the amount of labor that would have been necessary to build and maintain the great houses, to undertake agricultural activities, to maintain water and soil control facilities, and to build the Chaco roads. Nevertheless, the scale of these undertakings, along with their often simultaneous scheduling, required a substantial and well-organized labor force.

Research has revealed that Chaco had a very diverse genetic population. Analysis of human burials from Pueblo Bonito, in particular, has shown at least two distinct populations based on skeletal studies.[12] This research has also shown that the residents of Pueblo Bonito were taller and healthier and had better nutrition than contemporary residents of small house sites. This suggests a hierarchy, with "richer," perhaps higher-status individuals living in the great houses.

A more recent study has confirmed the diversity of Chaco Canyon and Pueblo Bonito specifically.[13] In this study, human remains from the western part of Pueblo Bonito showed a close relationship with Rio Grande populations, while burials from the north portion of Pueblo Bonito matched a Basketmaker group from Grand Gulch, Utah. Remains from several small house sites in Chaco revealed a relationship with transportation corridors, to bring people and goods from the hinterlands into the Canyon and back out to the outliers. But we must remember that the Puebloans did not have wheeled vehicles or draft animals. Thus, thirty-foot-wide roads were not a necessity for transportation; narrow footpaths, which have been documented across the Southwest, were certainly sufficient for travel. The overbuilt Chacoan roads would certainly have been useful paths to take into Chaco, or back into the hinterland, but it is unlikely that they were built for that purpose.

Thus, we have to look for another primary explanation for the roads. One productive hypothesis that has emerged from recent studies suggests that roads, like the great houses, are landscape monuments. Many of the roads do not appear to go anywhere in particular. The North Road runs almost due north and points in the direction of Salmon Pueblo (built around 1090 C.E.) and the Aztec Community (built beginning in 1105 C.E.). But, based on the evidence, the North Road does not go to Salmon or Aztec. Instead, it appears to represent a landscape monument—a great arrow that points north. In addition to serving a monumental purpose, roads also provided "public works" projects for the Chaco community that kept groups of men (presumably) occupied.

Archaeologists have proposed that the Chacoan roads were built wide for ceremonial processions that made their way into and out of Chaco Canyon during important ritual observances.[10] Other interpretations have suggested that some roads link great houses of different ages, serving as links through time, as well as space.[11]

Connected to the notion of the roads as landscape monuments is an inferred cosmological function. North, of course, has an obvious connection to the sun, because of the sun's northern position at noon. As discussed in Chapter 7, solar and lunar movements and observations were a critical part of Chacoan cosmology. Chacoan roads, then, mesh with this concept of Chacoan cosmology and Chacoan use and construction of a sacred landscape (including great houses, earthen architecture surrounding great houses, great kivas, and roads) that reflected cosmology.

POPULATION

Much of the land area of Chaco Canyon has been archaeologically surveyed. As a result, we have a good idea of how many total sites are some from the Village of the Great Kivas, to the south near Zuni Pueblo. Although these results represent only the beginning of what will be a much larger study, and made use of a limited sample from only specific regions in the Southwest, they are nevertheless significant. Chaco Canyon appears to have been the home of a very diverse group of people that probably represented a number of ethnic and linguistic populations. The presence of numerous macaws (parrots) in Pueblo Bonito suggests an ancestral connection to what became the macaw-parrot clans at Zuni and Hopi pueblos. The macaws found include primarily two species: scarlet macaws, with beautiful red, yellow, and blue feathers, and military macaws, which are predominantly green. Together, these findings indicate that Chaco Canyon was probably the ancestral home to people who live today at Hopi, Zuni, many of the Rio Grande pueblos, and probably other pueblos.

SOCIAL ORGANIZATION

What type of social organization did the Chacoans have? Were they organized like the Hopi and other Western Pueblos, with matrilineal and matrilocal (living near the woman's family) clans? Or were they more like the Eastern Pueblos, with weak or nonexistent clans and a village-wide bilateral moiety organization and various ceremonial societies or sodalities? Or were they governed with an organization that is not present among the contemporary Pueblos?

Various views of Chacoan social organization have been offered over the years. Here I cannot review all of these proposed explanations, but a few possibilities can be explored. One early suggestion regarding Chaco organization linked the inhabitants of the great houses with one type of social order and the small pueblo dwellers with a simpler form of organization.[14] Expanding on this view, Gwinn Vivian further proposed that two distinct ethnic groups built and lived in the great houses and small pueblos, respectively.

In the late 1970s and 1980s, models that viewed Chacoan society as hierarchical and ranked, with distinct differences among social classes, were proposed. In this view, Chacoan developments were led by a group of permanent leaders, who made important decisions and directed the course of Chaco's evolution. Putting Chaco into a typology developed to classify societies, proponents of this position described Chacoan society as a chiefdom.

By the late 1980s, it was clear to many archaeologists that simply classifying Chaco and trying to fit it into a rigid typology was not going to lead to enlightenment or understanding. The great houses in Chaco Canyon, as well as the outliers, had seemed different and unusual within the Pueblo world to archaeologists and laypeople alike, for more than 100 years. Maybe Chaco really was different and unique.

Getting away from conventional anthropological categories, Chacoan archaeologists interested in social organization began exploring a variety of issues, including power, competition, status, ritual, and complexity. From this reconsideration of issues, a number of new and innovative perspectives on Chacoan social relations emerged. Limitations of space preclude me from discussing all of these approaches. I will, however, highlight several contrasting views of Chacoan societal organization.

One recent school of thought among Chacoan archaeologists emphasizes the role of competition in driving the construction of great houses and other Chacoan developments.[15] To explain the presence of so many great houses in Chaco Canyon, competition among rival leaders is invoked. In this view, Chacoan leaders built great houses to improve their status, a type of self-aggrandizement, and to outcompete other aspiring leaders. To succeed, leaders needed to control prime agricultural lands and produce an agricultural surplus to feed supporters and for trading purposes, and they needed to attract a loyal group of followers. These leaders are not seen as situational—they were permanent, and they had higher social status than other individuals in the Pueblo.

Another recent reconstruction of Chacoan social organization also emphasizes the role of leadership but invokes a central, organized, and hierarchical system with Chaco as the center.[16] Great houses were planned and built by a central authority, not only in Chaco Canyon but also across the Pueblo Southwest. In this view, most (if not all) of Chaco's outliers were planned and built by the Chacoans, as part of an overall plan to colonize and control a large portion of the ancient Pueblo world.

In contrast to models that view Chacoan society as driven by competition and hierarchy, another new approach to social organization envisions a unified but cooperative endeavor. Chacoan society is seen as the result of an integrated, cooperative, and largely egalitarian effort without significant competition or social hierarchy.[17] In this view, ritual and ceremony are paramount concerns, and ritual specialists or priests are the leaders.

Between these two viewpoints lies significant middle ground, and not surprisingly, some archaeologists have drawn from both models, and others, to argue that neither extreme is correct. Marxist views of Chacoan archaeology reject the false dichotomy between hierarchical and egalitarian social relations. Instead, Marxist archaeologists view Pueblo society as a complex, communal organization with elements of hierarchy present but subsumed within the communal structure.[18]

We have barely scratched the surface with this brief exploration of Chacoan social organization. Clearly, Chacoan society was complex and is not easily classified or explained with the typologies usually used by archaeologists.

NOTES

1. Stephen H. Lekson, *Great Pueblo Architecture of Chaco Canyon, New Mexico* (Albuquerque: University of New Mexico Press, 1986).

2. George Pepper, *Pueblo Bonito* (New York: Anthropological Papers of the American Museum of Natural History, vol. 27, 1920; reprint, Albuquerque: University of New Mexico Press, 1996); Thomas C. Windes, "Blue Notes: The Chacoan Turquoise Industry in the San Juan Basin," in *Anasazi Regional Organization and the Chaco System*, edited by D. Doyel, Anthropological Papers no. 5 (Albuquerque: Maxwell Museum of Anthropology, 2001), p. 159; F. Joan Mathien, "The Organization of Turquoise Production and Consumption by the Prehistoric Chacoans," *American Antiquity* 66 (2001): 103–118.

3. Windes, "Blue Notes," pp. 159–170, passim.

4. Peter N. Peregrine, "Matrilocality, Corporate Strategy, and the Organization of Production in the Chacoan World," *American Antiquity* 66 (2001): 42; Pepper, *Pueblo Bonito*.

5. Pepper, *Pueblo Bonito*; Neil M. Judd, *The Material Culture of Pueblo Bonito*, Smithsonian Miscellaneous Collections, vol. 124 (Washington, DC: Smithsonian Institution, 1954).

6. Theodore R. Frisbie, "High Status Burials in the Greater Southwest: An Interpretative Synthesis," in *Across the Chichimec Sea: Papers in Honor of J. Charles Kelley*, edited by C. L. Riley and B. C. Hedrick (Carbondale: Southern Illinois University Press, 1978), pp. 202–227; J. C. Kelley, "The Mobile Merchants of Molino," in *Ripples in the Chichimec Sea: New Considerations of*

Southwestern-Mesoamerican Interactions, edited by F. J. Mathien and R. H. McGuire (Carbondale: Southern Illinois University Press, 1986), pp. 81–104; Robert H. Lister, "Mesoamerican Influences at Chaco Canyon, New Mexico," in *Across the Chichimec Sea: Papers in Honor of J. Charles Kelley*, edited by C. L. Riley and B. C. Hedrick (Carbondale: Southern Illinois University Press, 1978), pp. 233–241.

7. Christy G. Turner II and Jacqueline A. Turner, *Man Corn: Cannibalism and Violence in the Prehistoric American Southwest* (Salt Lake City: University of Utah Press, 1999).

8. A number of recent research papers address the issues of production in Chaco Canyon including H. Wolcott Toll, "Organization of Production in the Chaco Era" (draft manuscript prepared for Chaco Capstone Conference, Albuquerque, NM, October 2002); F. Joan Mathien, "Artifacts from Pueblo Bonito: One Hundred Years of Interpretation," in *Pueblo Bonito: Center of the Chacoan World*, edited by Jill E. Neitzel (Washington, DC: Smithsonian Books, 2003), pp. 127–142; and Cathy M. Cameron, "Pink Chert, Projectile Points, and the Chacoan System," *American Antiquity* 66 (2001): 79–102.

9. H. Wolcott Toll, Eric Blinman, and C. Dean Wilson, "Chaco in the Context of Regional Ceramic Systems," in *Anasazi Regional Organization and the Chaco System*, edited by David E. Doyel, Anthropological Papers no. 5 (Albuquerque: Maxwell Museum of Anthropology, 2001), pp. 147–158.

10. John R. Stein and Stephen H. Lekson, "Anasazi Ritual Landscapes," in *Anasazi Regional Organization and the Chaco System*, edited by David E. Doyel, Anthropological Papers no. 5 (Albuquerque: Maxwell Museum of Anthropology, 2001), pp. 87–100; John Kantner, "Ancient Roads, Modern Mapping: Evaluating Chaco Anasazi Roadways Using GIS Technology," *Expedition* 39, no. 3 (1997): 49–61; Michael P. Marshall, "The Chacoan Roads—A Cosmological Interpretation," in *Anasazi Architecture and American Design*, edited by B. H. Morrow and V. B. Price (Albuquerque: University of New Mexico Press, 1997), pp. 62–74.

11. Andrew P. Fowler and John Stein, "The Anasazi Great House in Space, Time, and Paradigm," in *Anasazi Regional Organization and the Chaco System*, edited by David E. Doyel, Anthropological Papers no. 5 (Albuquerque: Maxwell Museum of Anthropology, 2001), pp. 102–122; Ruth Van Dyke, "The Chaco Connection: Evaluating Bonito Style Architecture in Outlier Communities," *Journal of Anthropological Archaeology* 18 (1999): 471–506.

12. Nancy J. Akins, *A Biocultural Approach to Human Burials from Chaco Canyon, New Mexico* (Santa Fe, NM: Reports of the Chaco Center no. 8, 1986).

13. Michael A. Schillaci, "The Development of Population Diversity at Chaco Canyon," *Kiva* 68 (2003): 221–246.

14. Originally proposed by Clyde Kluckhohn, the "Co-Tradition" model was revived by Gordon Vivian and later by Gwinn Vivian. Clyde Kluckhohn, "Discussion," in *Preliminary Report on the 1937 Excavations: Bc 50–51, Chaco Canyon, New Mexico,* edited by C. Kluckhohn and P. Reiter (Albuquerque: University of New Mexico Bulletin 345, Anthropological Series 3(2), 1939), pp. 151–162; Gordon Vivian, *The Three-C Site, an Early Pueblo II Ruin in Chaco Canyon, New Mexico* (Albuquerque: University of New Mexico Publications in Anthropology 13, 1965); R. Gwinn Vivian, *The Chacoan Prehistory of the San Juan Basin* (San Diego: Academic Press, 1990).

15. Archaeologists Lynne Sebastian and John Kantner, separately, are the primary proponents of the "competition" model. Lynne Sebastian, *The Chaco Anasazi: Sociopolitical Evolution in the Prehistoric Southwest* (Cambridge: Cambridge University Press, 1992); John Kantner, "Political Competition among the Chaco Anasazi of the American Southwest," *Journal of Anthropological Archaeology* 15, no. 1 (1996): 41–105.

16. Steve Lekson is the primary advocate of the centralized model of Chaco, although other archaeologists have proposed similar models. Lekson has written numerous articles expressing these views. The primary reference is Stephen H. Lekson, *The Chaco Meridian: Centers of Political Power in the Ancient Southwest* (Walnut Creek, CA: Alta Mira Press, 1999).

17. Many Chacoan archaeologists have proposed hypotheses regarding social organization that fall into this general view. This view seems to represent a consensus or, at least, a majority opinion of the scholars gathered for the Chaco Synthesis Conferences.

18. Randall McGuire and Dean J. Saitta, "Although They Have Petty Captions, They Obey Them Badly: The Dialectics of Prehispanic Western Pueblo Social Groups," *American Antiquity* 61 (1996): 197–216; Dean J. Saitta, "Power, Labor, and the Dynamics of Change in Chacoan Political Economy," *American Antiquity* 62, no. 1 (1997): 7–26.

CHAPTER 6

CHACO CANYON'S OUTLYING COMMUNITIES: THE OUTLIERS

Moving beyond the confines of Chaco Canyon proper, we see that the flourishing society centered at Chaco was quite far-flung. Archaeologists are literally finding new Chacoan-affiliated sites, outliers, every few years in increasingly remote areas. But, at the present time, perhaps 150 Chaco outliers dating between 1050 and 1125 C.E. are known. As a group, these sites are similar to those found in Chaco but are *generally* smaller in size, have fewer rooms, fewer kivas, many do not meet Chacoan standards for architecture, and most are surrounded by clusters of smaller sites (villages, smaller pueblos, and nonresidential farming and other special-use areas). Notable exceptions include the ancient Aztec and Salmon Communities in the San Juan region (see Figure 1.1), both of which were large and well constructed enough to easily pass for a Chaco Canyon town. These two sites are discussed separately below, because of their special role in the northern portion of the ancient Chacoan world.

In extent, Chacoan outliers are found across four modern American states. Chimney Rock Pueblo lies several miles west of Pagosa Springs, Colorado, and represents the northeastern outpost of Chacoan (and of all Puebloan) settlements. Guadalupe Pueblo lies far to the south of Chimney Rock in New Mexico and anchored the southeastern portion of the Chacoan world. Moving across New Mexico to the northwest, the Cottonwood Falls great house in southeast Utah lies near the northwest edge of Chacoan influence. Lastly, Wupatki in northeast Arizona is the western-most example of a site that shows evidence of Chacoan contact and influence. This far-flung area is larger than New England and illustrates the vast spread of Chacoan material culture (things like architecture and pottery) and religious-ceremonial influence in the late eleventh and early twelfth centuries.

Of the roughly 150 known Chacoan outliers, perhaps 30 have been investigated systematically and are fairly well understood. This leaves more than 80 percent of the outliers insufficiently studied to understand the timing of their occupations (only excavation produces the tight clustering of tree-ring dates necessary to truly date a large site) and the nature of the remains that lie hidden within their buried rooms and kivas. The known outliers vary considerably. The great house at Bluff, Utah, for example, appears to represent a local version of a Chacoan great house.[1] In contrast, Salmon and Aztec ruins both would fit well in Chaco Canyon itself. Chimney Rock Pueblo, as another example of a unique great house, is a spectacular site built on a high mesa in Colorado. In addition to lying on the northeastern Puebloan and Chacoan frontier, Chimney Rock is also unique because of the reason for its construction. In short, the great house was located precisely on the mesa to make use of Chimney Rock and an accompanying rock spire, Companion Rock, to view the major standstill of the moon.[2] The architecture of Chimney Rock is distinctively Chacoan, compared to the local and non-Chacoan masonry employed at the Bluff great house.

Although they share traits in common with each other, and with great houses in Chaco Canyon, almost every outlier identified thus far has unique characteristics. Thus, understanding the relationship between Chaco Canyon and outlying sites of Chacoan age and affiliation is one of the challenges for Puebloan archaeologists. In fact, the very word itself—*outlier*—implies a relationship between a center (Chaco Canyon) and a site outside the center (an outlier) that was probably highly variable from site to site. In recent years, Chacoan archaeologists have begun to question these relationships and concentrate more of their research on the outlying sites. This new work has led some to question the existence of an integrated Chacoan system. In place of an integrated, centrally controlled society, some archaeologists have proposed that the Chacoan world is better described as a loose confederation of independent political entities. Outside the Canyon itself, and an area referred to as the Chaco Core, this is the view adopted here: that the larger Chaco System was a loose confederation of affiliated but mostly independent Pueblo villages that looked to Chaco Canyon as a religious-ceremonial center.

The primary criterion for understanding the level of Chacoan affiliation is architecture. Chacoan architects had a very specific set of criteria that they adhered to in constructing great houses. These characteristics included, at a minimum: (1) core-veneer construction with walls between 0.60 and 1.0 meter thick (2 to 3.3 feet); (2) monumental multistory (at least two stories and often three, four, or five) construction; (3) careful selection and use of predominantly tabular, high-quality sandstone; and (4) use of distinctive veneer facing patterns (Chaco masonry types I, II, III, IV, or V [McElmo style]).

Many of the so-called Chacoan outliers have one or more of these characteristics. But many do not exhibit all of the necessary traits. Some sites were located in areas with inferior sandstone, whereas others had only river cobbles close at hand. Large sites that are contemporaneous with Chaco, and many that date before or after Chaco, were built with these materials. However, sites that are distinctly Chacoan made use of fine tabular sandstone in construction. Salmon Pueblo (discussed in detail below), for example, is located adjacent to the San Juan River, and the Chacoan inhabitants had an ample supply of river cobbles at the site. The sandstone local to Salmon is blocky and friable (breaks easily) and not "up to standard" for Chacoan construction. Because of these factors, the Chacoans had to procure higher-quality sandstone at some distance from Salmon Pueblo. Two likely quarry sites have been identified for Salmon—one lies about three miles north of the pueblo; the other, three miles south. Both quarry sites provided good quantities of hard, workable sandstone from the geologic formation identified as the Nacimiento formation. Thus, in order to build Salmon Pueblo with the proper materials, the Chacoans had to scout the countryside, identify good sources of fine sandstone, then laboriously transport the millions of pieces of tabular sandstone required to build the site.

Other large sites that date to the period of Chacoan influence, for example, Morris site 39 in the greater San Juan area, were built of largely local materials, including blocky sandstone, river cobbles, and some tabular sandstone. These sites are typically described as Chacoan outliers because they date to the Chaco Era and are the largest sites in local areas. Should such sites, then, be called Chacoan? In my opinion, great houses that do not exhibit the characteristics of Chacoan architecture and masonry were not built by Chacoans. Thus, these sites are not colonies of Chaco but are, instead, local versions of great houses.

Outliers have been found in every direction around Chaco, with the greatest concentrations to the south-southwest and north. We'll briefly examine outliers in these two areas below, to gain an understanding of this diverse group of sites and their relationships to Chacoan society. Then, this leads into a more detailed exploration of the two largest outliers: Aztec and Salmon.

SOUTHERN SAN JUAN BASIN OUTLIERS

A large group of ancient Pueblo sites with Chacoan characteristics is located south and southwest of Chaco Canyon. At least fifty sites described as outliers are found in this region, which goes west across the New Mexico–Arizona state line and to the south for a distance greater than 125 kilometers (about 78 miles) from Chaco Canyon. This group of sites reveals variation in masonry and construction style, site layout and structure, and dating. Many of the southern outliers date to the middle c.e. 900s and early 1000s, prior to the initiation of much of the great house construction and expansion in Chaco Canyon.

One specific locale in which this pattern is apparent is the Red Mesa Valley, which lies about seventy-five kilometers (forty-seven miles) south of Chaco Canyon. Archaeological research has revealed perhaps a dozen great house communities, many with ceramic dates from 950 to about 1050 c.e. Many of these sites lack the distinctive masonry veneers that characterize Chacoan great houses in Chaco Canyon and elsewhere. Study of artifacts from the Red Mesa Valley sites reveals less nonlocal materials than in other Chacoan areas. Together, these findings suggest that the great houses in the Red Mesa Valley were primarily a local development, perhaps in emulation of the Chaco Canyon communities.[3]

OUTLIERS IN THE NORTHERN AND MIDDLE SAN JUAN REGION

Beginning about 75 kilometers (47 miles) north of Chaco Canyon, numerous outliers are scattered about the greater San Juan region (all the way across southwestern Colorado and into southeastern Utah). Examining the region at 1120 c.e. in a hypothetical time machine would reveal at least forty occupied great houses. These sites varied in size from about 20 rooms (including several small Chaco-style great houses in southwest Colorado and southeast Utah) to the Aztec Ruins complex, with several great houses and more than 600 rooms in use.

There are too many sites for individual discussion here. But the two largest Chacoan sites outside Chaco Canyon merit greater exploration: the Aztec Community and Salmon Pueblo. These sites represent probable examples of direct Chacoan colonization of the San Juan region in the late eleventh and early twelfth centuries.

THE AZTEC COMMUNITY

The ruins of the ancient Aztec Community lie on the north bank of the Animas River, about ten miles due north of Salmon Pueblo. Outside of the Pueblo Bonito–Chetro Ketl–Pueblo del Arroyo complex in Chaco Canyon, "downtown" Chaco as some archaeologists call it, no community in the pre-Hispanic Pueblo world was larger than Aztec at 1130 C.E. Aztec "West" was built between 1105 and 1115 C.E. and, when finished, consisted of more than 400 rooms, a dozen small kivas, and a great kiva. Aztec "East" was begun in the C.E. 1120s, and when it reached its final form in the 1200s, the pueblo had more than 200 rooms and numerous kivas. Rounding out the Aztec complex were at least two and perhaps three of the unusual ceremonial structures known as triwall features, the Earl Morris house (a smaller twenty-room great house), and a variety of smaller habitation locales within a one-kilometer (six-tenths of a mile) area around the central complex.

The roots of the Aztec Community extend to at least 1050 C.E., and perhaps earlier. Aztec "North" is a great house built of river cobbles and adobe and was occupied roughly between 1050 and 1100 C.E., and perhaps later.[4] Aztec North was not constructed in Chacoan style and seems to represent an earlier "San Juan"–style great house.

Although the Spanish inhabitants of what became New Mexico were probably aware of Aztec Ruins, much like Chaco, "discovery" and documentation of the ancient Aztec Community did not occur until the mid-nineteenth century. The ruins at Aztec were "discovered" in 1859 by geologist J. S. Newberry on a trip through the area, and the first documentation of Aztec was completed by Lewis Henry Morgan in

1878.[5] Earl Morris apparently knew of Aztec from the time he was a boy growing up in adjacent Farmington, New Mexico. Morris was hired in 1915 to supervise excavations at Aztec for the American Museum of Natural History in New York, and by 1921, most of the West Ruin at Aztec had been excavated.[6]

The amazing complex of great houses, great kivas, and ritual features at Aztec was in use until about 1290 or 1300 C.E. Then, like Salmon and other sites in the area, Aztec was abandoned, and the population migrated to other Pueblo villages and locales to the east, to the south, and perhaps some families, to the west.

The Aztec Community has been described by archaeologist Steve Lekson as the transplanted northern capital of Chacoan society in the C.E. 1200s.[7] Not all Chacoan archaeologists agree with this description, mostly because of extensive changes in the middle C.E. 1100s that resulted in the end of what most archaeologists recognize as Chacoan society. What emerged in the late C.E. 1100s and 1200s can perhaps best be described as post-Chacoan. Aztec and its complex of great houses and ceremonial features is the largest clustering of Chacoan sites outside of Chaco Canyon by 1130 C.E. But, beyond its architecture, Aztec is problematic as the new Chacoan capital. In short, most of the artifacts and other remains from the sites have not been intensively analyzed; most of the Aztec collection has hardly been studied since Earl Morris's work in the 1920s. Thus, while Chaco Canyon's geographic position, road system, clustering of specialized architecture, ceremonial traits, and material culture have all been studied and support the concept of a Chaco Canyon–focused Puebloan society, Aztec is poorly studied and has only its architecture to support its "descendant" Chacoan capital designation.

On the basis of recent research, archaeologist Gary Brown and his colleagues have suggested a modified interpretation of Aztec. Whereas Aztec certainly was the Chacoan center in the thirteenth-century San Juan region, study of the Aztec Community reveals numerous local influences that indicate that the Chacoan pattern was modified and reinterpreted by the local population over time.[8] Additional study of Aztec and its extensive artifact and sample collection is necessary to understand its role in the post-Chacoan, northern San Juan region of the late twelfth and thirteenth centuries.

SALMON PUEBLO

Named after the local man (Peter Salmon) who homesteaded the area in the 1870s and not the fish, Salmon (pronounced 'sal mən) Pueblo was constructed on the north bank of the San Juan River around 1090 C.E. by a group of planners, builders, and colonists, who migrated some forty-five miles from the Puebloan center at Chaco Canyon.[9] As laid out, Salmon Pueblo formed a huge E-shape on the landscape, with 150 ground floor rooms, 100 second-story rooms, and as many as 50 third-story rooms. The 300-room structure was home to perhaps 300 residents at the peak of its occupation, around 1100 C.E. Primary ceremonial facilities at Salmon included a Great Kiva (a huge subterranean structure fifty feet in diameter) in the central plaza and a smaller but equally impressive elevated Tower Kiva built into the exact middle of the Pueblo structure. Together, these two large kivas are believed to have provided the physical and spiritual environment necessary for many of the communal ceremonial and ritual activities that were part of Puebloan life at Salmon.

The Chacoans probably recruited local San Juan people to reside at the pueblo. After about a generation of residence, between 1115 and 1125 C.E., the Chacoans left Salmon, leaving the pueblo in the hands of the indigenous San Juan groups. Although willing residents in the Chacoan building, these folks were not satisfied with the internal design of Salmon. They made a number of minor and major architectural changes. These renovations included sealing off many of the first-floor doorways between adjacent rooms and adding architecture and other features to rooms to convert them into the ceremonial rooms known as kivas. By the end of the San Juan period at Salmon, more than twenty small kivas had been added to the pueblo. These changes at Salmon Pueblo, which occurred over a number of decades between 1120 and 1200 C.E., resulted in a very different physical environment. Many of the large Chacoan rooms were divided in two, kivas were added to rooms, to the front of the pueblo, and to the large plaza formed by Salmon's "E" shape. These changes reflect political, social, economic, and ceremonial differences between the Chacoans, the primary builders of Salmon, and the San Juan people, who subsequently modified the Salmon building. The San Juan inhabitants of Salmon were less centrally organized with regard to social and ceremonial activities than the Chacoans. Hence, the need for

a greater number of smaller kivas, which I interpret to reflect more de-
cision making at the family and extended-family level. This process,
which we might describe as local empowerment after the Chaco Era had
ended, was widespread across the greater San Juan–Mesa Verde region in
the late twelfth and thirteenth centuries.

The San Juan groups who remade Salmon were joined by other mi-
grants in the late 1100s and early 1200s, and no later than 1225, Salmon
was again thriving as one of the largest Puebloan communities in the
greater San Juan region and, indeed, anywhere in the ancient Southwest.

Around 1285 c.e., tragedy struck Salmon, and the pueblo was completely abandoned by 1290. Conflict with either neighboring Puebloans
or an outside group brought trouble to Salmon. The Tower Kiva structure was burned and the remains of almost twenty children and several
adults were found within and around the burned structure. Several of
the individuals were apparently cremated, perhaps as part of a ritural
abandonment of the site. Much of the remainder of the Pueblo was also
consumed by fire at this time. Archaeologists have found no evidence
of occupation at Salmon after this calamitous fire occurred. The living
history of Salmon Pueblo, then, came to an abrupt halt.

Largely burned, abandoned, and slowly crumbling under the ravages
of time and nature, Salmon Pueblo was absent from the archaeological
and historical record until 1874. Visits by itinerant Native Americans
and Spanish travelers undoubtedly occurred during this 600-year interval, but we have no records of any such visits. In October 1874, photographer Timothy O'Sullivan of the Wheeler Survey visited Salmon.
O'Sullivan identified the site as a "characteristic ruin of the Pueblo San
Juan" and made a number of wet-plate photographs of the site, from
various angles.[10] The earliest photographs of the site in the twentieth
century are from the mid-1960s, and none of the standing architecture
visible in O'Sullivan's photographs is present. Clearly, the highest portions of the pueblo collapsed or were knocked down in the intervening
ninety years.

Salmon reemerged into the historical record in the late 1960s. The
land containing the ancient pueblo was put up for sale and purchased
by the San Juan County Museum Association. The Association subsequently sold the land to San Juan County and entered into a lease
agreement to manage the property. High on the list of priorities for
Salmon was recruitment of a renowned archaeologist to direct excava-

tions at the site. Cynthia Irwin-Williams was this person. She began work at Salmon in 1970 and developed the San Juan Valley Archaeological Program (the Salmon Project) to understand Chacoan society in the northern Southwest. Excavations, analysis, and writing on the Salmon Project continued until 1980. Currently, work is under way to finish the effort begun by Irwin-Williams and her colleagues. A series of technical archaeological volumes and a comprehensive, synthetic book on Salmon will be finished in 2005.

Chacoan Life and Society at Salmon

Reconstructing life at Salmon Pueblo around 1100 c.e. in the absence of written records is challenging but not impossible. More than 100 years of archaeological research and ethnographic study of Puebloan peoples has allowed for an understanding of the basic aspects of the Puebloan lifestyle.

The Chacoan inhabitants of Salmon Pueblo depended principally on a trio of domesticated crops for their diet: corn, beans, and squash. These plants were grown in fields adjacent to Salmon, along the floodplain of the San Juan River, on terraces above the river and next to tributary streams, and probably in upland, dry locations dependent on rainfall. In addition to these domesticated crops, the Salmonites made use of a broad variety of natural plants for food including tansy mustard, goosefoot, spurge, purslane, and pigweed seeds and greens, yucca fruits, prickly pear pads, piñon nuts, juniper berries, chokecherry berries, and wild onions. Plants used as medicines or in ritual or ceremonial matters often overlap those used for food. Corn pollen, for example, is used ritually and sometimes medicinally by the modern Pueblos and probably by the Chacoans at Salmon and other great houses. Spruce and ponderosa tree bark, along with juniper boughs, were used ceremonially or medicinally at Salmon. Ephedra, commonly known as Mormon tea, was probably brewed as a hot beverage and used as a cure for intestinal and other disorders.

Plants were also used for clothing, with fragments of cotton garments recovered during excavations at Salmon. We have no evidence to indicate that cotton was grown at Salmon. Rather, it was probably traded in from areas to the south. Yucca was used to make sandals and a variety of other items including baskets, bags, belts, tumplines (for carrying heavy head loads), and twine. Hollow reed stems as well as straightened tree branches were used for arrow shafts.

Animals, both domestic and wild, were of great importance to the Chacoans at Salmon. First and foremost, game animals provided much of the protein critical to the diet. Deer, elk, antelope, jackrabbit, cottontail rabbit, and a variety of smaller mammals, birds, and rodents were all consumed at Salmon. Suckerfish from the San Juan River were caught and eaten. Lastly, animal skins, bird feathers, bear and raptor claws, and even live macaws were a necessary element of Chacoan ritual and ceremonialism at Salmon.

The only domestic animals in the Puebloan world were dogs and turkeys. Turkeys were domesticated as early as 600 C.E. and were important sources of feathers, bone tools, and meat. Particularly in the later occupation at Salmon after 1150, turkeys were kept in pens and eaten frequently. Dogs are a ubiquitous presence in most human settlements, past and present. Pueblo villages were no exception, and Salmon had its share of dogs. Dogs were used to help in hunting, carrying loads, and as general companions. Dogs in Native America were used for food only as a last resort in times of starvation, and there is no evidence of such use at Salmon. Canine bones were recovered from Salmon, and it seems clear that dogs were important companions as well as sources of labor for the people.

Daily life for Salmon residents involved a number of activities including working agricultural fields in the spring, summer, and continuing until the fall harvests. Heavy work in the fields, such as initial clearing, probably involved both men and women. Women and children probably did most of the daily weeding and watering of fields. Harvest time meant, as it does for all agricultural groups, an occasion for all members of the family to pitch in and fill the Pueblo storerooms with corn and other produce.

In fall and early winter, organized hunting trips were taken by men and boys. Most Pueblos historically had hunting societies, sometimes led by a hunting chief. Although we cannot be certain, Salmon and other Pueblos of the Chaco Era probably had institutionalized hunting societies of a similar nature.

Winter was the most difficult time at Salmon Pueblo. Outdoor activities were curtailed by cold and wet weather, and survival depended on substantial stores of corn and other plant foods and dried meat. Indoor activities, though, would have assumed greater importance, including various arts and crafts such as weaving, basketry, and stone and bone tool making.

Spring was undoubtedly a time of celebration at Salmon Pueblo, as the world emerged from the cold, gray winter. Activities shifted back to the outside, fields were prepared again for corn and other crops, ceremonies were probably held to commemorate the spring solstice, and the seasonal cycle began anew.

June is the most likely month during which the Salmon residents (probably the women) manufactured pottery. With spring planting completed, and a month or more before the monsoonal rains of July to August were to begin, the first month of summer was available. Clay and tempering materials (sand and crushed rock) were obtained locally. Ceramics paints were manufactured by boiling beeweed plants and grinding hematite and other minerals. Ceramic vessels of various sizes and shapes—large and small serving bowls, large water jars or ollas, large cooking jars, pitchers, ladles, and canteen-shaped jars—were formed using coils of clay. Once dry and scraped smooth, some vessels were painted. Other pots, destined for use as cooking or culinary pottery, were finished with fingernail impressions to create a corrugated appearance. All vessels were then fired in pit kilns, probably located at some distance from the village, at temperatures up to 600 degrees Celsius. Once cooled, ceramic vessels were ready for everyday use.

Several varieties of stone raw materials were used at Salmon, as everyday tools and building materials. The pueblo was constructed with at least two types of durable sandstone, available within three miles. Many stone tools were made of locally available raw materials including chert, siltstone, basalt, granite, and quartzite. Exotic, imported stone included the use of obsidian, from the Jemez Mountains to the east, and Narbona Pass chert, a high-quality tool stone that was traded all over the Four Corners area. Using these stone materials and with great skill in flint-knapping, people (probably the men) of Salmon manufactured beautiful projectile points, arrowheads, drills, perforators, axes, hoes, and a variety of other scraping, cutting, and chopping tools.

Corn was ground into meal on large slabs called metates, using hand stones that archaeologists identify as manos. Cornmeal was then shaped into flat cakes, similar to what we call tortillas today, and cooked on or near hearths on flat stones (called comals by archaeologists). Beyond their primary dependence on corn, the Chacoans at Salmon also grew a different type of corn from later occupants. Chacoan corn was mostly of flint or popcorn varieties that were larger, more uniform, and produced more kernels per cob than the flour varieties favored by the post-Chacoan, San Juan inhabitants. Further, Chacoan grinding facilities held more of the basal grinding slabs known as metates and were able to produce more ground cornmeal. These findings suggest a more intensive and organized approach to Chacoan corn production.

In the making of beautiful jewelry and other ornaments, Salmon artisans reached perhaps the peak of their skill. Several species of marine shell, minerals such as hematite and jet, turquoise, and even common materials like bone and siltstone were worked into amazing ornaments, pendants, necklaces, and bracelets. Beads were painstakingly carved from stone, bone, and shell and strung together into different pieces of jewelry. Some of these items were purely for personal enrichment and adornment, while others were perhaps more ceremonial in nature.

Several objects of inferred ceremonial importance were found during the excavation and study of Salmon Pueblo. Most significant, perhaps, was the finding of a carved, green sandstone lizard effigy near the floor of the Tower Kiva. Research into Puebloan ethnography suggested that the effigy represented Lizard Woman, an important mythological figure. Other ceremonial items from Salmon include two carved stylized frogs of turquoise, a bird effigy made of carved hematite (a red mineral), and several bird and animal effigies of fired pottery. Very similar frogs were found at Pueblo Bonito and Aztec Ruins. One researcher suggested that the frogs may have been made by a single craftsman, given the high degree of similarity in form and manufacturing technique.[11]

What about leadership at Salmon? Discussions of Puebloan leadership, past and present, have provided lots of controversy over the years. The general anthropological view, developed out of almost a century of ethnographic fieldwork among the Pueblos (from the 1870s through the 1970s), identifies the Pueblos as egalitarian (characterized by equality in social relations). In other words, Pueblos are viewed by many anthropologists as lacking evidence of significant social, economic, or political divisions or stratification. This view acknowledges the existence of leaders, chiefs or caciques (an adopted Spanish word for chief or headman), but suggests that the chiefs relied on persuasion and did not truly command the people.

Another view, proposed more recently, suggests that Puebloan society, past and present, is characterized by definite leaders and that hierarchical relations were present. Further, these leaders were able to command, as well as persuade, their people to follow certain courses of action. In this view, the great houses in Chaco Canyon and in some outlying communities like Salmon were built by leaders, chiefs—if we use that term—who directed the builders, masons, and other workers. Once built, these communities were directed by permanent leaders, who may have passed the reigns of leadership within their families (that is, chief or leadership positions may have been inherited, passed father to son).

Salmon Pueblo was constructed in a deliberate and planned fashion, and it is clear that leaders, perhaps religious leaders, were responsible for organizing the effort. Excavations at Salmon revealed one burial from the Chacoan occupation that represents an unusual individual. This elderly man was buried with a bow; nine cane arrows not designed for use (based on Pueblo ethnographic, nine is a sacred number); four bone awls probably originally in a bag (four is another sacred number); a wooden *paho* (prayer feather holder); a robe of fur or feather cloth; four ceramic bowls, all of San Juan manufacture but of unique design; and a wrapping of finely woven mats. Salmon archaeologist Cynthia Irwin-Williams proposed that this man was a priest in a Bow Society at the pueblo.[12] Bow Societies are present in many of the modern Pueblo villages, and it is not perhaps unreasonable to infer that such organizations existed in the past. Given the special treatment this individual received upon his death, it is logical to assume that he was an important man in the pueblo.

SUMMARY

Chaco Canyon's outliers were a critical component of Chacoan society. These sites were built across four modern American states in the tenth through twelfth centuries. Whereas affiliation and connection with Chaco Canyon united these sites, a number of other traits, including architecture and site size and layout, show considerable diversity across the Chacoan region. Some sites, such as Salmon, Aztec, and Chimney Rock, reveal exquisite architecture and masonry, the hallmark of the Chacoans, and were probably constructed by Chacoan architects and planners. Other sites, such as Bluff and Morris 39, appear Chaco-like with core-veneer construction and have artifacts indicating participation in the Chacoan economic realm but do not exhibit good Chacoan masonry. These sites, then, are interpreted as local versions of Chacoan great houses that allowed for participation in a Chaco exchange network but do not indicate colonization by Chacoan peoples.

NOTES

1. Joseph Peter Jalbert and Catherine Cameron, "Chacoan and Local Influences in Three Great House Communities in the Northern San Juan Region," in *Great House Communities across the Chacoan Landscape*, edited by John Kantner and Nancy M. Mahoney, Anthropological Papers of the University of Arizona no. 64 (Tucson: University of Arizona Press, 2000), pp. 79–90.

2. J. McKim Malville and Claudia Putnam, *Prehistoric Astronomy in the Southwest* (Boulder, CO: Johnson Books, 1993). Also, J. McKim Malville and Gary Matlock, *The Chimney Rock Archaeological Symposium* (USDA Forest Service General Technical Report RM-227) (Fort Collins, CO: Forest Service, Rocky Mountain Forest and Range Experiment Station, 1993).

3. Ruth Van Dyke, "Chacoan Ritual Landscapes: The View from the Red Mesa Valley," in *Great House Communities across the Chacoan Landscape*, edited by John Kantner and Nancy M. Mahoney, Anthropological Papers of the University of Arizona no. 64 (Tucson: University of Arizona Press, 2000), pp. 91–100. See also John Kantner, "Political Competition among the Chaco Anasazi of the American Southwest," *Journal of Anthropological Archaeology* 15, no. 1 (1996): 41–105.

4. John R. Stein and Peter J. McKenna, *An Archaeological Reconnaissance of a Late Bonito Phase Occupation, near Aztec Ruins National Monument, New Mexico* (Santa Fe: Southwest Cultural Resources Center, National Park Service, 1988); Gary M. Brown, Thomas C. Windes, and Peter J. McKenna, "Aztec Anamnesis: Aztec Ruins, or Anasazi Capital" (paper presented at the 67th annual meeting of the Society for American Archaeology, Denver, March 2002).

5. J. S. Newberry, "Geologic Report," in *Report of the Exploring Expedition from Santa Fe, New Mexico, to the Junction of the Grand and Green Rivers of the Great Colorado of the West, in 1859*, by Capt. J. N. Macomb (Washington, DC: Government Printing Office, 1876), pp. 70–109; Lewis Henry Morgan, *Houses and House-Life of the American Aborigines* (Washington, DC: Government Printing Office, 1881), pp. 154–197, passim.

6. Earl H. Morris, *The Aztec Ruin* (New York: Anthropological Papers of the American Museum of Natural History, vol. 26, pt. 1, 1919).

7. Stephen H. Lekson, *The Chaco Meridian: Centers of Political Power in the Ancient Southwest* (Walnut Creek, CA: Alta Mira Press, 1999).

8. Brown, Windes, and McKenna, "Aztec Anamnesis," p. 9.

9. Paul F. Reed, "Salmon Ruins: From Cynthia Irwin-Williams's Vision to a Central Place in the Totah," *Archaeology Southwest* 16, no. 2 (2002): 7–9.

10. Timothy O'Sullivan, "Caption for Plate 59," in *Report upon the United States Geographical Surveys West of the One-Hundredth Meridian, Volume VII—Archaeology*, by Lt. George M. Wheeeler (Washington, DC: Government Printing Office, 1879).

11. Jimmy D. McNeil, "Ornaments at Salmon Ruin, San Juan County, New Mexico" (master's thesis, Department of Anthropology, Eastern New Mexico University, 1986).

12. Cynthia Irwin-Williams, "A View of the Chaco from Salmon Ruins: Update 1980" (paper presented at the 1980 Pecos Conference, Mesa Verde, CO), ms. on file, Salmon Ruins Library, 1980, p. 23.

CHAPTER 7

CHACO CANYON AS A RITUAL CENTER OF THE ELEVENTH-CENTURY PUEBLO WORLD

Closely connected to the emergence of Chacoan society and its flores-cence in the late eleventh century is its importance as a center of ritual and ceremony. Several specific lines of evidence studied by archaeolo-gists over the years identify Chaco as ritually important and, beyond this, as the ceremonial center of the Puebloan world during the eleventh and early twelfth centuries. First is the presence of large numbers of ritually important artifacts in the great houses in Chaco, particularly in Pueblo Bonito. Several rooms in this site contained large numbers of artifacts of a ritual or ceremonial nature. Second, the construction style, architecture, and layout of the great houses encode and signal ritual behavior. Most of the eleventh-century Chacoan great houses were con-structed in alignment with either the sun, the moon, or some combi-nation of the two. Third, the number of ritual-ceremonial structures in Chaco Canyon signifies its importance, not only to internal Canyon populations but also for large numbers of people who lived outside the Canyon and visited regularly.

In this chapter, we will explore Chaco as a ritual center, examining the revealing structures, artifacts, and other characteristics. Next, we will briefly document solar and lunar observation in the Chacoan world and its connection to ritual. Finally, we will assess models of Chacoan ritual and its relation to other aspects of Puebloan society.

RITUAL STRUCTURES IN CHACO CANYON

Great kivas are the most apparent ritual structures in Chaco Canyon and throughout the ancient Pueblo world. Mid-eleventh-century great kivas in Chaco number at least thirteen and perhaps fifteen or more. Archaeological work over the last 100 years has confirmed the special nature of great kivas as well as identifying a number of characteristics that suggest their use for ceremony. The kiva structure itself, of whatever size, occupies a special and sacred place in Pueblo architecture. Modern Pueblo people consider the kiva representative of the point of emergence, the *sipapu*, of people into this world.[1] The round shape of the kiva and the construction of the roof represent the sky and the cosmos. Most great kivas contain floor vaults, internal features located symmetrically on either side of the central fire hearth. Excavation of some of these vaults suggests that they were covered with planks and hides and used as foot drums—similar drums are used in modern Pueblo kivas. Archaeologists have suggested that these foot drums provided cadence for dances and ceremonies held in the great kivas. Ceremonial niches or crypts built into kiva walls are another feature found in many great kivas. Within the niches, various types of artifacts have been recovered, including inlaid turquoise, shell, and jet pendants, necklaces, and other jewelry. Niches were often sealed after religious objects were placed within. Contents of the niches have been interpreted as ceremonial offerings, similar to a practice of the modern Pueblos.

A recent study by archaeologist Ruth Van Dyke shows remarkable consistency in the size and basic layout of great kivas across the Chacoan world.[2] Even in larger Chacoan communities that might have required larger ritual facilities, most of the great kivas fall within the norm for size. This suggests a commonality in ritual and ceremonial practice across the region. Hypothesizing that Chacoan great kiva rituals were under the control of a small group of religious practitioners, priests as we might call them, it is perhaps not surprising that great kivas were constructed in a highly uniform manner. In general, Chacoan sites and structures exhibit a greater degree of organizational consistency, which, in turn, suggests central control in the hands of some kind of hierarchical order.

Biwall and triwall structures are another type of specialized ritual structure found in Chaco Canyon (at Pueblo del Arroyo) and at outlying sites (the ancient Aztec Community, for example, has perhaps three triwalled structures). These structures are similar to other kivas and great kivas found outside great house structures. They differ in having one (biwall) or two additional concentric walls (triwall) encircling the primary kiva structure in the center. These encircling walls enclose small rooms that probably served a specialized purpose related to the ceremonialism of the structure.

Some of the least obvious ceremonial structures in the Chaco world are the monumental roads built across large areas of the San Juan Basin. Although the roads certainly served some utilitarian transportation needs, the best explanation suggests that they were constructed as monuments and were part of the Chacoan cosmologic geography.

Finally, the Chacoan great houses have been recently interpreted as largely ritual-ceremonial facilities. Archaeologists have observed the lack of domestic features (such as corn mealing bins) in Pueblo Bonito and other great houses and what seems to be a scarcity of fire hearths (cooking and heating features). Further, great house rooms were built inordinately large (some as big as 7 × 7 meters—23 × 23 feet square), well beyond the largest rooms used by both earlier and later Pueblo peoples. Such findings, combined with the amazing numbers of ritual objects in Pueblo Bonito and Chetro Ketl, suggest a nonresidential and predominantly ritual function for at least some of the great houses.

Archaeologists John Stein and Steve Lekson have argued that all of these ritual features—great kivas, great houses, roads, and earthen mounds—together constitute a sacred, created landscape.[3] These ritual landscapes, intentionally created by the Chacoans, reflected and embodied the underlying cosmological principles.

CEREMONIAL ARTIFACTS IN CHACOAN SITES

Another primary indication of the importance of ritual and ceremony for the Chacoans is the presence of ceremonial artifacts. We have already discussed some of these artifacts associated with great kivas. But a number of other types of ritual artifacts have been recovered from excavations at Chacoan great houses.

Excavations at Pueblo Bonito have produced more ceremonial artifacts than any other Chacoan site. In brief, this inventory includes a carved frog made of jet with inlaid turquoise eyes and an inlaid turquoise necklace, carved and painted wooden sticks (perhaps *pahos* or prayer sticks), thousands of carved shell objects including pendants, bracelets, discs, and beads, bifurcated ritual baskets, about forty copper bells or bell fragments, hundreds of Chaco black-on-white cylindrical vessels, hundreds of crooked sticks, several deer bone scrapers with inlaid turquoise and jet decoration, and several carved turquoise bird effigies. Ceremonial artifacts are not limited to Pueblo Bonito by any means. Other Chacoan great houses contain ritual artifacts, as well. In fact, as we have discussed, the presence of exotic artifacts, often of a ceremonial nature, is one of the hallmarks of Chacoan society. Artifacts similar to those found at Pueblo Bonito, including animal forms, such as carved turquoise frogs, inlaid turquoise, jet, and shell items, human fertility effigies (carved stone or fired pottery representations of pregnant women), copper bells, ceramic animal effigies, painted wooden prayer sticks, and corn mothers (corncobs mounted on small wooden sticks) have been recovered and studied at many of the Chacoan outliers.

In addition to human-derived artifacts, excavations at Pueblo Bonito also revealed an amazing number of macaw (parrot) skeletons. Thirty-one whole or partial macaws were present, with many of these in just a single room.[4] Other Chacoan great houses also contained whole macaw skeletons (indicating that they were maintained alive) including Pueblo del Arroyo, Salmon Pueblo, and Aztec's West Pueblo. The northern Chihuahua, Mexican, site of Casas Grandes is the likely source for the southwestern macaws. Given the constraints and the costs of transporting these birds many thousands of miles from their natural habitat in central Mexico to Casas Grandes, and into the American Southwest, it is clear they were very important to the Chacoans. The modern Hopi and Zuni Pueblos have macaw or parrot clans today, and it is not unreasonable to trace the roots of these organizations to Pueblo Bonito. Further, it seems logical to suggest that macaws were ritually very important to the Chacoans.

Emergency excavations at Chetro Ketl in 1947 produced an unparalleled assemblage of ritual artifacts. Among the artifacts recovered from the upper story of a floodwater-damaged room were 200 carved and painted wooden objects. These objects included various depictions of birds (heads, beaks, tails, feathers, entire birds), scalloped discs of various sizes, decorated wooden slats and sticks, a plume circle (painted group of wooden pieces in a semicircular pattern), painted arrow shafts, and *pahos* (prayer sticks).[5] Interpretation of these esoteric items focused on the comparison of similar items from other archaeological sites and made use of ethnographic analogy from modern Pueblo villages such as Hopi and Zuni. Drawing on these data, archaeologist Gwinn Vivian and his colleagues concluded that most of the carved and painted wooden objects were probably part of ceremonial altars or similar constructions.[6] Other items, such as the *pahos* and painted arrow shafts, were probably used in Puebloan rituals.

Direct reconstruction of past ceremonial events is, of course, not possible. Nevertheless, archaeologists can infer usage of these ritual artifacts, and many others that have not been found or studied, in the numerous ceremonies observed at sites in Chaco Canyon and in the outlying communities. Some of the items are so rare, the carved frogs, for example, that they may have been used only once yearly or less for specific ceremonies in great kivas. Other, more common artifacts like the animal effigies and prayer sticks may have been used in nearly every kiva ritual. It is difficult to be sure. We can be sure that these items were significant and had importance for the Chacoans.

SOLAR AND LUNAR OBSERVATION BY THE CHACOANS

Concern with the movements of the sun and moon are common among human groups worldwide, particularly for people dependent on agricultural cycles and associated rituals. So it was with the Chacoans and all Pueblo people. Beginning in the 1930s, if not earlier, archaeologists studying Chaco became aware of the role that solar and lunar observation played in Pueblo cosmology. Systematic research into Pueblo astronomy and its linkage to ceremonialism was initiated in the late 1960s, and the last twenty years, in particular, have produced a veritable explosion of new research.

Briefly, Chacoan concern with astronomical movements manifested itself in several ways. First, alignment to the sun and the moon was important in the design and construction of great houses and other structures and the overall layout of several Chacoan great house structures. Pueblo Bonito was built facing south, on a north–south largely symmetrical axis, with its front section of rooms aligned east–west. Other sites in Chaco Core reflect similar concerns with alignment and symmetry. Pueblo Alto, north of Pueblo Bonito, and Tsin Kletzin, to the south, are located on the same north–south line. At opposite ends of Chaco Canyon, several miles to the east and west, the sites of Penasco Blanco and Una Vida are aligned on the major lunar standstill baseline (as observed from Pueblo Bonito).[7]

Another aspect of the Chacoan concern with astronomy is the construction and use of features designed to observe and track celestial and other phenomena. The most well known of these features in Chaco is the Sun Dagger or Three-Slab site, located on the east face of the highest cliff on Fajada Butte. Using light that passes through three parallel, upright slabs (that unfortunately collapsed recently) and two spirals carved into the rock, the Sun Dagger tracks the equinoxes and solstices and the minor and major standstills of the moon. Because of its nearly inaccessible location, the site probably did not serve a calendrical function for groups of people. Rather, it was probably used by a Chacoan religious leader (perhaps similar to a modern Pueblo sun priest) in private to make determinations about the ritual calendar.[8]

Corner windows built into the structure of Pueblo Bonito provide additional evidence of Chacoan sky-watching activities. Such corner windows are very rare in Pueblo structures, and two appear to be positioned to allow for observation of the sun at winter solstice.[9] Although intervening structures and walls may have blocked use of the windows at certain times, these structures have come to be identified as solstice windows. Aztec West has at least one such corner window, as well. However, Aztec is aligned differently from Pueblo Bonito, and viewing the solstice was apparently not the purpose of the window.

Chimney Rock: A Chacoan Observatory

Among all Chacoan sites, Chimney Rock, Colorado, stands out as unique. The full moon rises between the two pillars of rock that comprise Chimney Rock, as seen from the Chimney Rock great house, during the northernmost movement and then standstill of the moon—what is referred to as "the major lunar standstill." The lunar standstill is comparable to the winter solstice of the sun—its northernmost position in the sky. This event occurs only once every 18.6 years when the moon rises at the same point on the horizon for a period between two and four years.[10] Clearly, this rare astronomical occurrence, happening only once per Pueblo generation, was sufficiently important for the Chimney Rock great house to be precisely constructed on the mesa adjacent to the rock pillars to observe the rising of the full moon. No other known Chacoan site was built for such a specific purpose. Furthermore, no other Chacoan great houses are believed to have been geographically located specifically for a ceremonial observation.

Tree-ring samples taken from wood timbers at the great house reveal two dates for construction: 1076 and 1093 c.e. These dates correspond to periods when the moon was at standstill and "captured" at moonrise between the Chimney Rock pillars. Although the sample of dates is small and other construction events may have occurred, there seems little doubt that Chimney Rock great house was built as an observatory. In addition to the lunar standstill, the winter solstice was probably a yearly event of great importance to the inhabitants, and the co-occurrence of the lunar standstill with the winter solstice (on December 21) was undoubtedly a time of great celebration. The modern Pueblo people commemorate the winter solstice to this day, and this tradition has deep roots that extend to the Chacoans and, perhaps, earlier Puebloan ancestors.

Pueblo rituals of today include ceremonies linked to the summer and winter solstices and the spring and fall equinoxes. Sun-watching is very important in determining the proper times to schedule events and ceremonies. Lunar rituals are of less importance to the modern Pueblos. Given the concern of the Chacoans and other ancient Puebloans for lunar standstill cycles, we can infer that these rituals were lost with the end of the Chacoan world or, perhaps, at a later point in time.

CHACO CANYON AS A RITUAL CENTER FOR THE PUEBLO WORLD

Given the evidence discussed above, in terms of ceremonial structures, artifacts, roads as landscape monuments, and use of Chimney Rock and other sites to observe and track astronomical phenomena, it is not difficult to envision ritual and ceremony as critical concerns for the Chacoans. Beyond this, what can we say at a more general, theoretical level about Chaco Canyon as a ritual center?

From the beginnings of archaeological work and exploration in the Canyon, the uniqueness of the Chacoan great houses has been clear. Various researchers have discussed the importance of ritual and ceremony. Beyond relatively simple comparisons to the modern Pueblos, however, no comprehensive models or theoretical explanations have been offered until the last few years. Without sufficient space here to discuss every theory proposed, I instead focus on a recently developed view of Chaco as a "rituality."[11] It should be clear at the outset of this discussion that other views of Chaco ritual have been proposed and that the model presented here is by no means the only possibility.

The term *rituality* is used by archaeologist Jim Judge (and others) in contrast to the term *polity*. *Polity* denotes an organized and more permanent leadership structure, whereas *rituality* allows for a more fluid, situational leadership scenario. In terms of Chaco Canyon, the "ritual nature of Chaco cannot be reduced to its being the handmaiden of economic and/or political institutions. The term 'rituality' also implies that Chacoan society cannot readily be typed in neo-evolutionary terms, as being somewhere on its way to statehood."[12] In other words, Chacoan society is difficult to classify along the typical evolutionary sequence that anthropologists and archaeologists employ. We should not look at Chacoan society and assume that something happened to cut short its progress along an inevitable path to greater complexity, to the eventual emergence of the complicated form anthropologists describe as a state-level society. Chacoan society appears to represent a unique form, with some elements of societies identified as tribal and other traits associated with more complex organizations.

As a rituality and the ritual-ceremonial center for a large geographic area in the American Southwest, we can make several inferences about Chaco Canyon and the Chacoans. First, with its concentration of monumental public architecture, Chaco was the center of religious-ceremonial activities, probably on a seasonal calendar similar to those in use by modern Pueblo villages. These periodic ceremonies were probably linked to winter and summer solstices, spring and autumnal equinoxes, and other unknown seasonal events. These regular events were not only open to the residents of Chaco Canyon but also to Chaco-affiliated (and even nonaffiliated) groups across a large area of the northern Southwest. Thus, it is likely that hundreds and even thousands of non-Canyon residents traveled into Chaco during these occasions.

Although we can infer that ceremonial activities were the primary purpose for these seasonal events, other important social and economic functions occurred. Trade and commerce were undoubtedly ongoing throughout these events. Various great houses in Chaco served as marketplaces, with local venders offering food, craft goods, and services for barter to out-of-town visitors. Travelers, in turn, brought their wares into Chaco for exchange with distant family members, trading partners, and strangers. Among the goods we can envision trading hands were ceramic vessels from the Chuska Valley and elsewhere, high-quality stone raw materials, such as Narbona Pass chert and Jemez Mountains obsidian, carefully woven cotton textiles and yucca sandals, and perhaps some exotic items such as live macaws from Mexico and beautifully crafted jewelry of turquoise, shell, jet, and other luxuriant materials.

The second point on our list of inferences about the Chaco rituality relates to the nature of leadership. If the ritual model is correct, then we might infer that the leaders of Chaco were priests or medicine men. Certainly, the individual buried in Pueblo Bonito with many thousands of turquoise artifacts and other special, ritual items is a good candidate for a religious leader. Similarly, the man buried at Salmon Pueblo with trappings suggestive of Bow Society membership might have been a spiritual leader. But could we conclude that these men were the overall Pueblo leaders? A careful reading of Puebloan ethnographic research of the last 130 years suggests otherwise. Whereas the Pueblo village studied had religious leaders, the village also had secular positions that constituted the primary leaders—caciques, as they were named by the Spaniards. Before proceeding with this discussion, we must keep in mind that the Spanish caused considerable disruption in Puebloan society when they conquered New Mexico in the late sixteenth century and again in the late seventeenth century. Spanish administrators in colonial New Mexico wanted a single individual, today the governors of the Pueblos, to serve as the ultimate leader for each village. Thus, secular leadership positions among the Pueblos may be the product of Spanish influence. However, the social-ceremonial organizations of the Pueblos have leadership positions that are not religious in nature—the summer and winter chiefs of the Tewa, for example.[13] On balance, then, I would conclude that the available ethnographic and archaeological data suggest that leadership positions among the Chacoans and other pre-Hispanic Puebloans were not limited to medicine men, priests, or other religious-ceremonial practitioners. What we could call secular leaders existed and probably coordinated with religious leaders.

Several other concepts round out the notion of a Chaco rituality. First, ritual and ceremony are viewed as the dominant, overarching principles of organization. Other concerns in the economic, political, and social realms are important as discussed but secondary. Second, the rituality model presented includes a largely egalitarian and nonhierarchical view of Chacoan society. Social relationships are viewed as mostly equal, without any significant divisions, and leadership is seen as emerging situationally, as required. With Chacoan great houses viewed as ritual structures, a low resident population is inferred for these structures and extended to the Canyon as a whole. As ritual structures, great houses are variously envisioned to have provided temporary housing for pilgrims coming to Chaco (a "hotel" model), as storage structures, or some combination.

Criticisms of the Rituality Model

The idea of a Chacoan rituality explains some previously inexplicable aspects of the archaeology in Chaco Canyon. But the model has some problems, and an exploration of these issues is appropriate. First, if Chaco Canyon was primarily a ritual-ceremonial center, and not occupied by a large population, and if pilgrims came into Chaco on a regular basis for ceremonies, we could expect to find a greater number of great kivas. Chaco does have at least a dozen great kivas, but most are associated with great houses. Because of this association, we could infer that these great kivas were used primarily by the people who built and lived in the great houses. If large numbers of pilgrims were streaming into Chaco on a seasonal basis, we might expect that more isolated great kivas would have been built and used. As it stands, only three isolated great kivas are known in Chaco Canyon.

Second, looking at the pilgrimage model in a cross-cultural context is revealing. Historical data from Rome, Jerusalem, and Mecca, for example, indicate that pilgrims visiting these cities did not enjoy the best housing (certainly nothing like the Chacoan great houses) and were subject to poor treatment at the hands of local merchants and innkeepers.[14] Housing conditions for hypothetical Chacoan pilgrims could have been better, but pilgrims are usually among the lower socioeconomic classes of societies. One response to this criticism proposes that at least some of the great houses, Pueblo Alto, for example, were built by Puebloans who lived outside Chaco Canyon. Perhaps Pueblo Alto was built by a group from the Chuska Valley, west of Chaco, to serve as their primary residence during ceremonies and festivals held in the Canyon.[15] In this view, then, some of the "pilgrims" were landlords in Chaco.

SUMMARY

Chaco Canyon in the eleventh and early twelfth centuries was the ritual and ceremonial center of the Puebloan world. The concentration of great houses, great kivas, and ceremonial objects, as well as the symmetrical layout and astronomical alignments of the great houses, all point to Chaco's unique position in Pueblo culture. Chimney Rock great house, a Chacoan outlier, was constructed by the Chacoans as an astronomical observatory for the lunar standstill. Viewing Chacoan society organized as a rituality helps explain the presence of so many great houses in Chaco Canyon. As a society organized through ritual and ceremony, and demonstrating success in agricultural pursuits and construction projects (such as great houses, roads, and agricultural facilities), the Chacoans were able to recruit outside people and continue to grow. The possibility of outside groups constructing great houses (for example, Pueblo Alto) as ritual residences in Chaco Canyon is intriguing and might also help to explain the presence of so many large structures in a relatively small portion of the Canyon.

NOTES

1. Linda S. Cordell, *Archaeology of the Southwest* (San Diego: Academic Press, 1997).

2. Ruth Van Dyke, "The Chacoan Great Kiva in Outlier Communities: Investigating Integrative Spaces across the San Juan Basin," *Kiva* 67, no. 3 (2002): 231–247.

3. John R. Stein and Stephen H. Lekson, "Anasazi Ritual Landscapes," in *Anasazi Regional Organization and the Chaco System*, edited by David E. Doyel, Anthropological Papers no. 5 (Albuquerque: Maxwell Museum of Anthropology, 2001), pp. 87–100.

4. Kathy Roler Durand, "Function of Chaco-Era Great Houses," *Kiva* 69, no. 2 (2003): 141–169.

5. R. Gwinn Vivian, Dulce N. Dodgen, and Gayle H. Hartmann, *Wooden Ritual Artifacts from Chaco Canyon, New Mexico*, Anthropological Papers of the University of Arizona no. 32 (Tucson: University of Arizona Press, 1978), pp. 9–16.

6. Ibid., p. 37.

7. Several researchers over the last twenty-five years have studied astronomy at Chaco. The ideas presented here are extracted from several sources: John M. Fritz, "Paleopsychology Today: Ideational System and Human Adaptation in Prehistory," in *Social Archaeology*, edited by C. L. Redman et al. (New York: Academic Press, 1978), pp. 37–59; Anna Sofaer, "The Primary Architecture of the Chacoan Culture: A Cosmological Expression," in *Anasazi Architecture and American Design*, edited by B. H. Morrow and V. B. Price (Albuquerque: University of New Mexico Press, 1997), pp. 88–132; John R. Stein, Judith E. Suiter, and Dabney Ford, "High Noon in Old Bonito," in *Anasazi Architecture and American Design*, edited by B. H. Morrow and V. B. Price (Albuquerque: University of New Mexico Press, 1997), pp. 133–148.

8. J. McKim Malville and Claudia Putnam, *Prehistoric Astronomy in the Southwest* (Boulder, CO: Johnson Books, 1993), p. 33.

9. Jonathan E. Reyman, "Astronomy, Architecture, and Adaptation at Pueblo Bonito," *Science* 193 (1976): 957–962.

10. Malville and Putnam, *Prehistoric Astronomy in the Southwest*, p. 49.

11. Several researchers have discussed ritualities over the last few years. Robert D. Drennan, "Analytical Scales, Building Blocks, and Comparisons," in *Great Towns and Regional Polities*, edited by Jill E. Neitzel (Albuquerque: University of New Mexico Press, 2000), p. 257; Norman Yoffee, "The Chaco 'Rituality' Revisited," in *Chaco Society and Polity: Papers from the 1999 Conference*, edited by Linda S. Cordell, W. James Judge, and June-el Piper, Special Publication no. 4 (Albuquerque: New Mexico Archaeological Council, 2001); W. James Judge, "A Trial Timeline for Chacoan Society and Polity" (draft manuscript prepared for Chaco Capstone Conference, Albuquerque, NM, October 2002).

12. Yoffee, "The Chaco 'Rituality' Revisted," p. 266.

13. Alfonso Ortiz, *The Tewa World* (Chicago: University of Chicago Press, 1969).

14. Joseph A. Tainter and Fred Plog, "Structure and Patterning: The Formation of Puebloan Archaeology," in *Themes in Southwest Prehistory*, edited by G. J. Gumerman (Santa Fe, NM: School of American Research Press, 1994), p. 180.

15. H. Wolcott Toll, "Organization of Production in the Chaco Era," draft manuscript prepared for Chaco Capstone Conference, Albuquerque, New Mexico, October 2002.

CHAPTER 8

CHACOAN SOCIETY:
WHAT WE KNOW AND WHAT WE DON'T

In this book, we have explored the Puebloan society of Chaco Canyon. We have gained insight into Chaco's history by reviewing the period of discovery and exploration of the Chacoan great houses. We have examined those characteristics that made the Chacoan society unique in the Pueblo world. Our journey has taken us into the world of the outlying communities associated with Chaco Canyon—the outliers. We have taken a step back in time and visited Salmon Pueblo, figuratively, to see how its people lived and what was important in their lives.

To complete our literary and archaeological journey and close the circle, I want to review two sets of important considerations in our study of Chaco Canyon and the Chacoans. The first, in summary fashion, is what we know about this ancient society. The second is the harder of the two to discuss—what archaeologists do *not* know about Chacoan society. It's more difficult to shine a light on this topic because archaeologists, as well as historians and other scientists, rarely enjoy discussing that which they do not understand. This is particularly true in a publicly funded pursuit such as southwestern archaeology. Typical reaction to the disclosure of these "unknowns" is rarely favorable and runs along the lines of: "We provided thousands of dollars of funding and you still can't tell us. . . ." Public officials and the administrators of funding and granting agencies (as well as the general public) often fail to understand or appreciate the uncertainties inherent in archaeological research. They assume that X number of dollars equals X new findings and the answers to all the questions. In reality, this is rarely the case. Much remains unknown, and some of it unknowable, at the end of any archaeological research endeavor. So it is with Chaco Canyon and its eleventh- and twelfth-century society.

My structure for this exploration of the "knowns" and the "unknowns" about Chaco comes through discussion of several different characteristics of Chacoan society.

SIZE, POPULATION, AND DISTRIBUTION OF CHACOAN SOCIETY

The population supported by Chaco Canyon is a source of much debate. What can we say with certainty about the population of Chaco? With absolute certainty, we know that at least hundreds of people lived in Chaco Canyon. Most archaeologists would agree that between 1,500 and 5,000 people made Chaco their home at 1100 C.E.

Chacoan society, broadly defined, was spread across the San Juan Basin, predominantly in the modern state of New Mexico but extending into Colorado, Utah, and Arizona. Outlying communities, the outliers, associated with Chaco Canyon were built across this large area. At least 150 such communities are known, and we can infer that thousands (or tens of thousands) of people living in these communities were "affiliated" with Chaco Canyon in some fashion. Of these, we know that only a relatively small group of great houses beyond the Chaco Core (including Salmon, Aztec, Chimney Rock, Lowry, and a few others) have the specific architectural characteristics that indicate construction by Chacoan builders. Most of the outliers have some Chacoan characteristics but do not appear to have been built by Chacoan colonists. These sites were part of the broad Chacoan society, however, and were connected to Chaco through social and economic ties. We know that the Chaco System brought together a diversity of people and that multiple ethnic groups were involved.

We move along to our list of questions, the "unknowns" of Chacoan population. We cannot specify the precise number of people who lived in any of the Chaco Canyon great houses, in the Canyon as a whole, or in the outliers. The data simply do not exist for exact estimates. Similarly, we do not know how many of the outliers were contemporary with Chaco. Some have been dated with tree-ring dating or other absolute means, but for most, all we have for dating is surface architectural and ceramic data. Although many outliers have been documented, others undoubtedly lie "undiscovered." Archaeologists use available data to make reasonable inferences, but the bottom line is that we do not know the extent of contemporary outliers. Finally, archaeologists debate the nature of the relationship between central Chaco and the outliers. Some outliers, like Salmon and Aztec, seem to represent colonies of Chaco; but most do not. And although most outliers share a few characteristics with Chaco and with each other, most also have unique traits that indicate local origin and influence. Clearly, additional research is needed to understand the relationship between Chaco and its outliers.

LEADERSHIP

Starting with the most obvious point, we know the Chacoans had leaders. We know they had religious-ceremonial leaders, and we can infer that they had secular leaders not specifically connected to ritual and ceremony. The accomplishments of Chacoan society tell us that their leaders were strong and effective. Further, we know that Chacoan leaders had foresight and great skill in planning. Without these talents, the attainments of Chacoan architecture and other aspects of their culture would not have been possible.

Many questions and uncertainties remain about Chacoan leadership. We do not know if religious leaders or secular leaders had the ultimate authority, or if this power was shared or balanced. We do not know if Chacoan leaders were permanent, or if their authority was situational and thus transitory. We do not know if leadership in Chaco was achieved (earned through merit or hard work), if it was ascribed (passed from generation to generation), or if some combination of both occurred.

TRADE AND EXCHANGE

The durable record of Chacoan material culture—their ceramics, stone tools, wooden construction beams and artifacts, masonry walls, bone tools, corn and other foodstuffs, jewelry, room furnishings, clothing—gives us much information about the nature of trade, exchange, and interaction in the Chaco medieval world. We know that the Chacoans traded with their neighbors to obtain raw materials for stone tools, ceramic vessels, and perhaps clay, corn, and other agricultural products, cotton clothing, several species of wood for use in pueblo construction, and exotic shell, jet, and other minerals (as finished ornaments and as raw materials for use in craft production). Chacoan ceramics are found on sites around the Pueblo world, so we know they exchanged their own ceramics on occasion for other goods.

We know much about *what* the Chacoans bartered and obtained in trading activities. But we do not know *how* the Chacoans conducted trade. Drawing on economic theory in anthropology and other disciplines, archaeologists have proposed different trade mechanisms for the Chacoans and other Puebloans. The simplest, and most often proposed, is simple exchange of goods of equal or nearly equal value. This approach was probably used to bring most of the goods into Chaco and to move materials out of Chaco, through what is called "down-the-line" exchange. Goods move from trading partner to trading partner and can cross great distances over time. Other mechanisms have been proposed, such as long-distance trade of valuable exotic goods (such as macaws or shell jewelry) between elite members of Chacoan society and outside groups. Clearly, trade brought in such exotic items, but archaeologists do not know precisely how this process unfolded.

CEREMONIALISM AND RITUAL

The rich archaeological findings related to ritual, along with the presence of great kivas and the importance the Chacoans attached to astronomical movements of the sun, moon, and other celestial bodies, leave little doubt that ceremony and ritual were of critical importance to the Chacoans. Items like the likely altar furniture (consisting of carved and painted wooden objects) found in Chetro Ketl and Pueblo Bonito suggest ceremonial practices that were at least similar to those of the modern Pueblos. Ritual is, in fact, believed by many Chacoan archaeologists to be the primary raison d'être for the rise of Chacoan society in its unique form. We can say unequivocally that ritual and ceremony were an important part of Chacoan society and were important factors in its evolution. Archaeologists are confident that ritual specialists, whom we might call priests, were responsible for conducting ceremonies, for maintaining ritual artifacts and paraphernalia, and for tracking the ritual calendar and scheduling events.

Our list of "unknowns" regarding Chacoan ceremonialism is substantial. We cannot specify accurately the nature of Chacoan ritual and ceremony. We do not know what ceremonies were like or how they were conducted. We have no information on the words that were spoken, the songs that were sung, and the music and drumming that probably occurred during ceremonies. More specifically, we do not know the names of the deities important in Chacoan religion.

SOCIAL ORGANIZATION

Social organization is among the most debated of topics in Chacoan archaeology. The list of known facts is short—simply because there is no consensus on many issues. All or nearly all Chacoan archaeologists would probably agree that Chacoan social organization does not fit any other known pattern or type in the Southwest or elsewhere in the world. Chacoan society was complicated and involved multiple ethnic groups. Some elements of Western Pueblo–like clan organizations and Eastern Pueblo–like sodalities were probably present in Chaco. The term used by archaeologists recently to encapsulate Chacoan society is "rituality"— a society organized with ritual and ceremony as determining elements and lacking a persistent, hierarchical political system.

The list of uncertainties in this area is great. We cannot directly observe social relations while excavating archaeological sites or by analyzing the material remains of the Chacoans. With all the possibilities that have been proposed, we still simply do not know what exact form Chacoan social organization took. We cannot say with certainty that the Chacoans had a hierarchical social order, that egalitarianism (equality in social relations) was the rule, or what combination of these elements might have prevailed.

CONCLUDING THOUGHTS

Lest the reader come away believing that Chacoan archaeology is hopelessly mired in uncertainty and debate, or that the rendering of Chacoan archaeological data into "history" is futile, I offer some words of encouragement. Much has been learned over the last 150 years about Chaco archaeology and history. We have gathered a tremendous amount of data and conducted significant research on many aspects of Chacoan and Puebloan life. Today, we know much more than Lt. James Simpson did in 1849. We know that the Chacoans are the ancestors of the contemporary Pueblos, and we no longer need to invoke the Aztecs or another vanished empire to explain the magnificence of Chacoan architecture. We understand and appreciate the great houses of Chaco Canyon and the outliers both as unique phenomena and as ancestral precursors to the later Pueblo people. Chaco arose, collapsed, and left a legacy of diverse traditions whose threads we still see among the modern Pueblo people. Chacoan society is perhaps best viewed as a short-lived, ancient American social and ceremonial phenomenon during the worldwide medieval period.

Artist Richard Kern's rendering of Hungo Pavi, Chaco Canyon. Kern drew the pueblo as it might have looked when the Chacoans occupied it. Kern was part of Lt. James Simpson's trip through Chaco Canyon. Courtesy of the National Archives.

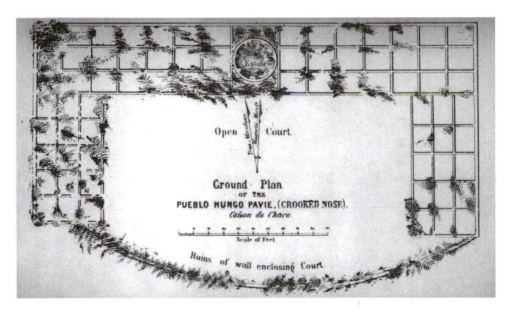

Richard Kern's site map of Hungo Pavi, Chaco Canyon, 1849. The only detail not apparent to Kern, but obvious in later expeditions to the site, was the great kiva in the plaza of the great pueblo. Courtesy of the National Archives.

Richard Kern's drawing of Pueblo Bonito, in the distance, in ruins. Note Threatening Rock looming over the site. Chaco Canyon, 1849. Courtesy of the National Archives.

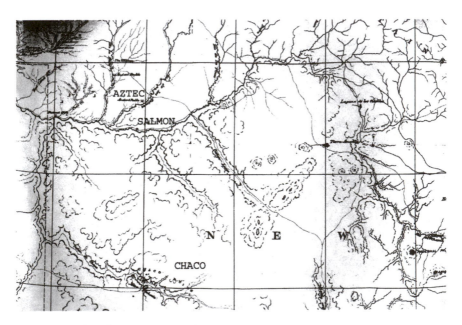

A portion of William Henry Jackson's 1878 map of ancient ruins in the American Southwest. The map shows Chaco Canyon, Aztec Ruins, and an unidentified ruin on the San Juan River that came to be known as Salmon Ruins. (Text added to identify great houses more clearly.)

Aerial photograph of "downtown" Chaco, looking north, including the ruins of Pueblo Bonito (*left center*), Chetro Ketl (*right*), Pueblo del Arroyo (*far-left center*), and Pueblo Alto (*upper center*) and the great kiva at Casa Rinconada (*lower center*). © Adriel Heisey.

Close-in aerial photograph of Pueblo Bonito, Chaco Canyon. Note the great kiva in the center of the pueblo and crumbled remains of Threatening Rock behind. © Adriel Heisey.

One of Timothy O'Sullivan's photographs of Salmon Pueblo, New Mexico, taken in 1874 during the Wheeler Survey. The view is to the southeast and shows the long back wall of Salmon and remnants of third-story architecture. Courtesy of the National Archives.

One of Timothy O'Sullivan's photographs of Salmon Pueblo, New Mexico, taken in 1874 during the Wheeler Survey. The view is the west and shows the interior of a second-story room, with part of the roof visible in the foreground. O'Sullivan is seated in the center of the frame next to a camera, with an unidentified assistant standing next to him. Courtesy of the National Archives.

Aerial photograph of Salmon Pueblo, New Mexico. The view is to the east, showing the great kiva prominently in the pueblo's plaza. © Adriel Heisey.

Excavation of the north wing of the West Ruin of Aztec Ruins using hand-drawn carts in 1917. Earl Morris directed the excavations at Aztec for the American Museum of National History. Courtesy of Aztec Ruins National Monument (AZRU 82).

View of excavated section of West Ruin at Aztec, New Mexico, 1920. Courtesy of Aztec Ruins National Monument (AZRU 1377).

Aerial photograph of the excavated West Ruin at Aztec Ruins, New Mexico. Note restored and roofed great kiva (*upper center*) in the plaza of the pueblo. © Adriel Heisey.

Photograph of Chacoan site of Pueblo Pintado, viewed from the northeast. This photograph captures well the medieval castle–like appearance of the site. Photo by author.

BIOGRAPHIES

Florence Hawley Ellis (1906–91)

Florence Hawley Ellis left a lasting legacy on Chacoan archaeology and more generally on southwestern American anthropology. She was one of the first women to complete graduate studies in archaeology and anthropology and be awarded a Ph.D. As a professor in the Department of Anthropology at the University of New Mexico from 1934 until 1971, she contributed to the intellectual development of thousands of students. Beyond this, Ellis is remembered as a valued teacher, colleague, and friend.

Ellis was born in 1906 in a small mining town in Sonora, Mexico, where her father worked as the chief chemist for a mine. The family relocated to the United States a few years later, and Ellis completed public school by the age of sixteen. She entered the University of Arizona, intending to study art. She completed her A.B. in English in 1927 and finished a Master of Arts degree in 1930. Enchanted with archaeology, Ellis taught at the University of Arizona for two years, then attended the University of Chicago. Ellis wrote her Ph.D. dissertation in 1934, studying the dendrochronology of the Chacoan site of Chetro Ketl. She then accepted a position at the University of New Mexico in the Department of Anthropology.[1]

For her dissertation, Ellis applied the newly developed techniques of dendrochronology (tree-ring dating) and stratigraphic dating of archaeological deposits to understand the history and evolution of Chetro Ketl. Her program of wood sampling at Chetro Ketl and other great houses in the Canyon was the largest effort of the time, eventually amassing more than 550 samples. The bulk of these samples came from Chetro Ketl—about 250 from beams within the mass of the pueblo and the remaining 200 from the massive trash mound located in front and east of the site. In particular, dating of wood from trash mounds was unprecedented. This approach allowed her to assign absolute dates to distinct soil layers in the big midden, thus dating the pottery types found in those layers. Ellis's work at Chetro Ketl pioneered this methodology and demonstrated its usefulness. As a result, such large-scale sampling of structural wood has been the standard approach for decades in Pueblo archaeology. Ellis also developed the first typology of the intricate Chacoan masonry. Although it has been modified over the years, her basic progression of masonry patterns is still used by archaeologists.[2]

Ellis worked in the field at Chaco Canyon for more than ten seasons in the 1930s and 1940s. Much of this work concentrated on small house sites, typically located on the south side of Chaco Canyon. Under Ellis's direction, several small house sites were excavated. The data recovered from these sites complemented and balanced what was known about great houses in Chaco. In addition, small house excavations led to a greater understanding of the chronology of Chaco, demonstrating contemporaneous use of many small house and great house sites.

In addition to work in Chaco Canyon, Ellis was very interested in Northern Rio Grande archaeology and conducted excavations at a number of sites in northern New Mexico including Pojoaque, Sapawe, Tsama, and San Gabriel del Yunque. In the 1950s and 1960s, Indian Land Claims became a primary concern for Ellis. She conducted extensive archaeological and ethnographic research on behalf of numerous Pueblo villages and the Navajo Nation. Her work broke new ground and demonstrated the value of combining archaeological and ethnological approaches to understanding culture.[3] She also conducted research into the Gallina Anasazi culture of northwest New Mexico. Later in life, the focus of Ellis's energy was the Ghost Ranch Museum in northern New Mexico.

Florence Hawley Ellis had a positive impact on the lives of thousands of students. At the University of New Mexico she is remembered as an inspiring and beloved teacher. She was very active late in her life, continuing to write about sites she had investigated until her death in 1991 at age eighty-four.

NOTES

1. Theodore Frisbie, "A Biography of Florence Hawley Ellis," in *Collected Papers in Honor of Florence Hawley Ellis*, edited by T. R. Frisbie (Norman, OK: Hooper Publishing Company, 1978), pp. 1–11. Much of the general information in this biography was drawn from this article.

2. Florence M. Hawley, *The Significance of the Dated Prehistory of Chetro Ketl, Chaco Canyon, New Mexico* (Santa Fe, NM: Monographs of the School of American Research, no. 2, 1934).

3. Frisbie, "A Biography of Florence Hawley Ellis," pp. 1–11, passim.

Alden Hayes (1916–98)

During the course of his long life and decades of archaeological work in Chaco Canyon, Alden C. Hayes bridged several eras of Chacoan research. He came up as a camp boy in the University of New Mexico (UNM) field schools in the 1930s and finished his career as a key player in the National Park Service's Chaco Project of the 1970s and 1980s. In a way that few others have, Hayes embodied Chacoan archaeology.

Alden Hayes was born in 1916 in Englewood, New Jersey. His family moved west, and Hayes was first exposed to Native American culture in Montana via contact with the Salish Indians.[1] Growing up, he developed the initial interest that would carry him through a lifetime of work as an archaeologist and anthropologist. Hayes met Edgar Hewett at a summer field camp and decided to attend the University of New Mexico. Studies and fieldwork were completed with Donald Brand, Florence Ellis, W. W. Hill, and Leslie Spier, among others. He graduated in 1939 with a Bachelor of Arts in anthropology and went no further with his education. Hayes later described himself as "one of the last uneducated archaeologists."[2] This statement reveals the modesty that characterized Alden Hayes throughout his life, despite his overwhelming archaeological knowledge and strong publication record.

Hayes first came to Chaco Canyon in 1935, working along with Robert Lister as a camp boy for the UNM field school. He followed this with summer field schools in Chaco in 1936 and 1937. Work in other areas of the West and Mesoamerica ensued, along with time in the army during World War II and the Korean War. Hayes also spent time in the 1940s and 1950s ranching in Arizona.

In 1957, Hayes returned to archaeology, after a four-year drought drove him out of the ranching business in Arizona.[3] He took a position with the National Park Service at Casa Grande in Arizona. The next year he became Supervisory Archaeologist on the Wetherill Mesa Project at Mesa Verde National Park in Colorado.[4] For most of the next decade, Hayes devoted his time to the Wetherill Project and greatly advanced knowledge and understanding of Mesa Verde archaeology. Work at Pecos National Monument occupied his time until early 1971.

In 1971, the Park Service initiated the Chaco Project under the leadership of Robert Lister and, later, James Judge. Hayes joined the project and took charge of a comprehensive survey of all land within the boundary of Chaco Canyon National Monument. Through this effort, more than 2,200 sites were recorded in an area of forty-three square miles by 1975.[5] The Hayes survey provided a complete inventory of cultural sites in Chaco for the first time and provided the baseline data that allowed for later synthetic studies of population, land use, and settlement. The survey data collected reflect Hayes's meticulous and comprehensive approach to archaeological fieldwork. Hayes retired from the National Park Service in 1976, after completing a number of Chaco Project reports.

Alden Hayes referred to himself as a "failed farmer, bankrupt cattleman, sometime smoke-chaser, one-time park ranger, and would-be archaeologist"—typically tongue-in-cheek for a multifaceted man who had many scholarly archaeological publications to his credit.[6] Alden Hayes died in 1998 and left a lasting legacy of archaeological fieldwork and writing about Chaco Canyon and the greater Southwest.

NOTES

1. Marjorie F. Lambert, "Alden C. Hayes," in *Prehistory and History in the Southwest: Collected Papers in Honor of Alden C. Hayes*, edited by Nancy Fox, Papers of the Archaeological Society of New Mexico no. 11 (Santa Fe: Ancient City Press, 1985), pp. 1–4. Much of the general information in the biography was drawn from this article.

2. Ibid., p. 2.

3. Mark Varien, "Alden Hayes Passes, 1998," www.swanet.org/zarchives/gotcaliche/alldailyeditions/98sep/228.html.

4. Lambert, "Alden C. Hayes," p. 2.

5. Alden C. Hayes, "A Survey of Chaco Canyon Archaeology," in *Archae-*

ological Surveys of Chaco Canyon, New Mexico, by Alden C. Hayes, David M. Brugge, and W. James Judge (Albuquerque: University of New Mexico Press, 1981), pp. 1–68.

6. "A Portal to Paradise, 2001," www.uapress.arizona.edu/books/bid1272.htm.

Edgar Hewett (1865–1946)

An ambitious and controversial figure in early American archaeology, Edgar Lee Hewett left a lasting legacy, training several generations of students and founding two of the Southwest's most enduring institutions. Born as the Civil War ended in 1865, Edgar L. Hewett was a man of his time. Early in his career in Missouri and Colorado, he taught school while working toward a Master of Pedagogy in Education (awarded in 1898 by Colorado State College of Education).[1] Degree in hand, Hewett was appointed president of New Mexico Normal University in Las Vegas (known today as Highlands University). Southwestern archaeology, in its infancy at the start of the twentieth century, would be changed forever through Hewett's efforts. Hewett worked throughout the world as an archaeologist, in Mexico, Central and South America, Italy, the Middle East, and of course, the American Southwest. Here the focus is on his southwestern work involving Chaco Canyon.

Leaving college administration behind, Hewett completed his doctorate at the University of Geneva. Later, he founded the Museum of New Mexico and School of American Archaeology (later known as the School of American Research), both in Santa Fe. Hewett was instrumental in passage of the Antiquities Act of 1906, the landmark legislation that provided for the protection of threatened archaeological and historic sites throughout the United States. In large part, Hewett was spurred to action by the activities of the Hyde Exploring Expedition, which conducted excavations at Pueblo Bonito between 1896 and 1901, under the direction of George Pepper and Richard Wetherill. Hewett believed the Hyde work to be little more than organized plundering and was instrumental in getting the excavations permanently suspended by 1902. Furthermore, he was one of the principal advocates for creation of Mesa Verde National Park in 1905 and Chaco Canyon National Monument in 1907.[2]

As a result of his firm-handed and sometimes domineering leadership, Hewett came to be known as "El Toro" (the bull).[3] Although he counted many friends among American archaeologists and members of Santa Fe society, he also acquired many enemies because of his determination and single-mindedness.

Beginning in the late 1920s, Hewett developed a program of excavation and research in Chaco Canyon, in conjunction with the University of New Mexico. The university had recruited Hewett to head up the newly created Department of Archaeology and Anthropology, and the resulting summer archaeological field schools trained hundreds of students. Fieldwork focused initially on the spectacular ruins of Chetro Ketl, second only to Pueblo Bonito in size. Work continued at Chetro Ketl for eight seasons. Other, smaller pueblos were excavated by archaeologists from the University of New Mexico (with Hewett's broad oversight) over the next fifteen years at Chaco. In addition, Hewett's School of American Research sponsored excavations at two great kivas in the canyon: Casa Rinconada and Kin Nahasbas. Through Hewett's efforts and enthusiasm, many prominent southwestern archaeologists and anthropologists of the middle twentieth century received their initial training. One major shortcoming of the work Hewett oversaw in Chaco was the publication record. Although theses, dissertations, and short papers and articles were completed, many of the important multiyear projects, such as the excavations at Chetro Ketl, were incomplete, and comprehensive archaeological reports were not finished.

Hewett also founded departments of archaeology and anthropology at the University of Southern California and the University of New Mexico in the 1920s. Hewett died in 1946 and left a legacy as one of the founding archaeologists in the Southwest, as a major supporter of archaeological research in Chaco Canyon for decades, and with lasting contributions to world archaeology and history.

NOTES

1. William S. Wallace, "Edgar L. Hewett: Archaeologist–College Administrator," *Southwestern Lore* 21, no. 1 (1955): 1–4.

2. Robert H. Lister and Florence C. Lister, *Chaco Canyon: Archaeology and Archaeologists* (Albuquerque: University of New Mexico Press, 1981).

3. "SAR: A Historical View," www.sarweb.org/home/history.htm. This Web page provided background information used in writing the biography.

Cynthia Irwin-Williams (1936–90)

In her short fifty-four years of life, Cynthia Irwin-Williams achieved a great deal and left a positive and lasting impression on a generation of archaeology students. She made significant contributions to archaeological research, relating not only to Chacoan studies but also to Paleoindian and Archaic adaptations and the transition to agriculture and sedentism in the ancient Puebloan world.

Irwin-Williams was born in Denver, Colorado, in 1936. She was interested in archaeology from a very young age. As a high school student, she excavated her first site under the direction of Marie Wormington. Irwin-Williams completed her bachelor's degree in anthropology at Radcliffe College in 1957. Although other women had completed advanced degrees in anthropology decades before, Irwin-Williams was one of the first women to be awarded the doctorate by Harvard University in 1963.[1] Her dissertation reported excavations at Magic Mountain, Colorado, an Archaic through Early Ceramic period site.

Cynthia Irwin-Williams first came to the ruins of Salmon Pueblo in 1969. In the mid-1960s, she had initiated the Anasazi Origins Project, with the goal of understanding the transition from Archaic period non-agricultural hunter-gatherers to the agricultural, sedentary Puebloans. But most of Irwin-Williams's prior archaeological research focused on Paleoindian and Archaic period human adaptations. With the beginning of the San Juan Valley Archaeological Research Project (with a primary emphasis on the excavation and study of Salmon Pueblo) in 1970, she was immediately immersed in the waters of complex Chacoan and Puebloan archaeology. To her credit and coming as no surprise to her colleagues and students, Irwin-Williams embraced the new challenge.

In 1972, she coined the phrase "Chaco Phenomenon" and designed a program of research at Salmon Pueblo and across the greater San Juan Valley. Not content to excavate and understand Salmon Pueblo merely as a single large site (this "single-site study" approach was the prevailing methodology in American archaeology at the time in the 1950s and 1960s), Irwin-Williams adopted a regional approach. She considered Salmon Pueblo, a Chacoan outlier along the San Juan River, to be a useful lens through which to view and understand the Chaco Phenomenon.

With this research focus in mind, Irwin-Williams directed fieldwork at Salmon Pueblo from 1970 through 1978. Approximately one-third of the Pueblo ruin was excavated, and more than 1.5 million artifacts and samples were collected. Analytic laboratories were operated at the site, and more than 700 students, volunteers, and professionals were involved in the Project. In 1980, Irwin-Williams co-edited a Final Report on the work at Salmon. She continued to work on a publishable manuscript for the site until her premature passing.

Beyond the excavations at Salmon, Irwin-Williams was very committed to the success of the San Juan County Museum Association, the managing body for the Salmon Ruins property. She successful lobbied the New Mexico legislature and other funding agencies and helped bring about the 1972 bond election that funded construction of a permanent research and laboratory facility on the Salmon premises.

Irwin-Williams died in 1990, and the career of one of southwestern archaeology's great thinkers was cut short. "Throughout her career, Cynthia Irwin-Williams displayed an energy and dedication to archaeology that few can equal. She was also a loyal friend, sometimes an extraordinarily generous friend, to people that she met as colleagues and as students."[2]

NOTES

1. Lynn Teague, "Cynthia Irwin-Williams: A Profile," *Archaeology Southwest* 16, no. 2 (2002): 5. In addition to this citation, Teague's article provided general information used here.

2. Ibid.

William Henry Jackson (1843–1942)

Of all the Chaco Canyon researchers and explorers profiled in this volume, William Henry Jackson, above all the others, is most well known for accomplishments that are unrelated to Chacoan archaeology. Jackson is one of the most renowned early American photographers. He took photographs all over the American West, including land that would become the states of Wyoming, Colorado, Idaho, Utah, Arizona, and New Mexico. He shot photographs along the Union Pacific Railroad route and was the official photographer of the U.S. Geologic Survey of the Territories, informally known as the Hayden Survey, in the 1870s.

His work documented Native Americans, in formal portraits and in "real life" in their villages at Hopi, Arizona, and on Ute Indian lands in Colorado. Central to our interest here, Jackson completed extensive descriptions of the ruins in Chaco Canyon in 1877 (published in 1878), and his work helped introduce the American public to the monumental Chacoan great houses.

William Henry Jackson was born in 1843 in Keeseville, New York. He became interested in the developing art of photography as a very young man. After graduating from high school, he worked as a photographic retoucher (with the predominant daguerreotype photography of the time). Jackson served on the Union side in the Civil War until 1865. In 1867, he opened a photography studio in Omaha, Nebraska, and equipped himself to do wet-plate photography in the field.[1]

Jackson's work as official photographer of the Hayden Survey covered most of the 1870s. Initial work of the Survey in 1872 documented the breathtaking geologic wonders of Yellowstone and helped bring about Yellowstone's designation as the country's first national park. The next years of Jackson's life involved geologic documentation and photography in Colorado. Colorado's Mount of the Holy Cross was "discovered," and Jackson photographed it for the first time. More significant for archaeology, the Survey came across ancient Indian ruins at Mesa Verde in 1874—several years before Wetherill found and named the spectacular Cliff Palace ruin at Mesa Verde.

In 1877, as part of the Hayden Survey, William H. Holmes and Jackson made a tour of most of the known Anasazi-Pueblo sites, including San Juan, Canyon de Chelly, Chaco Canyon, Pueblo Pintado, and the existing Moqui (Hopi) Villages near the Colorado River. This expedition brought Jackson to Chaco, allowing for his extensive contributions and, perhaps, one of his worst experiences as a photographer. Experimenting with a new method that differed from the wet-plate approach, Jackson made dozens of negatives of Chaco Canyon sites and scenery. None of the plates developed properly, and Jackson was horribly disappointed. Nevertheless, Jackson's descriptions of the Chacoan ruins were outstanding, and he found several sites not previously documented, including Pueblo Alto. He also identified several prehistoric stairways cut into the rock, including one north of Chetro Ketl that bears his name—the Jackson Stairway.[2]

In the 1880s and 1890s, Jackson worked across the West and traveled to India to take photographs. He photographed a number of railway routes, and his work was exhibited at the 1893 World Columbian Exposition. He retired from active work in 1924 but continued to take pictures, write, and draw. Jackson died in 1942, at the age of ninety-nine, in New York City.

Before he died, Jackson visited Chaco again in 1941, at the age of ninety-eight, and climbed up the stairway to the Canyon rim to look down again on Pueblo Bonito. He is the oldest person in the history of Chaco Canyon to make the ascent to the canyon rim. Jackson's legacy of site documentation in Chaco Canyon, while not linked to his well-known photography elsewhere, is nevertheless his lasting archaeological contribution.

NOTES

1. William Henry Jackson, *The Pioneer Photographer* (New York: World Book Company, 1929).

2. Robert H. Lister and Florence C. Lister, *Chaco Canyon: Archaeology and Archaeologists* (Albuquerque: University of New Mexico Press, 1981).

Neil Judd (1887–1976)

Neil M. Judd brought a detailed, analytical, and organized approach to fieldwork at Chaco Canyon in the 1920s. His reports on Pueblo Bonito and Pueblo del Arroyo still serve today as the primary source documents for these important sites.[1]

Judd was born in 1887. Little additional information is available about his childhood. Judd was a student at the University of Utah in 1907 when Professor Byron Cummings invited him on a trip to ruins in southeast Utah and northeastern Arizona. The trip resulted in Judd's lifelong fascination with archaeology and anthropology. In 1909, he was a member of the Cummings–William B. Douglass expedition to Rainbow Natural Bridge. Two years of work as a volunteer with Cummings ensued and led to a job at the Smithsonian National Museum in Washington. As an assistant in the museum, Judd sorted, catalogued, and classified thousands of artifacts and became very well acquainted with the laboratory end of the archaeology spectrum.[2] By 1913, Judd had completed a master's degree at George Washington. World War I interrupted Judd's studies, as he enlisted for duty but never served in Europe.

Judd's first southwestern employment came in 1917, when he accepted a position at the newly created Navajo National Monument in Arizona. He excavated and stabilized Betatakin Ruins, which he had helped discover with Cummings in 1907. Judd's work in stabilizing the ruins at Betatakin provided excellent training for the challenges he would later face at Pueblo Bonito.

Judd came to Chaco in 1921 to begin excavations at Pueblo Bonito. Judd's primary research interest was tracking the origin, evolution, and termination of Chacoan culture.³ At the outset, Judd believed that the society in Chaco was the result of local development through a long sequence of accrued traits and changes. Understanding this evolution required fine-tuned chronological data on Pueblo Bonito and Pueblo del Arroyo, the two Chacoan sites under investigation. Judd worked with A. E. Douglass, providing ancient timbers for tree-ring analysis. As work proceeded, Judd's crews completed the first efforts to stabilize exposed walls, roofs, and other features in the Chacoan sites. He recognized the importance of the prehistoric environment to the Chacoans and initiated some of the first studies designed to reconstruct past climate and environment. As work proceeded and data accumulated, Judd became convinced that the indigenous development model was incorrect. Instead, Judd proposed that later development (after 1050 C.E.) at Pueblo Bonito and in the rest of Chaco Canyon was the result of a migration of northern San Juan Basin peoples into the Canyon. Thus, Judd coined the terms *Old Bonitians,* for the original builders at Chaco, and *New Bonitians,* for the latecomers who took over the older sites, as well as building newer sites, such as Pueblo del Arroyo.⁴

After the National Geographic–sponsored fieldwork at Chaco ended in 1927, Judd returned to Washington, ostensibly to begin work on a series of reports. Ironically, however, Judd succumbed to the same problems that delayed George Pepper's report on Pueblo Bonito for twenty years: Curation, administration, and fieldwork on other Smithsonian projects diverted his attention.⁵ Although he filed progress reports on a regular basis and wrote short articles on the work at Pueblo Bonito, Judd's first comprehensive report on Chaco was not published until 1954, almost thirty years after the fieldwork ended.

Judd was appointed curator in archaeology at the National Museum in 1930. In the 1930s and 1940s, Judd completed fieldwork in a variety of locales across the West, some in the eastern United States, as well as work to the south in Guatemala. He studied ancient Hohokam canals in the Salt and Gila river basins in Arizona. Judd served a one-year term as president of the American Anthropological Association in 1945. As his active responsibilities declined with retirement in 1949, Judd was able to devote more time to his Chaco publications in the 1950s and 1960s. By 1964, three major volumes on the work in Chaco Canyon had finally been published.

Judd died in 1976, at the age of eighty-nine, after a decades-long career of archaeological fieldwork and research. His legacy is the completion of the first scientific and multidisciplinary research project at Chaco Canyon in the 1920s.

NOTES

1. R. Gwinn Vivian and Bruce Hilpert, *The Chaco Handbook: An Encyclopedic Guide* (Salt Lake City: University of Utah Press, 2002), p. 137.

2. Neil M. Judd, *Men Met Along the Trail* (Norman: University of Oklahoma Press, 1968).

3. R. Gwinn Vivian, *The Chacoan Prehistory of the San Juan Basin* (San Diego: Academic Press, 1990).

4. Neil M. Judd, *The Architecture of Pueblo Bonito*, Smithsonian Miscellaneous Collections, vol. 147, no. 1 (Washington, DC: Smithsonian Institution, 1964).

5. Robert H. Lister and Florence C. Lister, *Chaco Canyon: Archaeology and Archaeologists* (Albuquerque: University of New Mexico Press, 1981), p. 73.

Robert Lister (1915–94)

Robert Lister was born in Las Vegas, New Mexico, in 1915. Much of his youth was spent on a nearby cattle ranch, where Lister learned the value of hard work. He graduated from high school in Las Vegas and attended the University of New Mexico at Albuquerque beginning in 1933. Four year later, Lister had completed a bachelor's degree in anthropology. By 1938, he had finished a master's degree in anthropology and was teaching at the University of New Mexico.[1]

Fieldwork in Mexico and New Mexico helped convince Lister that archaeology was the career to pursue. Preparing to attend Harvard University, Lister instead was drafted into the army at the beginning of World War II. With the war over in 1945, he began a doctoral program at Harvard. His Ph.D. finished in 1950, Lister accepted a position in the newly created Department of Anthropology at the University of Colorado, Boulder. Over the next twenty years, Lister developed and shepherded the anthropology program. A primary emphasis was archaeological field schools, held at Mesa Verde National Park for many years. Lister also played a key role with the University of Utah's Glen Canyon archaeological program in the 1950s and served as a consultant to the National Park Service.

In 1971, Lister's life and career shifted, as he retired from teaching in Colorado. He took on the director's job for the National Park Service's Chaco Canyon Project. Lister thus returned to Chaco, where he had trained as a student with Florence Hawley Ellis in the 1930s. Lister and his colleagues created the research program designed to answer some of the long-standing questions about Chaco. When, how, and why were the great houses built? What is the relationship between great houses and small houses in Chaco? How did the environment and climate influence cultural activities and developments in Chaco?

During the 1970s, Lister also became chief archaeologist for the National Park Service, overseeing thousands of employees and projects nationwide. By 1978, Lister had retired from his Park Service positions. In retirement, he continued to write and lecture about Chacoan archaeology. He and his wife Florence wrote books about Chaco Canyon and Aztec Ruins in the 1980s.

Robert Lister died in 1994 on a trip to Moon House, a Puebloan cliff dwelling in southeastern Utah. Out of the old American West comes the expression "They died with their boots on." Lister passed on in perhaps the best fashion for an archaeologist—in the field while visiting archaeological sites.

NOTE

1. Robert C. Euler and David A. Breternitz, "Bob and Florence Lister: In Retrospect," in *From Chaco to Chaco: Papers in Honor of Robert H. Lister and Florence C. Lister*, edited by M. S. Duran and D. T. Kirkpatrick (Albuquerque:

Archaeological Society of New Mexico Papers 15, 1989), pp. 1–10. This article
was the source for much of the material in this biography.

Earl Morris (1889–1956)

Earl Morris, New Mexico archaeologist of the first half of the twentieth century, is believed to have been the model for the Indiana Jones
movie character created by Steven Spielberg. Morris cut a dashing figure
with his signature hat (although not a fedora, as Indiana Jones wore)
and trowel. Perhaps more than any other person, Earl Morris captures
the essence of early-twentieth-century archaeology in the American
Southwest.

Earl Morris was born in Chama, New Mexico, in 1889. His father,
Scott Morris, worked as a teamster in the frontier town of Farmington,
running freight for miners and farmers and occasionally prospecting for
and selling Native American, mostly Puebloan, artifacts. Earl excavated
his first site in 1893 as a toddler wandering about his family's property.
From this point on, his passion for archaeology burned hot, and Morris
would pursue this passion for the next fifty years. Whereas Morris's early
work can certainly be described as looting or pot hunting by modern
standards, most of the materials he excavated (primarily whole ceramic
vessels from various sites) were donated to various museums.[1]

Morris completed bachelor's and master's degrees at the University of
Colorado and by 1916 was ready to embark on what would become one
of his life's great works: the excavation of Aztec Ruins, New Mexico.
Morris excavated at Aztec for several years, eventually clearing many of
the rooms comprising the west pueblo of Aztec—the entire site is preserved as Aztec Ruins National Monument. The inaccurately named
Aztec Ruins[2] was initially discovered and damaged by local relic hunters
and casual visitors in the 1880s. Later, the site was purchased and protected by H. D. Abrams, who agreed to excavations by the American
Museum of Natural History. Work began under the academic supervision of archaeologist Nels Nelson, with Morris in charge of the fieldwork. Land containing the Aztec pueblos and several other sites was
donated, and Aztec Ruins became a national monument in 1923.

Morris and his crews labored at Aztec for six field seasons between
1916 and 1921. Excavations revealed more than 350 rooms and almost
thirty small kivas (ceremonial structures), as well as a great kiva in the

plaza (the open space in the court of the pueblo).[3] To accommodate his work at the site and to fulfill his appointment as on-site custodian of Aztec, Morris constructed a southwestern-style house (using discarded and salvaged materials from the ruin) close to the pueblo in 1919. After Morris finished work, the house became the visitor center for the new monument. Morris returned to work at Aztec in 1934 to reconstruct the great kiva for visitation. Although critics (then and now) nitpick at the details, Morris's reconstruction represents a major accomplishment and helps visitors gain a firsthand sense of the power and mystery of Puebloan ceremonial life.

Morris's work at Aztec Ruins was important, but perhaps ironically it came at an early point in his career before he fully understood the ebb and flow of Pueblo history. The report Morris wrote on Aztec is descriptive and focuses on the Pueblo's architecture and material culture (pottery, textiles, and stone tools). Morris offers some interpretation of Aztec but did not discuss its place within the broader frame of Puebloan history.

After he finished work at Aztec, Morris spent the next twenty-five years excavating sites across the American Southwest and in the Yucatan studying Mayan sites. Next to Aztec, Morris's biggest investment of fieldwork was the archaeology of the La Plata Valley, just a few miles west and north of Aztec. This research resulted in a synthetic interpretation of early Pueblo history—Morris's report: *Archaeological Studies in the La Plata District* in 1939.[4] In the La Plata report Morris drew fully upon his decades of archaeological fieldwork in the Southwest, including his time at Aztec.

Earl Morris died on June 24, 1956. With his passing, southwestern archaeology lost one of its pioneering giants. Morris was an amazing fieldworker, completing more than forty field seasons during his lifetime. His enduring legacy is the picture he painted through his writings of early Puebloan history and culture.

NOTES

1. Florence C. Lister and Robert H. Lister, *Earl Morris and Southwestern Archaeology* (Albuquerque: University of New Mexico Press, 1968). Much of the information in this biography came from this source.

2. Aztec Ruins was thought by the pioneers of the late nineteenth century

and some archaeologists of the day to have been constructed by the Aztecs, who lived far to the south in Mexico and several hundred years later in time. Although limited contact may have occurred between the early Pueblos of the Southwest and Mexican cultures, there is no evidence that the Aztecs ever visited the Southwest.

3. Robert H. Lister and Florence C. Lister, *Aztec Ruins on the Animas* (Albuquerque: University of New Mexico Press, 1987).

4. Earl H. Morris, *Archaeological Studies in the La Plata District* (Washington, DC: Carnegie Institution of Washington Publication no. 519, 1939).

George Pepper (1873–1924)

George H. Pepper is probably the least well known in this group of biographies. Two primary factors account for Pepper's anonymity relative to others in this group. First, Pepper worked at Chaco as a young man in his twenties and did most of his later anthropological studies outside the American Southwest. Second, Pepper worked with the Hyde Exploring Expedition to Chaco, which was shut down after an investigation by the U.S. government. Although Pepper is recognized for contributions to Chacoan archaeology, the chance for greater accomplishments and recognition was lost with the end of the Hyde Expedition in 1902.

Pepper was born in 1873 on Staten Island, New York. Growing up, Pepper became very interested in the Indian sites around the family home. Upon graduating from high school in 1895, Pepper began studies at the Peabody Museum of Harvard University with the encouragement of Professor Frederic Putnam. This training led to his appointment as assistant curator in the Department of Anthropology at the American Museum of Natural History in New York.[1] By 1896, the Hyde Exploring Expedition to Pueblo Bonito was gearing up. Putnam sent Pepper, who at that time had no field experience, to Chaco to serve as field supervisor. Richard Wetherill, who had visited Chaco in 1895 and convinced the Hyde brothers to fund an expedition, served as field foreman.[2]

Pepper thus came to Chaco Canyon early in his career, at the age of twenty-three and with no prior fieldwork under his belt. Nevertheless, Pepper was a meticulous note-taker and kept detailed records of the excavations at Pueblo Bonito. These skills nicely complemented those of Wetherill, who was an able and effective field foreman. Under Wetherill's direction, crews of Navajo men moved amazing quantities of dirt and rubble during five seasons of work through the summer of 1900. Pepper excelled at documenting and cataloguing the materials recovered from excavation. Once the fieldwork was terminated, he published several articles on the ceremonial artifacts recovered from Pueblo Bonito. Although the report was delayed twenty years, Pepper completed a monograph on the Hyde Expedition work at Pueblo Bonito.[3]

Beyond Chaco Canyon, Pepper made important contributions to American anthropology. He undertook an ethnological reconnaissance of the modern Pueblo villages after the work at Pueblo Bonito ended and studied Navajo weaving. Pepper conducted archaeological work in Mexico and Ecuador before moving to the University Museum in Philadelphia in 1909. In this new assignment, Pepper made perhaps his most lasting contribution to the field of anthropology. The museum collection Pepper assembled evolved into the core of the Heye Foundation's Museum of the American Indian. He continued at the museum for the next fifteen years, working mostly on collections with occasional fieldwork including a 1918 trip to the Zuni site of Hawikuh with the Museum of the American Indian's Hendricks-Hodge Expedition.[4]

George Pepper died in 1924 at the age of fifty-one. His legacy to Chacoan archaeology encompasses meticulous record keeping and the understanding of the great importance of ritual and ceremony in the Chacoan worldview. Chacoan archaeologists have come full circle over the last 100 years and are again trying to understand and explain Chacoan ritual and ceremonialism.

NOTES

1. "Anthropology Notes: George Hubbard Pepper," *American Anthropologist* 26 (1924): 566–567. This source provided much of the information used in this biography.

2. R. Gwinn Vivian, *The Chacoan Prehistory of the San Juan Basin* (San Diego: Academic Press, 1990).

3. George Pepper, *Pueblo Bonito* (New York: Anthropological Papers of the American Museum of Natural History, vol. 27, 1920; reprint, Albuquerque: University of New Mexico Press, 1996).

4. "Anthropology Notes," pp. 566–567.

Lt. James Simpson (1813–83)

James H. Simpson spent only a few short years of his life in the West. Yet it was during those years that his most lasting contributions to history were made.[1] His descriptions of ruined great houses in Chaco Canyon stand not only as the first known documentation but also in the great perception and appreciation revealed.

Simpson was born in 1813 in New Jersey. Little is known of his days as a youth. His parents were devout Episcopalians, and he was named James Hervey after an English clergyman.[2] Simpson was a gifted student and given an appointment to West Point at the age of fifteen, in 1928. He saw military action in the late 1830s in the Seminole War in Florida. At the age of twenty-five, he was transferred to the Corps of Topographical Engineers and began the work that would occupy most of his military career. Over the next two decades, he designed and supervised the construction of bridges, roads, lighthouses, and other projects up and down the East Coast and Midwest.

In 1849, Simpson was a first lieutenant in the Corps of Topographical Engineers. Newly arrived in New Mexico, Simpson was assigned to military governor Col. John Washington's 1849 Expedition. Washington's overt goal was to make contact with the Navajo Indians and sign a peace treaty. In truth, however, Washington wanted to impress upon the erstwhile hostile Navajos the power and military capability of the United States. The party left Santa Fe, New Mexico, and traveled west, intending to meet up with the Navajos at Canyon de Chelly, Arizona.

East of the main group of Chacoan great houses, tracking the Chaco drainage as it ran west, Washington's column spotted the high walls of the ruins of Pueblo Pintado. Of all the Chacoan sites, Pueblo Pintado truly projects a monumental image. It is visible for literally miles when approaching from the northeast, as did the 1849 Expedition, and is analogous to the medieval castles of Europe. The military party's guides related the knowledge they possessed of the ancient ruins. Pueblo Pintado, in particular, had spawned numerous tales and was given a different name by almost every guide in the group.

Several miles down the Chaco, as the outfit prepared to leave the canyon for a more direct course west, the guide mentioned the presence of several more large Puebloan ruins. Simpson received leave to take a small party, including artist Richard Kern and Mexican guide Carravahal, and investigate the ruins. His report provided the first documentation of the amazing, spectacular, and well-preserved multistory great houses of Chaco Canyon.

Finishing his work on the ruins, Simpson and his small party rejoined the military expedition. After a calamitous encounter in which Navajo headman Narbona and six other Navajos were killed, the group made its way to Canyon de Chelly. A council between the Americans and Navajos was held, and a treaty to end hostilities between the Navajos and the Mexican, American, and Puebloan peoples of New Mexico was signed.

After finishing his journal in 1850, Simpson remained in the West on various surveying parties until 1851, when he was transferred to Minnesota Territory and later put to work on the East Coast. He returned to the West in 1858 and stayed until the beginning of the Civil War in 1861. During the war, Simpson fulfilled various duties and ended the war as chief engineer for the Department of the Interior in Washington. Near the close of the Civil War in 1865, Simpson was promoted to the rank of brevet brigadier general. Simpson died in 1883 at the age of seventy.

Simpson's description of the Chacoan ruins has inspired many people, past and present. Ironically, as author Frank McNitt related:

> Simpson abominated the Southwest, as he so grimly confessed. [Nevertheless,] few writers most ardently attuned to the region have conferred such favor upon it. Alone in Colonel Washington's command, Simpson comprehended what was remarkable in broken walls of ancient stone, the depths and distances of a canyon gorge, and of old names carved on a lonely rock. His record of discovery, fresh and sometimes naive, still illuminates as though for the first time silent places and vanished people of our past.[3]

NOTES

1. James H. Simpson, *Navaho Expedition: Journal of a Military Reconnaissance from Santa Fe, New Mexico to the Navajo Country*, edited and annotated by Frank McNitt (1850; reprint, Norman: University of Oklahoma Press, 1964), p. lix. This source provided most of the information for this biography.

2. Ibid., p. lx.

3. Ibid., p. 174.

Gordon Vivian (1908–66)

More than any other single individual, Gordon Vivian was instrumental in the development of policies and procedures for the protection and stabilization of Chacoan sites. Because of his early association with Edgar Hewett and a long period of work for the National Park Service at Chaco, Vivian excavated and stabilized a broad range of sites from the great kiva at Casa Rinconada to small houses scattered around the canyon. With some modification, Vivian's stabilization program is still the standard for work at architectural sites across the American Southwest.

Richard Gordon Vivian was born in Michigan in 1908. His family moved to Albuquerque, New Mexico, in 1918, where his father established a dairy business. As a high school student, Vivian explored much of the area around Albuquerque on bicycle and became very interested in the local archaeology.[1]

Vivian enrolled in the University of New Mexico in 1927 and studied under Edgar Hewett. He first came to Chaco in 1929, to work as a field school participant at Chetro Ketl. He worked in a variety of capacities for Hewett until 1935. In 1931, Vivian began excavations at Casa Rinconada, one of several isolated great kivas in Chaco Canyon. Once the structure was cleared of debris and fully excavated, preserving and stabilizing the structure became the next priority. Vivian took on this task with enthusiasm and evolving skill, which led to his involvement with stabilization and ultimate development of the National Park Service's program in 1937.[2]

Vivian received a B.A. in archaeology in 1931 and completed a master's degree at the University of New Mexico in 1932. His thesis reported excavations at the abandoned Pueblo village known as Bandelier's Puaray.

Over the next twenty years, until the late 1950s, Vivian worked in Chaco for the National Park Service on numerous projects. Beyond this, he lived in Chaco Canyon for many years and became a storehouse of knowledge about the ruins and the history of the canyon. Vivian directed stabilization and limited excavation at many of the large sites such as Pueblo Bonito and Chetro Ketl. Small site excavation, such as Vivian's work at the Three-C Site, was also completed. Vivian oversaw the excavations in Room 93 in Chetro Ketl, which produced an amazing collection of ritual wooden artifacts unparalleled in Puebloan archaeology.[3]

In 1953, Vivian completed excavations at the Hubbard site at Aztec Ruins. The site consisted of a triwall structure with the remains of at least two earlier small pueblos underneath. Based on ceramics and the depositional context, Vivian dated the Hubbard site to the C.E. 1200s, coincident with the later San Juan–Mesa Verde occupation at Aztec.

During his time in Chaco, Vivian became interested in the remains of agricultural systems in the canyon. He laid the groundwork for the extensive studies of water and soil control completed by his son Gwinn Vivian in the 1960s and 1970s. Through his work at Kin Kletso and in the ensuing report, Vivian presented his hypothesis (following the work of anthropologist Clyde Kluckhohn) that Chaco was occupied by three distinct cultural groups. These distinct groups were represented in the canyon by the three primary types of architecture: (1) early great house or Bonito style; (2) small house or Hosta Butte style; and (3) late great house or McElmo style. Because of the proposed existence of three distinct traditions, this view is known as the Chaco Co-Tradition model.[4]

Gordon Vivian died in 1966, and Chacoan archaeology lost one of its most knowledgeable practitioners. Perhaps Vivian's most lasting contribution was his development of a ruins stabilization program that preserved and protected the unique remains in Chaco Canyon and elsewhere in the Pueblo Southwest.

NOTES

1. Roland Richert, "Richard Gordon Vivian, 1908–1966," *American Antiquity* 32 (1967): 100.

2. R. Gwinn Vivian and Bruce Hilpert, *The Chaco Handbook: An Encyclopedic Guide* (Salt Lake City: University of Utah Press, 2002), p. 260.

3. R. Gwinn Vivian, Dulce N. Dodgen, and Gayle H. Hartmann, *Wooden Ritual Artifacts from Chaco Canyon, New Mexico*, Anthropological Papers of the University of Arizona, no. 32 (Tucson: University of Arizona Press, 1978).

4. R. Gwinn Vivian, *The Chacoan Prehistory of the San Juan Basin* (San Diego: Academic Press, 1990).

Richard Wetherill (1858–1910)

Richard Wetherill, cowboy, explorer, and trader, is credited (along with cowboy Charlie Mason) with discovering and publicizing the spectacular ruins of Mesa Verde, Colorado, specifically the site of Cliff Palace, in 1888. He went on to explore many of the cliff ruins of the area and other caves in Utah and Arizona. In 1895, Wetherill guided a party to Chaco Canyon and became enamored. He went on to conduct excavations in Pueblo Bonito and open a trading post near the ruin. Among his contributions, Wetherill popularized the term Anasazi, derived from a Navajo phrase meaning either "ancient ones" or "ancient enemies of our ancestors."[1] He also coined the term *Basket Maker*, to describe the cave-dwelling ancestors of the builders of Cliff Palace and other Puebloan sites. Wetherill's archaeological explorations generated significant controversy because most of the work was focused on obtaining artifacts for museum and private collections. Too little attention was paid to understanding the context of the remains and artifacts collected as sites were quickly excavated.

Wetherill was born on June 12, 1858, in Chester, Pennsylvania. His parents were Quakers, and while an infant, his father took employment with the U.S. government as an Indian agent. Wetherill had little formal education but learned the basics of mathematics and geography. He never attended college. Formal writing was not a skill he acquired, and this proved to be limiting in later years as some of his archaeological pursuits necessitated good written communication skills. The Wetherills moved west in the 1870s, eventually settling in Mancos, Colorado, in 1880. Their Alamo Ranch was built in 1882 and became the family home for decades.[2]

Largely by accident, Wetherill became involved in archaeological discovery and exploration and evolved into a self-taught archaeologist. He and Charley Mason stumbled onto Cliff Palace in Mesa Verde, Colorado, while hunting stray cattle in December 1888. For the next few years, Wetherill and his four brothers explored and prospected in the Mesa Verde ruins. They amassed a sizable collection of intact pottery and other museum-quality items (complete textiles, rabbit-fur blankets, baskets, sandals), which were sold to museums and private collectors in the United States and overseas. These collections, obtained without benefit of controlled excavations or documentation, represent the questionable legacy of Wetherill's prospecting activities, particularly from a conservation viewpoint. We must remember, however, that this "collection mentality" was rampant in late-nineteenth- and early-twentieth-century America, and much of the material held today in American museums was gathered during that time with questionable methodology. In this fashion, Richard Wetherill, like Earl Morris and other early archaeologists, was a man of his time.

In 1895, Wetherill came to Chaco Canyon while guiding the Palmer family. Wetherill immediately recognized Pueblo Bonito as a treasure trove of archaeological specimens. He probed the ruin in 1895, explored the other great houses in the canyon, and became determined to pursue large-scale excavation at Pueblo Bonito. For financial backing, Wetherill enlisted the Hyde brothers of New York, who had previously purchased archaeological collections. The Hyde Exploring Expedition teamed up with Frederic Ward Putnam of the American Museum of Natural History to undertake excavations at Pueblo Bonito. Wetherill served as field foreman for several seasons of work at Pueblo Bonito. In 1900, Wetherill filed for a 160-acre homestead that included the four largest Chacoan great houses in the canyon. To supply his group of Navajo workers, Wetherill built a trading post and store adjacent to Pueblo Bonito, utilizing a well-preserved 900-year-old back room in the pueblo as a storeroom. Excavations at Pueblo Bonito were temporarily terminated in 1900 by a U.S. government investigation that included the legitimacy of Wetherill's homestead claim. As a result of Agent Holsinger's investigation and 1901 report, the Hydes' work was permanently ended, and Wetherill's homestead claim was suspended in 1902 and ultimately rejected.[3]

With the archaeological work ended, the Hydes and Wetherill concentrated on trading activities in the canyon and beyond. At their peak, they were operating twelve trading posts across the Southwest. Wetherill had a falling out with the Hydes in 1903 and bought the Pueblo Bonito trading post.[4] He continued to pursue his suspended homestead claim, trying to make a living farming and ranching on the land. Wetherill also promoted Navajo weaving, a declining craft in the early 1900s, encouraging weavers to expand beyond the traditional blanket style that prevailed at the time. Along with George Pepper, who purchased many rugs and supported local weavers, Wetherill helped to reinvigorate and redirect the Navajo weaving tradition in New Mexico.

Richard Wetherill was killed in a June 1910 encounter with a Navajo man. Almost 100 years later, the events surrounding his death remain complicated, and it is unclear if the man intended to kill Wetherill. Controversy seemed to follow Wetherill throughout his life.[5] Nevertheless, he made lasting contributions to American archaeology and should be remembered for that legacy.

NOTES

1. Frank McNitt, *Richard Wetherill Anasazi: Pioneer Explorer of Southwestern Ruins* (Albuquerque: University of New Mexico Press, 1957). This source provided general material for this biography.

2. Ibid., pp. 21–40, passim.

3. S. J. Holsinger, "Report on Prehistoric Ruins of Chaco Canyon, New Mexico" (Chaco Canyon: Manuscript on file, Chaco Culture National Historic Park, 1901).

4. Robert H. Lister and Florence C. Lister, *Chaco Canyon: Archaeology and Archaeologists* (Albuquerque: University of New Mexico Press, 1981).

5. McNitt, *Richard Wetherill Anasazi*, pp. 269–271.

PRIMARY DOCUMENTS

Josiah Gregg's 1844 Description of Pueblo Bonito

In Commerce of the Prairies, *trader and explorer Josiah Gregg describes
his adventures along the Santa Fe Trail between Missouri, Arkansas,
and New Mexico from 1831 to 1840. Of interest here, he describes
several of the Pueblo villages of the day and the ruins of Pueblo Pintado,
near the head of Chaco Canyon. Gregg used the name Pueblo Bonito
for this ruin. Lieutenant Simpson later referred to the site as Pueblo
Pintado, one of the names the Jemez governor Hosta provided, and it is
by the name Pueblo Pintado that the ruin is currently known and described. It is unclear if Gregg was guided to the site by Hosta or another
individual or if he was told a secondhand account, with the name Pueblo
Bonito applied to the ruin in question.*

*Gregg refers to the writing of Mexican Jesuit priest and historian Fran-
cisco Saverio Clavigero, who apparently was responsible for popularizing
the myth of the northern wanderings of the Aztecs (Gregg renders the
name as Azteques) with his* Historica antica del Messico *(Ancient
History of Mexico) in 1780. As other documents in this section illustrate, nearly every early explorer of the Chaco and San Juan regions
heard a version of the Aztec myth told by Native American or Spanish
Mexican guides. Many of the early explorers accepted the idea that the
Aztecs of central Mexico had built the fabulous houses in Chaco Canyon, and Gregg was no exception. He believed the ruins of Pueblo Pintado to have been built by a people "far more enlightened" than any that*

still inhabited the region. We know today that this is not the case. Rather, the great houses in Chaco Canyon represent a unique part of ancient Pueblo history.

Gregg's account is historic because it is the first-known written account of Chaco Canyon and Pueblo Pintado. There is considerable debate among scholars as to whether or not Gregg actually visited Chaco Canyon. Some have speculated that he drew upon earlier Spanish and Mexican military accounts in his descriptions. It is certainly possible that Gregg found and read one or more prior accounts of Chaco. But those documents were certainly not readily available. Furthermore, Gregg spent enough time in Santa Fe during the decade of the 1830s to have easily allowed for a visit to Chaco.

Gregg's description of Pueblo Pintado, with walls built of "fine-grit sandstone," certainly anticipates later studies of the amazing masonry and architecture of Chaco Canyon sites. He comments on the excellent condition of some of the rooms, with roofs still intact. Lieutenant Simpson made similar observations in 1849; by 1877 William Henry Jackson's visit made it clear that significant impacts to the ruins in Chaco Canyon had begun.

DOCUMENT 1
Commerce of the Prairies, 1844
Josiah Gregg

All of the Indians of New Mexico not denominated Pueblos—not professing the Christian religion—are ranked as *wild tribes*, although these include some who have made great advances in arts, manufactures and agriculture. Those who are at all acquainted with the ancient history of Mexico, will recollect that, according to the traditions of the aborigines, all the principal tribes of Anahuac descended from the North: and that those of Mexico, especially the Azteques, emigrated from the north of California, or northwest of New Mexico. Clavigero, the famous historian heretofore alluded to, speaking of this emigration, observes, that the *Azteques*, or Mexican Indians, who were the last settlers in the country Anahuac, lived until about the year 1160 of the Christian era in Aztlan, a country situated to the north of the Gulf of California; as is inferred from the route of their peregrinations, and from the information afterwards acquired by the Spanish in their expeditions through these countries.

Even allowing that the traditions upon which Clavigero founded his theoretical deductions are vague and uncertain, there is sufficient evidence in the ruins that still exist to show that those regions were once inhabited by a far more enlightened people than are now to be found among the aborigines. Of such character are the ruins of *Pueblo Bonito* [Pintado], in the direction of Navajo, on the borders of the Cordilleras; the house being generally built of slabs of fine-grit sand-stone, a material utterly unknown in the present architecture of the North. Although some of these structures are very massive and spacious, they are generally cut up into small, irregular rooms of which yet remain entire, being still covered, with the *vigas* or joists remaining nearly sound under the *azoteas* of earth; and yet their age is such that there is no tradition which gives any account of their origin. But there have been no images or sculptured work of any kind found around them. Besides these, many other ruins (though none so perfect) are scattered over the plains and among the mountains. What is very remarkable is, that a portion of them are situated at a great distance from any water; so that the inhabitants must have depended entirely upon rain, as is the case with the Pueblo of Acoma at the present day.

The general appearance of Pueblo Bonito [Pintado], as well as that of the existing buildings of Moqui [Hopi villages] in the same mountainous regions, and other Pueblos of New Mexico, resembles so closely the ruins of Casas Grandes, that we naturally come to the conclusion that the founders of each must have descended from common stock. The present differences between their languages and that of the Indians of Mexico, when we take into consideration the ages that have passed away since their separation, hardly presents any reasonable objection to this hypothesis.

Josiah Gregg, *Commerce of the Prairies*, edited by Max L. Moorehead. Norman: University of Oklahoma Press, 1954, pp. 197–198. Originally published in 1844.

Lt. James Simpson's 1849 Narrative of Chaco Canyon

The following excerpt from Lt. James Simpson's journal of the 1849 expedition to the Navajo is longer than most of the documents included in this volume. Simpson's journal is significant because it is the first written account with descriptions of the Chacoan great houses. Its historic nature thus merits greater presentation.

In his descriptions and observations, Simpson identified many of the Chacoan traits that archaeologists today almost take for granted. These traits represent the unique signature of Chacoan architecture and construction: (1) massive, multistory construction; (2) terracing of rooms, from highest in the back of the pueblos to lowest in the front; and (3) the overall quality of architecture, in terms of fine, tabular sandstone selected and careful finishing of wooden support beams. Simpson observed that Pueblo Bonito was probably the best preserved, although he found Pueblo Pintado to be more beautiful in the details of its arrangement and layout.

Simpson discussed the probable origin of the ruins, relating what two of his guides told him. The Jemez Pueblo governor Hosta and the Navajo chief Sandoval told different versions of the story but reached the same conclusion: that the Chaco great houses were built by Montezuma and his Aztec people. As noted above, Josiah Gregg discussed the proposed Aztec origin of the Chacoan sites, citing the Mexican historian Clavigero's discussion of the mythic wanderings of the Aztec. Given the widespread knowledge and dissemination of the "Aztec myth of Chaco origins" in the mid-nineteenth century, it seems likely that an original origin story was modified by Native Americans through contact with Euro-Americans who were acquainted with Mexican history. Thus, a story that may have originally referred to a mythic Pueblo ancestor who founded the sites in Chaco and elsewhere was perhaps modified over time and substituted Montezuma, the king of the Aztecs, as the ancestral founder who eventually migrated south to build the great Aztec civilization.

DOCUMENT 2
Journal of a Military Reconnaissance from Santa Fe, New Mexico to the Navaho Country
Lt. James H. Simpson

August 28—This morning, the route of the command deviating from the Cañon of Chaco, in which were represented to be some more ruins of an interesting character, I obtained permission from the colonel commanding to visit them—it being my intention to join the command upon the Chaco, which it was said the troops would strike again before halting for the night. I took with me Mr. R. H. Kern and the guide Carravahal, seven mounted Mexicans accompanying us as an escort. Mr.

E. M. Kern was directed to continue with the troops and keep up the topography of the route.

Proceeding down the cañon one and a half miles (its general course northwest by west), we came to an old ruined structure, called by Carravahal *Pueblo Una Vida*. The circuit of this pueblo we found on measurement to be nine hundred and ninety-four feet. The structure had been built, like those I have already described, of very thin tabular fine-grained sandstone—the highest present elevation of the main walls being about fifteen feet. Two stories are now discernible, but the mass of *debris* at the base of the walls certainly shows that there must originally have been more. The remains of four circular *estuffas* are still apparent. . . .

A mile further down the cañon we came to another pueblo in ruins, called by Carravahal *Hungo Pavie*, which he interprets as Crooked Nose. These ruins show the same nicety in the details of their masonry as those I have already described. The ground plan shows an extent of exterior development of eight hundred and seventy-two feet, and a number of rooms upon the ground floor equal to seventy-two. The structure shows the existence of but one circular *estuffa*, and this is placed in the body of the north portion of the building, midway from either extremity. This *estuffa* differs from the others we have seen in having a number of interior counterforts. The main walls of the building are at base two and three-quarter feet through, and at this time show a height of about thirty feet. The ends of the floor beams, which are still visible, plainly showing that there was originally, at least, a vertical series of four floors, there must then also have been originally at least a series of four stories of rooms; and as the debris at the base of the walls is very great, it is reasonable to infer that there may have been even more.

Continuing down cañon one and three-quarters miles further, we came to another extensive structure in ruins, the name of which, according to the guide, is *Pueblo Chetro Kettle*, or as he interprets it, the Rain Pueblo. These ruins have an extent of exterior circuit, inclusive of the court, of about thirteen hundred feet. The material of which the structure has been made, as also the style of the masonry, is the same as that of the ruined pueblos I have already described—the stone a sandstone, and the beams pine and cedar. The number of stories at present discoverable is four—there having been originally a series of windows (four and a half by three and a half feet) in the first story, which are now walled up. The number of rooms on the first floor, all of which were distinguishable excepting those in the west wing, must have been as many as one hundred and twenty-four. The circular *estuffas*, of which there are six in number, have a greater depth than any we have seen, and differ from them also in exhibiting more stories, one of them showing certainly two, and possibly three, the lowest one appearing to be almost covered up with *debris*.

Two or three hundred yards down the cañon we met another old pueblo in ruins, called *Pueblo Bonito.* . . . This pueblo, though not so beautiful in the arrangement of the details of its masonry as *Pueblo Pintado*, is yet superior to it in point of preservation. The circuit of its walls is about thirteen hundred feet. Its present elevation shows that it has had at least four stories of apartments. The number of rooms on the ground floor at present discernible is one hundred and thirty-nine. In this enumeration, however, are not included the apartments which are not distinguishable in the east portion of the pueblo, and which would probably swell the number to about two hundred. There, then, having been at least four stories of rooms, and supposing the horizontal depth of the edifice to have been uniform from top to bottom, or in other words, not of a retreating terrace form on the court side, it is not unreasonable to infer that the original number of rooms was as many as eight hundred. But, as the latter supposition (as will be shown presently) is probably the most tenable, there must be a reduction from this number of one range of rooms for every story after the first; and this would lessen the number to six hundred and forty-one.

The question now arises, as we have seen all the ruins in this quarter, What was the form of these buildings?—I mean as regards the continuity or non-continuity of its front and rear walls. Were these walls one plain surface from bottom to top, as in the United States, or were they interrupted each story by a terrace, as in the case with modern pueblo buildings in New Mexico?

The front or exterior walls were evidently one plain surface from bottom to top; because, whenever we found them in their integrity, which we did for as many as four stories in height, we always noticed them to be uninterruptedly plain.

The rear walls, however, were, in no instance that I recollect of, found to extend higher than the commencement of the second story; and the partition walls were, if my memory is not at fault, correspondingly step-like in their respective altitudes. The idea then, at once unfolds itself, that in elevation the inner wall must have been a series of retreating surfaces or, what would make this necessary, each story on the inner or court side must have been terraced. This idea also gathers strength from the fact that we saw no indications of any internal mode of ascent from story to story, and therefore that some exterior mode must have been resorted to—such as, probably, ladders, which the terrace form of the several stories would make very convenient. Again, the terrace form of the stories would best conduce to light and ventilation for the interior range of apartments. The idea, then, which Mr. R. H. Kern was the first to suggest—that these pueblos were terraced on their inner or court side—is not without strong grounds of probability; and it is in consequence with this idea that, in his restoration of the *Pueblo Hungo Pavie* (see Plate 31), he has given it the form exhibited in the drawing.*

In regard to the position of the several structures in respect to the four true cardinal points of the heavens, it deviated in every instance more or less from them; but in no instance was the variation from the *magnetic* cardinal points more than five degrees, except in the case of the *Pueblo Una Vida*, where it was as great as fifteen degrees east. . . .

In regard to the origin of these remains, there is nothing that I can learn conclusive in relation to it. Hosta, one of the most intelligent Pueblo Indians I have seen, says, as I have before remarked, that they were built by Montezuma and his people, when on their way from north to the region of the Rio Grande and to Old Mexico. Sandoval, a very intelligent Navaho chief, also says they were built by Montezuma, but further states that the Navahos and all the other Indians were once but one people, and lived in the vicinity of the Silver [La Plata] mountain; that this mountain is about one hundred miles north of the Chaco ruins; that the Pueblo Indians separated from them (the Navahos) and built towns on the Rio Grande and its tributaries, but that "their house continues to be the hut made of bushes." Nothing more satisfactory than this have I been able to get from either Indians or Mexicans.

*Unwittingly Mr. Kern has fallen one story short of the number the ruins exhibited. In their recorded state, four stories should appear. [Footnote from original document]

Lt. James H. Simpson, *Journal of a Military Reconnaissance from Santa Fe, New Mexico to the Navaho Country, Made with the Troops under Command of Lt. Col.*

John M. Washington in 1849 Washington, DC: Report of the Secretary of War, 31st Cong., 1st sess., Senate Executive Document 64, 1850, pp. 78–83, passim.

Professor Newberry's 1859 Encounter with Aztec and Sites on the San Juan

Professor John S. Newberry came through the greater San Juan region in 1859 as part of an exploration party heading to the Green River, Utah, with the Corps of Topographical Engineers of the U.S. Army. Newberry spent several days studying the ruins that came to be known as Aztec Ruins. He made a number of original observations about Aztec Ruins, including its great size, architectural details, and the amazing preservation in several of the interior rooms. Most important, from our perspective, Newberry correctly identified the builders of the ruined pueblos as the ancestors of the modern Pueblo Indians. By examining the details of broken pottery and the architecture of the site, Newberry concluded that continuity existed between the site and the occupied pueblos of the Southwest.

In addition to Aztec Ruins, Newberry also made the first recorded visit to and mention of the site that came to be known as Salmon Ruins, on the San Juan River. "Near Camp 43 also are the remains of several large structures, of which portions of the walls of stone are still standing, twenty or more feet in height." The structures described are, indeed, part of Salmon Ruins. Another large, ancient pueblo site, identified by Newberry at the confluence of the Animas with the San Juan River, was later investigated briefly by Earl Morris in the early 1900s. This site, called by Morris the "Old Fort," was a Pueblo III period (dating from 1150–1300 c.e.) village associated with a long irrigation ditch that runs up the Animas River toward Aztec. This ditch, along with at least two others identified in the vicinity of Aztec Ruins, provides evidence of ancient Pueblo irrigation activities. Accounts of early settlers in the Aztec, Bloomfield, and Farmington, New Mexico, areas also mention irrigation ditches, many located in ideal settings for the settlers' own water needs.

DOCUMENT 3
Geology of the Banks of the San Juan, 1859
Professor J. S. Newberry

It is in this part of the valley that the ruins are situated. The principal structures are large pueblos, handsomely built of stone, and in a pretty good state of preservation. The external walls are composed of yellow Cretaceous sandstone, dressed to a common smooth surface without hammer-marks; in some places they are still 25 feet in height. As usual in buildings of this kind, the walls were unbroken by door or window to the height of 15 feet above the foundation. The interior shows a great number of small rooms, many of which are in a perfect state of preservation, and handsomely plastered. These larger structures are surrounded by mounds and fragments of masonry, making the sites of great numbers of subordinate buildings; the whole affording conclusive evidence that a large population had its home here. The fragments of highly ornamented and glazed pottery which cover the surface in the vicinity of these buildings, as well as the peculiar style of architecture in which they were constructed, show that the people who built and occupied these structures belonged to the common aboriginal race of this region, now generally known as the Pueblo Indians. . . .

Though now entirely deserted, these valleys were once occupied by a dense population, as is shown by the extensive ruins with which they are thickly set. Those on the Animas, twenty miles above its mouth, have already been noticed.

At the junction of this stream with the San Juan the remains of a large, but very ancient, town are visible, the foundations of many buildings of considerable size still remaining, and traces of an acequia through which water was brought from a point some miles above on the Animas.

Near Camp 43 also are the remains of several large structures, of which portions of the walls of stone are still standing, twenty or more feet in height. Indeed, it may be said that from the time we struck the San Juan we were never out of sight of ruins, while we were following up its valley.

J. S. Newberry, M.D., LL.D., "Geologic Report," in *Report of the Exploring Expedition from Santa Fe, New Mexico, to the Junction of the Grand and Green Rivers of the Great Colorado of the West, in 1859,* by Capt. J. N. Macomb. Washington, DC: Government Printing Office, 1876, pp. 80, 109.

Frederick Ward Putnam's Summary of the Pueblo Ruins, 1879

The following excerpt from Harvard curator F. W. Putnam's report appeared in 1879, after some of the other Wheeler accounts that follow it here. This document is provided before other accounts of Wheeler Survey participants (those of O'Sullivan, Birnie, and Loew below) because it provides a good introduction to the archaeological and ethnological activity on the Wheeler Surveys from 1869 to 1878.

Of interest here, the questions Putnam outlined more than 100 years ago—including "Whence came this once numerous people?" and "How long since they reached the high position of village and agricultural life?"— are still of interest to archaeologists and have not been fully addressed. A considerable amount of data has been collected, and archaeologists of today certainly have a lot more facts with which to work.

One such "properly equipped expedition" that Putnam wrote of did, in fact, occur not long after he made the case. The Hyde Exploring Expedition (discussed in Chapter 3) was launched in 1896, with Putnam in overall charge from his Harvard office. Of course, understanding Pueblo history proved to be a tall order, and many expeditions followed the Hyde, with variable results.

Putnam's account reveals the "collection strategy" of the early days in American archaeology and ethnology. Much of this early work was driven by the conception of the "disappearing Indian," whose objects of art and life, indeed, whose very culture, had to be collected and preserved before they vanished forever. This approach had some factual basis in the extreme decline of Native American populations in the centuries since first contact with Europeans. But this collection approach removed numerous objects of ceremonial importance from Native American nations, disturbed countless numbers of graves and burials, and allowed the people most effected absolutely little or no opportunity to participate in the process of "saving their cultures."

Lastly, Putnam discusses the "Montezuma myth" of Pueblo origins that was told and retold numerous times during the late nineteenth and early twentieth centuries in the American Southwest. Putnam essentially concludes that contact with Spanish or Mexican folks led to a substitution of Montezuma and the Aztecs into what was an original Pueblo origin story. This conclusion is reasonable, but Putnam's suggestion that the story was not of ethnological merit because of its lack of native purity seems quite biased.

DOCUMENT 4
"The Pueblo Ruins and The Interior Tribes," 1879
Frederick W. Putnam

During the progress of the survey of the territory west of the 100th meridian, several of the officers connected with the field parties in New Mexico, Arizona, and Colorado had opportunities for collecting a number of objects pertaining to the Indian tribes. They were also able to record many observations of considerable archaeological and ethnological importance and interest in relation to the ancient and present pueblos. . . .

As there is yet wanting a full correct account of the people who, while formerly more numerous than now, still inhabit the great interior portion of our country, principally included between the 32 and 38 degrees of north latitude and from 104 to 113 degrees west longitude, every addition that is made to the meagre history of this, ethnologically considered, important development of village life on the western continent is of interest.

Whence came this once numerous people? How long since they reached the high position of village and agricultural life? What has been their influence on the history of American tribes? All these are questions which are yet without satisfactory answers. Of speculations there have been many, but until a more thorough record of facts is obtained all theories are comparatively worthless. As yet we are hardly possessed of anything more than preliminary observations which lead us to the belief that there is here an extensive field for research.

When an expedition, properly equipped, with no other than ethnological and archaeological work to perform, with plenty of time allowed for the work, shall have been over the region, it will be time to offer theories with some hope of their leading to satisfactory results. It is, therefore, with this feeling of importance of placing on record every reliable fact and observation possible, in relation to the present pueblo tribes, and the ruins of the former more or less extensive towns, and probably communal houses, that the observations of the officers of the Survey are here incorporated, with short descriptions of a number of stone implements, pottery, and other objects found in the pueblos and about the ruins.

Various objects were also obtained by the officers of the Survey from the Indian tribes of the interior and are briefly referred to in the following pages, though, owing to the rapid disappearance of these from Indian life, their importance is such as to justify a more extended notice than it is possible to give in this connection. . . .

As a general account of the Pueblo people would not be complete without a reference to the "Montezuma legend" in some one of its many forms, the above rendering of the myth is here retained, although the legend itself probably refers simply to one or more of the great leaders of the Pueblo tribes at a period proceeding the Spanish conquest. The name of the composite hero, and his final journey to Mexico, are so evidently due to early Spanish interpretations and additions to the original legend, that until the legend is known as it existed at the time of Spanish conquest, its consideration is not of the least ethnological importance. [From the footnote on p. 322 of the original work]

Frederick W. Putnam, "The Pueblo Ruins and The Interior Tribes," in *Report upon the United States Geographical Surveys West of the One-hundredth Meridian, Part II, Volume VII—Archaeology*, by Lt. George M. Wheeler. Washington, DC: Government Printing Office, 1879, pp. 315–318, 322, passim.

Timothy O'Sullivan's Short Description of Salmon Pueblo, 1874

> *Photographer Timothy O'Sullivan's description of what would come to be known as Salmon Ruins (O'Sullivan called the site Pueblo San Juan) is historic because it is the first detailed description of the site. Like almost every visitor to Salmon Pueblo, past and present, O'Sullivan was impressed with the stone architecture, comparing it favorably to the late-nineteenth-century English bond style. Through consultation with his Native American guide, accompanying O'Sullivan as part of the 1874 Lt. Wheeler Military Expedition (perhaps the Navajo or Apache man pictured in one of the photographs), O'Sullivan understood the great antiquity of the ruins and the presumed lack of connection to Native tribes of the area.*
>
> *Much of O'Sullivan's caption is devoted to speculation regarding the Aztecs, their purported wanderings through the San Juan area, and alleged construction of large sites (the Aztec pueblos, for example). It seems likely that a Native American guide or another individual told O'Sullivan*

a version of the same Aztec story relayed to Lieutenant Simpson as he examined the great houses in Chaco Canyon. In 1874, O'Sullivan was apparently not aware of the great houses of Chaco Canyon or, if he had heard of them, was not sufficiently familiar with the architecture to make the connection between Chaco and his "Pueblo San Juan." With W. H. Jackson's trip to Chaco Canyon still three years into the future (1877), and Lieutenant Simpson's journal languishing in obscurity, information about the Chacoan great houses was apparently not readily accessible.

DOCUMENT 5
"Caption for Plate 59," Pueblo San Juan, 1874
Timothy O'Sullivan

For "Colorado," in the title opposite, read "New Mexico," in the northwestern part of which Territory these remains were discovered in the expedition of 1874. They are situated on the north bank of the San Juan River, about 15 miles west of the Cañon Largo. The ruin is about 350 feet square, and is built of stone in its natural shape, joined by a mud cement. Observe the regularity of the courses of masonry, and the resemblance of the design to the *English bond* of our present style of architecture the large blocks of stone corresponding to the stretchers which, in our structures, retain the walls longitudinally. The measuring scale of 36 inches, to be seen in one angle of the room, is a criterion by which to estimate its dimensions. This ruin is characteristic of an ancient people and civilization of which the present tribes know nothing, not even in tradition. There is a belief that the Aztec race in its integrity, centuries ago, inhabited this San Juan region whence they were compelled to migrate by the absence of rainfall and the increasing aridity of their land. A portion of them, it is believed, journeyed to Mexico and built cities there, where they were found by Montezuma, who promised to return for the remaining tribes, and some of the living Pueblos, of New Mexico, who have by some been considered as the abandoned remnant of his people, still believe, or profess to do so, in the ultimate fulfillment of that promise.

Timothy O'Sullivan, "Caption for Plate 59," in *Report upon the United States Geographical Surveys West of the One-hundredth Meridian, Part II, Volume VII—*

Archaeology, by Lt. George M. Wheeler. Washington, DC: Government Printing Office, 1879.

Lt. Rogers Birnie Jr.'s Report on Ruins in New Mexico

The following excerpted section is from the report of Lt. Rogers Birnie, a member of the same 1874 Wheeler Survey during which Timothy O'Sullivan took historic photos of Salmon. Birnie apparently observed Salmon Pueblo but wrote nothing specific about the site (identified as Pueblo San Juan by O'Sullivan) for the report. Instead, Birnie contributed a sizable narrative on what came to be known as Aztec Ruins, quoted here in full. Although his report is not the first on Aztec, it is very detailed, and he seems to have "captured" the essence of the Aztec Ruins well. Birnie did not identify the pueblo he was describing by name, but there can be no doubt that his description is of Aztec Ruins.

Birnie describes both the East and West Ruins at Aztec and found entry into a well-preserved room in the East Ruin. He provided a wonderful description of a typical Pueblo roof construction with two or three big pine or spruce beams (called vigas) laid first across a room, followed by a series of smaller diameter pieces (latillas), then a layer of split wood and bark, and finally earth (dirt and mud). Birnie noted numerous inscriptions in the plaster and on the rock walls of the room—the first observation of what was revealed to be many inscriptions left over a large period of time at Aztec. Birnie also provided the first brief description of the unusual circular structure (what archaeologists call a tri-walled ceremonial structure) located directly between the East and West Ruins.

Curiously, Birnie references one of O'Sullivan's photographs of Salmon (cited as Plate IX in the report) to illustrate his description of the height of the walls at Aztec. It is unclear why Birnie confused the two sites, as his description of Aztec is correct to the level of minute details about the layout of the site and the East and West Ruins. O'Sullivan apparently did not take any photographs of Aztec, and it is possible that Birnie did not visit Salmon. Thus, he might have assumed that the photograph in question was taken at Aztec.

Like most of the early explorers, Birnie correctly surmised that Aztec was a site of considerable antiquity. The Native American guides with Birnie at Aztec probably indicated that the site was unknown in their lore. If he was told the "Aztec origin story" of the large abandoned pueblos, Birnie did not make note of it.

DOCUMENT 6
"Report on Certain Ruins Visited in New Mexico"
Lt. Rogers Birnie Jr., Thirteenth United States Infantry

The most extensive ruins met with were on the right bank of the Las Animas River, about twelve miles above its junction with the San Juan. I had been previously informed of this, my informant stating that he had counted 517 rooms in one pueblo. On visiting the ruins we found what had once been, apparently, quite a town, with two main buildings and numerous small ones about them. One of the main buildings, situated nearest the river, extended to and was built into a bluff separated a few hundred yards from the river by a flat. The plan was rectangular with a small court on the south side, the court flanked on either side by two circular rooms or towers at the corners of the building; two more of these rooms at the other corners, and three through the center and parallel to the longer side of the building; the walls supporting the towers on either side of the court were square-cornered but had re-entrant angles. The remainder of the building was divided into rectangular compartments apparently of three stories, the two upper ones nearly in ruins, on two sides of the building, which was about 150 by 100 feet; the wall was quite perfect and in place 25 feet in height still standing. (See Plate IX [this photograph actually shows Salmon Pueblo, not Aztec]). Entering a room nearly altogether in ruins, it was found connected with an interior one by a door-way 4 feet 4 inches and 2 feet 4 inches, cased with nicely-dressed soft sandstone about the size of an ordinary brick; the walls were 2 feet 4 inches thick, many of the stones being marked with crosses, (+) &c, and some with inscriptions, though these latter were nearly obliterated. The interior room was about 14 feet 4 inches by 6 feet 4 inches, and the roof fallen in. An entrance was found to a lower room, apparently one of the lower story, through a door of about the same dimensions as the other mentioned; the lintel was composed of small round pieces of wood well cleaned, titted, and bound together with withes; the dimensions of the room 14 feet 4 inches by 6 feet, and 7 feet high; the walls had been well plastered, and remained nearly intact, though covered on all sides with curious figures and signs scratched upon them. The floor must have been of earth; the ceiling was supported primarily by clean pine or spruce beams about 6 inches in diameter, and 30 inches apart; these were crossed by smaller ones of the same kind, and across these latter were split pieces, small and half-round, and fitting closely together, supporting the earth above. . . .

The other main building, which is the larger of the two, is about 200 yards to the west of this, and quite remarkable in plan. What was probably the principal part is on the north side, the roof fallen in and much debris about the exterior. We found a number of much larger rooms than in the other building, and interior walls at least 30 feet high. This portion of the building is about 200 feet long and regularly supported on the exterior by buttresses; from either end two connect and run out, making the interior angle about 100 degrees; these wings extend about 150 feet, then their extremities seem to have been connected by a circular wall, now entirely in ruins but showing the remains of a gate-way. Above the buttresses on the exterior wall of the main portion the wall is quite perfect, and shows some very pretty architectural design. The masonry is not only built with courses of different thicknesses of stone, but, also, of different colors. There is seen a projecting cornice, plain, composed of three or four courses of very thin reddish sandstones, and again a course of nearly white stone, perhaps a foot thick, both very even, and then other courses of different shades and thicknesses alternate. In this building there are the remains of three circular rooms, one at each of the angles above referred to, and one in the center of the court. A great deal of broken crockery was about, but confined to certain portions of the building, principally the extremities of the wings. Want of time prevented me from making measurements and obtaining much accurate data that I desired.

Many years have elapsed since these building were in ruins, but some of the walls, where supported, are well preserved. Very heavy sage-brush was growing in many places upon the mounds of the ruins. The remains of a circular building were found midway between the two main buildings, and it has been supposed these circular rooms were places of worship. But little analogy could be observed between these and the Indian pueblo at Taos [New Mexico] that I afterward visited; but stone ruins seen at Nacimiento and near other (now occupied) Mexican towns were very similar, except as to plan, to those described, the ruins about the towns being entirely different from any of the present habitations.

In many places along the San Juan River, pieces of old crockery were observed and remains of several small stone houses. In one of these I found a very fine specimen of a stone hammer, oval and of natural shape, with the ordinary groove cut about it for attaching the handle. A number of important ruins were also observed along the Cañon de Chaco. None of these so minutely described by Lieut. Simpson in 1849 were visited by us, as we did follow his route only perhaps a very short distance. The Navajo Indians ascribed some of the figures and signs seen in the lower room of the ruins to Apaches and Comanches; but their explanations were very vague, principally from the difficulty of understanding them.

Lt. Rogers Birnie Jr., "Report on Certain Ruins Visited in New Mexico," in *Annual Report of the Chief of Engineers to the Secretary of War for the Year 1875, Part II*, by George M. Wheeler. Washington, DC: Government Printing Office, 1875, app. J, pt. 3, pp. 1099–1100.

Oscar Loew's Discussion of Pueblo Ruins in Chaco Canyon

Oscar Loew toured several of the existing Pueblo villages and Puebloan ruins in 1874 as part of the Wheeler Survey. His description of Pueblo Bonito (excerpted below) actually refers to Pueblo Pintado. Like Josiah Gregg, Loew applied the name of Pueblo Bonito to Pueblo Pintado. The site is described as being at the head of Chaco Canyon, which fits the location of Pueblo Pintado and not Pueblo Bonito. Loew's detailed treatment of the ruin and its characteristics also match better the site known as Pueblo Pintado, including mention of three stories (Pueblo Bonito had at least four) and the square layout (Pueblo Bonito is crescentic in shape).

Loew's account of Pueblo Pintado is poetic, differing in style from many contemporary accounts that were more direct, "matter-of-fact," and dry. Loew found interest in the mute residents of the abandoned pueblo—the lizards, ants, and crying crows. He lamented the lack of inscriptions (written records of any type) providing any information about the lives, the joys, and the sorrows of the inhabitants. Although interest in and speculation about (some of which could be described as rampant and without merit) the lives of the ancient Pueblo dwellers were more common in the early days of southwest archaeology and anthropology, many early explorers provided only basic, physical narratives of the sites they encountered. Loew and a few others, including Lieutenant Simpson and William Henry Jackson, went beyond these basics and tried to understand other aspects of Puebloan society.

Interestingly, Loew identified the wood used in construction of the doors and windows at the pueblo as juniper. In fact, much of the wood from Pueblo Pintado has been identified through tree-ring studies over the last twenty years. Although some juniper was used for roofing timbers at the site, a diversity of wood species is in evidence, including piñon, cottonwood or aspen, ponderosa pine, spruce, and white fir.[1]

DOCUMENT 7
"Report on the Ruins of New Mexico," 1875
Oscar Loew, M.D.

During your expedition of last year [1874] I had occasion to visit the ruins of Pueblo Bonito [Pintado], at the head of Cañon de Chaco. The desolation of the surrounding land is in keeping with that of the inhabitants of the pueblo, while lizards and ants roaming amid the rubbish of the past, the crying crow nestling between the walls, and the fallen stone tell of the flight of time; but silent and mute is the ruin, no inscription telling the tales of former joys or sorrows within these crumbling walls. The ruins consist of one large building with a yard surrounded by a wall, which form a square whose sides are nearly 200 feet long; the doors of the building open on this yard. The walls 1½ to 2 feet thick, and are built of plates of sandstone, like those found in the immediate vicinity. The south and west sides of the square form the three-story building which descends in terraces toward the interior of the square, the second series of rooms forming two stories, third series one story. The lowest story is 7 feet high, the middle one 9, and the uppermost 6. The most exterior row has ten rooms in the length, and therefore thirty in the upper three stories; these rooms measure 20 feet long by 6 feet wide. . . . The wood used for the construction of the doors and windows was juniper, which grows profusely on the sandy mesas, requiring but little moisture; it is in a good state of preservation. As no steps were found leading to the upper story, the ascent was probably made by ladders, as is still the custom among the Pueblos of New Mexico. In the southern corner of the yard are the walls of two cylindrical buildings, 20 and 30 feet in diameter, having six pillars on the periphery, equidistant, most likely remnants of the *estufas*, or temples, in which the sun was worshipped. The bottoms of these buildings were about 3 feet lower than the surrounding yard. Pieces of painted pottery, an article seen in exceedingly many localities in New Mexico, were found scattered about profusely. . . .

No trace of former irrigating-ditches can be found in the neighboring valley of the Chaco, but there are traces of a former road to Abiquiu, sixty miles off, where ruins have also been found, two in the immediate vicinity and three between Abiquiu and El Rito.

NOTE

1. Thomas C. Windes, personal communication regarding wood at Pueblo Pintado, July 2002.

Oscar Loew, M.D., "Report on the Ruins of New Mexico," in *Annual Report of the Chief of Engineers to the Secretary of War for the Year 1875, Part II*, by George M. Wheeler. Washington, DC: Government Printing Office, 1875, app. J, pt. 2, p. 1096.

William Henry Jackson's 1878 Report on Chaco Canyon

The following excerpts, from William Henry Jackson's 1878 report on Chaco, illustrate the detail of Jackson's account and his desire to "update" the condition of the ruins, compared to the description of Lieutenant Simpson from 1849. Writing about Hungo Pavi, Jackson comments on the extreme height (four stories) of what is otherwise a medium-sized Chaco great house. Interestingly, although both Jackson and Simpson identify four stories for Hungo Pavi, official park service documentation of the great house in the mid-1980s mentions only three stories. Although it is true that only three stories were in evidence by the 1980s, one would think that the firsthand accounts of two astute observers like Simpson and Jackson might have allowed the archaeologists to at least mention the fourth story.

Also, in the quote on Hungo Pavi, Jackson introduces the translation "Crooked Nose" for the site name. No other source provides such a translation, and Jackson's source of information is not specified. Thus, this attribution must remain a mystery.

Jackson's description of Pueblo Bonito, quoted below, is basic and to the point, without much elaboration. The lasting impression conveyed, though, is that Pueblo Bonito suffered little deterioration or damage in the quarter century of time that passed between Simpson's (1849) and Jackson's (1877) visits. Unfortunately, knowledge of the site increased significantly after Jackson's report was published. Significant damage was done to Pueblo Bonito by relic hunters over the next twenty-five years, through 1900. However, awareness of and casual visitation to Pueblo sites across the American Southwest increased dramatically during the last quarter of the nineteenth century, and Jackson certainly was not solely responsible for the increased traffic to Chaco Canyon.

DOCUMENT 8
"Report on the Ancient Ruins Examined in 1875 and 1877"
William Henry Jackson

Pueblo Hungo Pavie

One mile farther, on the same side and also built close under the walls of the cañon, are the ruins of the Pueblo Hungo Pavie, or Crooked Nose, portions of which are yet in quite perfect condition. It is built like Weje-gi around three sides of a court, but this is enclosed by a semicircular wall reaching from one wing to the other. The north or main building is 309 feet long on the outside, and the two wings 136 feet each. The ground plan represents a depth of but three rows of rooms, and as the walls still indicate that there were at least four stories, it gives a much greater degree of height in comparison with breadth than any of the other ruins. The single estufa is situated midway in the north building and appears to have extended up to the top of the second story. In front of it is a projection or platform of masonry, nearly as high and of the same width as the estufa, which extends some 10 or 12 feet into the court. The interior, which is 23 feet in diameter, has six counter-forts or square pillars of masonry—like those of the Pueblo Pintado—built into the encircling wall at equal distances from each other, and which appear to have extended up to the top. In the northeast corner of the ruins the walls are not standing 30 feet high, showing a portion of the fourth floor. Many of the heavy pine logs that supported the flooring are still in position. The height of the second story rooms was about 9 feet and of the third story about 7 feet. The masonry is of the same character as that already noticed, but the walls of the first story are of unusual thickness—nearly 3 feet—otherwise it has not marked difference of features. The rooms of the central portion of the building are generally long and narrow, while those of the wings are of the same length but wider. There are no signs of masonry in the low mound which is all there is left of the wall which enclosed the court. Just outside of it, near the centre, is the usual mound of rubbish, and just inside, one of the great circular depressions generally in the same relative position in nearly all the ruins. . . .

Pueblo Bonito

Five hundred yards below and also close under the perpendicular walls of the cañon are the ruins of the Pueblo Bonito, the largest and in some respects the most remarkable of all. Its length is 544 feet and its width 314 feet. By referring to the plan it will be seen that it only roughly approximates the usual rectangular shape. The two side wings are parallel with each other, and at right angles to the front wall, for a distance of 70 feet; the west wing then bends around until a little past a line drawn through the centre of the ruin transversely, when it bears off diagonally to join the east wing, thus resembling in its outline a semi-oval. Instead of a semicircular wall, the court is enclosed by a perfectly straight row of small buildings running almost due east and west, and is intersected by a line of estufas, which divide it (the court) into two nearly equal portions. . . . Several of the interior parallel and transverse walls are also standing fully 30 feet high. Many of the vigas, which are in excellent preservation, still retain their places and protect a number of rooms on the first floor.

William Henry Jackson, "Report on the Ancient Ruins Examined in 1875 and 1877," in *Tenth Annual Report of the United States Geological and Geographical Survey of the Territories*, by F. V. Hayden (Washington, DC: Government Printing Office, 1878), pp. 438–441, passim.

Lewis Henry Morgan's Description of the Ruins of Chaco and Aztec

> As part of the Powell Survey (the U.S. Geographical and Geological Survey of the Rocky Mountain Region) of the late 1870s and early 1880s, Lewis Henry Morgan undertook a study of the houses and lives

of the people he described as American aborigines. Morgan was an attorney with considerable interest in the anthropological study of American Indians. Morgan wrote a historical synthesis of human society, Ancient Society, in which he laid out a unilineal theory of human sociocultural evolution through three broad stages: savagery, barbarism, and civilization. The Pueblo Village Indians were classified by Morgan into his Middle Barbarism stage. Morgan's sequence constituted a significant contribution to the anthropology of the late nineteenth century. But archaeologists of today reject the notion that all societies pass through a predetermined set of cultural stages; the individual development of the numerous, distinct human societies across time and space is viewed today as a very complicated process.

In his work on house types, as excerpted below, Morgan devoted considerable time to the Iroquois Confederacy of the Eastern United States and to the Aztecs of Old Mexico. He also committed two chapters in his monograph to the Pueblo Indians of the southwestern United States. A careful reading of his work suggests that Morgan never visited Chaco Canyon. His descriptions closely follow those of W. H. Jackson and Lt. James Simpson. The report reproduces earlier maps and quotes extensively from the two earlier reports by Jackson and Simpson. In contrast, Morgan is explicit regarding his visit to Aztec Ruins on July 22, 1878.

Anticipating later conclusions about Chaco Canyon, Morgan suggested that "Chaco must have possessed remarkable advantages for subsistence." He noted the period of highest stream flow in Chaco Wash occurred in July (based on Lieutenant Simpson's trip) and inferred an abundance of water during the critical summer months for agriculture. More recent research, such as that of archaeologist Gwinn Vivian, has documented extensive systems in Chaco Canyon for the collection and transport of runoff water from summer rainstorms. Further, Chaco Canyon has recently been assessed by Vivian and other archaeologists as a superior location within the San Juan Basin for agricultural pursuits.

Commenting on the scale and immense size of the Chacoan great houses, Morgan drew an analogy to the feudal castles of contemporary, medieval Europe. He believed that the great houses grew through time, as the population expanded and more habitation space was needed. This process of growth by accretion has been documented at several pueblos in Chaco, mostly notably Pueblo Bonito. However, most of the Chacoan great houses were built as planned structures, with construction occurring rapidly over only a few years.

Aztec Ruins was the primary focus of Morgan's work among the ruins of the Pueblo Indians, and he made a number of astute observations.

Morgan identified five stories along Aztec's back wall and four stories running down each wing. Later explorers would document no more than three stories at Aztec. Earlier explorers, such as Newberry and Birnie, did not specifically describe the number of stories. Morgan explicitly documented the use of Aztec Ruins as a stone quarry by local residents and was told by a settler that perhaps one-quarter of the rock from both the East and West pueblos at Aztec had been removed. Certainly, Aztec Ruins had seen significant impact from collection of building stone and random vandalism by the late 1800s. It is possible that these impacts had removed upper stories from Aztec's back wall, the location in which Morgan had commented on extensive rubble piles and where he indicated the fifth story was located.

In assessing the origin of the Pueblo structures of the San Juan, Morgan developed a broad interpretation, well beyond that of other researchers of his day. In the Pueblo villages of the ancient San Juan, Morgan found the roots of all village life in North and perhaps South America. He believed that the builders of the pueblos migrated east, to found the societies of the Mound Builders, and south, to build the great Aztec and Mayan cities and civilizations of Mesoamerica. Morgan believed that the ancient Pueblo Indians of the American Southwest were the originators of the advanced sedentary culture (Morgan's Middle Stage of Barbarism) that eventually spread to most of the New World. Archaeologists of today view this idea as naive and overly simplistic. It is clear that societies developed independently in many areas but that ideas and people circulated between these areas.

DOCUMENT 9
Ruins of the Houses of the Sedentary Indians of the San Juan, 1881
Lewis Henry Morgan

The finest structures of the Village Indians in New Mexico, and northward of its present boundary line, are found on the San Juan and its tributaries, unoccupied and in ruins. Even the regions in which they are principally situated are not now occupied by this class of Indians, but are roamed over by wild tribes of Apaches and the Utes. The most conspicuous cluster of these ruined and deserted pueblos are in the cañon or valley of the Rio Chaco, which stream is an affluent of the San Juan, a tributary of the Colorado. Similar ruins of stone pueblos are also found in the valley of the Animas River, and also in the region of the Ute Mountain in Southwestern Colorado. . . .

The supposition is reasonable that the Village Indians north of Mexico attained their highest culture and development where these stone structures are found. They are similar in style and plan to the present occupied pueblos in New Mexico, but superior in construction, as stone is superior to adobe or to cobble-stone and adobe mortar. They are also equal, if not superior, in size and in the extent of their accommodations, to any Indian pueblos ever constructed in North America. This fact gives additional interest to these ruins, which are here to be considered. . . .

It is a remarkable display of ancient edifices; the most remarkable in New Mexico. With the bordering walls of the cañon, rising vertically, in places, one hundred feet high, it presented long vistas in either direction, with natural and inclosing walls. Shut in from view of the table lands at the summit of these walls, this valley, at the time its great houses were occupied, must have presented a very striking picture of human life as it existed in the Middle Period of Barbarism. The greater part of the valley must have been covered with garden beds, from which the people derived their principal support, as the mesa lands without the canyon were too dry for cultivation. It no doubt presented an interesting picture of industrious and contented life, with a corresponding advancement in the arts of this period. There is still some uncertainty concerning the time when these pueblos were last occupied, and the fate of their inhabitants. There are a number of circumstances tending to show that they were the "Seven Cities of Cibola," against which the expedition of Coronado was directed in 1540–1542. There are seven pueblos in ruins in the cañon, without reckoning Nos. 8 and 9 [so numbered by W. H. Jackson], the smallest in the valley.

With respect to the manner of constructing these houses, it was probably done, as elsewhere remarked, from time to time, and from generation to generation. Like a feudal castle, each house was a growth by additions from small beginnings, made as exigencies required. When one of these houses, after attaining a sufficient size, became overcrowded with inhabitants, it is probable that a strong colony, like the swarm from the parent hive, moved out, and commenced a new house, above or below, in the same valley. This would be repeated, as the people prospered, until several pueblos grew up within an extent of twelve or fifteen miles, as in the valley of the Chaco. When the capabilities of the valley were becoming overtaxed for their joint subsistence, the colonists would seek more distant homes. At the period of the highest prosperity of these pueblos, the valley of the Chaco must have possessed remarkable advantages for subsistence. The plain between the walls of the cañon was between half a mile and a mile in width near the several pueblos, but the amount of water now passing through it is small. In July, according to Lieutenant Simpson, the running stream was eight feet wide and a foot and a half deep at one of the pueblos; while Mr. Jackson found no running water and the valley entirely dry in the month of May, with the exception of pools of water in places and a reservoir of pure water in the rocks at the top of the bluff. The condition of the region is shown by these two statements. During the rainy season in the summer, which is also the season of the growing crops, there is an abundance of water; while in the dry season it is confined to springs, pools, and reservoirs. From the number of pueblos in the valley, indicating a population of several thousand, the gardens within it must have yielded a large amount of subsistence; the climate being favorable to its growth and ripening. . . .

About sixty miles north of the pueblos on the Chaco, and in the valley of the Animas River, is a cluster of stone pueblos, very similar to the former. These I visited in 1878. The valley is broad at this point, and for some miles above and below to its mouth. At the time of our visit (July 22) the river was a broad stream, carrying a large volume of water. . . . The supply of water for irrigation at the pueblo was abundant.

The pueblo . . . is one of four situated within the extent of one mile on the west side of the Animas River, in New Mexico, about twelve miles above its mouth. Besides these four, there are five other smaller ruins of inferior structures within the same area. This pueblo was five or perhaps six stories high, consisting of a main building three hundred and sixty-eight feet long, and two wings two hundred and seventy feet long, measured along the external wall on the right and left sides, and one hundred and ninety-nine feet measured along the inside from the end back to the main building. A fourth structure crosses from the end of the wing to the end of the other, thus inclosing an open court. It was of the width of one and perhaps two rows of apartments, and slightly convex outward, which enlarged somewhat the size of the court. The main building and the wings were built in the so-called terrace form;

that is to say, the first row of apartments in the main building and in each wing on the court side were but one story high. The second row back of these were carried up two stories, the third row three stories, and so on to the number of five stories for the main building and four for each wing. The external wall rose forty or fifty feet where the structure was five stories high and but ten feet on the court side, including a low parapet wall, where the structure was but one story high. . . .

The external wall of the main building has fallen the entire length of the structure. As these ruins are resorted to by settlers in the valley as a stone quarry to obtain stone for foundations to their houses and barns, and for stoning up their wells, the loose material is gradually removed; and when the standing walls are more convenient to take they will be removed also. One farmer told me he thought that one quarter of the accessible material of this and the adjacent stone pueblo had already been removed. It is to be hoped that the number of these settlers inclined to Vandalism will not increase. . . .

The peculiar arrangement of the doorways tends to show that this great house was divided into sections by the partition walls extending from the court to the exterior wall; and that the rooms above were connected with those below by means of trap-doors and ladders. If this supposition be well founded, the five rooms on the ground floor, from the court back, communicated with each other by doorways. The four in the second story communicated with each other in the same manner, and with those below through trap-doors in the floors. The three rooms in the third story communicated with each other by doorways, and with those below as before. The same would be true of the two rooms of the fourth story. It seems probable that the connected rooms were occupied by a group of related families. . . .

Outside the front wall closing the court, and about thirty feet distance therefrom, are the remains of a low wall crossing the entire front and extending beyond it. The end structures were about sixty-five feet long by forty feet wide, while at the center was a smaller structure, fifty-four feet long by eighteen wide. All its parts were connected. It was evidently erected for defensive purposes; but it is impossible to make out its character from the remains. . . .

Those familiar with the remains of Indian Pueblos in ruins will recognize at once the resemblance between this pueblo and the stone pueblos in ruins on the Rio Chaco, in New Mexico, about sixty miles distant from these ruins, particularly the one called Hungo Pavie, so fully described by General J. H. Simpson. There is one particular in which the masonry agrees, viz., in the use of course of thin stones, about half an inch in thickness, sometimes three together, and sometimes five or six. There courses are carried along the wall from one side to other, but often broken in upon. The effect is quite pretty. These stones measure six inches in length by one-half an inch in thickness. General Simpson found the same course of thin stones, and even thinner, in the Chaco ruins, and comments upon the pleasing effect they produced. . . .

These pueblos, newly constructed and in their best condition, must have presented a commanding appearance. From the materials used in their construction, from their palatial size and unique design, from the cultivated gardens by which they were doubtless surrounded, they were calculated to impress the beholder very favorably with the degree of culture to which the people had attained. It is a singular fact that none of the occupied pueblos in New Mexico at the present time are equal in materials or in construction with those found in ruins. . . .

I wish to call attention again to the San Juan district, to its numerous ruins and to its importance as an early seat of Village Indian life. These ruins and those of similar character in the valley of the Chaco, together with the numerous remains of structures of sandstone, of cobblestone, and adobe in the San Juan Valley, in the Pine River Valley, in the La Plata Valley, in the Animas River Valley, in the Montezuma Valley, on the Hovenweep, and on the Rio Dolores, suggest the probability that the remarkable area within the drainage of the San Juan River and its tributaries has held a prominent place in the first and most ancient development of Village Indian life in America. The evidence of Indian occupation and cultivation throughout the greater part of this area is sufficient to suggest the hypothesis that the Indian here first attained to the condition of Middle Status of barbarism, and sent forth the migrating band who carried this advanced culture to the Mississippi Valley, to Mexico, and Central America, and not unlikely to South America as well. . . .

With such evidences of ancient occupation, here and elsewhere in the San Juan country, we are led to the conclusion that the Village Indians increased and multiplied in this area, and that at some early period there was here a remarkable display of this form of Indian life, and of house architecture in the nature of fortresses, which must have made itself felt in distant parts of the continent.

Lewis Henry Morgan, *Houses and House-Life of the American Aborigines*. Washington, DC: Government Printing Office, 1881, pp. 154–197, passim.

PUEBLO PEOPLES' ACCOUNTS OF CHACO CANYON

Origin Story of Acoma Pueblo and "White House"

> *These short quotations from the Matthew Stirling monograph* Origin Myth of Acoma and Other Records *are atypical in this set of documents because of their brevity. The unifying theme is the reference to "White House." Some archaeologists have inferred that the White House in Acoma (and other Keresan-speaking Pueblos) oral history refers to Chaco Canyon and specifically to Pueblo Bonito. Specific, clear references to Chaco Canyon are absent in the documented Pueblo ethnographic record. But these short vignettes are included to document what is the most likely written connection to Chaco. The Acoma word* chaianyi *in the first quotation is translated as "medicine men."*
>
> *Of particular interest here is Stirling's parenthetical comment in the first quotation, suggesting that the disease that befell the Acomans at White House was smallpox. Smallpox was introduced by Europeans in the early 1500s and was not present in the pre-Hispanic Southwest. If we take the passage at face value and infer that the disease was smallpox, then we cannot identify White House with Chaco Canyon, because Chaco was abandoned by 1300 C.E; more than 200 years prior to the first contact of any Native Americans with smallpox. Certainly, it is possible that the stories relating to White House incorporate historical elements from multiple time periods. Thus, an epidemic of smallpox that occurred centuries earlier could have become attached to an earlier story about the ancestral home at White House. Conversely, the disease identified at White House may have been an indigenous, American disease.*
>
> *The second quotation is instructive, as it indicates that famine accompanied disease at White House and no doubt contributed to the Acomans' departure from White House. Finally, the third quote may provide an oral history baseline for the development of the Katsina cult in the Pueb-*

loan Southwest. Again, taking the information at face value, we could infer that the Katsina cult, which radically changed Western Pueblo social organization in the 1300s c.e. (after abandonment of the greater San Juan region—the core of earlier Puebloan settlement), developed initially at Chaco Canyon (in the period from 1050 to 1250 c.e.) but did not emerge until several decades or centuries later. Clearly, much of this is speculative and not subject to verification. Nevertheless, incorporating Puebloan oral history into archaeological interpretations can only increase our appreciation for the Chacoan era.

DOCUMENT 10
"Origin Myth of Acoma Pueblo"
Matthew Stirling

Sometime afterward, a sickness fell upon the people at White House and for the first time sickness brought death to many people. The population decreased rapidly. The *chaianyi* called this sickness *ushporoni*. It was a disease with blisters all over the body (smallpox?). The *chaianyi* did their best to cure it, but it was too much for them.

After the famine at White House there was a woman living with her daughter.

This initiation goes back in place to White House where the real katsina left and the katsina society was organized. Acoma people do it exactly the same today.

Matthew W. Stirling, *Origin Myth of Acoma and Other Records*, Smithsonian Institution Bureau of American Ethnology Bulletin no. 135. Washington, DC: Government Printing Office, 1942, pp. 66, 92, 108.

Zuni Historian Andrew Napatcha's Narrative of Chaco Canyon

In this quote from Zuni historian Andrew Napatcha, a clear linkage is made between current Zuni practices and traditions and Chaco Canyon. The origin of one of the Zuni medicine societies, the Sword Swallowers, is tracked back to Chaco Canyon.

This migration story of the Sword Swallowers is corroborated by two other published accounts. Clearly, Chaco Canyon is an important an-

cestral place for Zuni Pueblo in general and particularly for the Sword Swallowers society.

DOCUMENT 11
Andrew Napatcha's Telling of the Sword Swallowers and Chaco Canyon
Kendrick Frazier

A lot about Chaco Canyon people fits in with the prayers and traditions of the people of Zuni. The influence of this Chaco Canyon has been felt among all the Pueblo Indians of the Southwest. . . .

[Napatcha] told a long story from the Zuni oral traditions. It told of a religious order that, while on a migratory quest for the "center of the earth," lived for a time in Chaco Canyon. This medicine society was called the Sword Swallowers because they were considered to have special powers and carried out magic rituals or performances in which they put wooden swords down their throats. After living at Chaco Canyon, they eventually made their way to Zuni. . . .

Napatcha said there were probably other groups from Chaco that had become part of the Zunis also. He personally felt that many of the Zuni religious and governmental traditions had come out of Chaco.

Kendrick Frazier, *People of Chaco*. New York: Crown Publishers, 1986, pp. 210–212.

TWENTIETH-CENTURY ACCOUNTS OF CHACO CANYON AND THE OUTLIERS

S. J. Holsinger's Report on Chaco Canyon, 1901

Samuel Holsinger was called into Chaco Canyon in 1901 to investigate the homestead claim made by Richard Wetherill. Holsinger went well beyond an examination of Wetherill's situation and made a substantial contribution to early-twentieth-century understanding of Chaco. Several sections of Holsinger's report are quoted below for several reasons. First, he provides a comprehensive assessment of the Chacoan ruins, as of 1901. Second, he has a good sense of the prior history of Chaco and offers useful insights.

In the first paragraph quoted below, Holsinger mentions William Henry Jackson's report and inexplicably refers to Jackson's photographs of Chaco, which unfortunately did not develop properly. He says that the Chacoan ruins are the most impressive north of the Aztec Empire, and he sidesteps one of the debated issues of the day: Were the Chacoan ruins built by the Aztecs? By 1900, this issue was still unresolved, and archaeologists and researchers of the day were probably pretty evenly divided in their views. Holsinger promotes the idea of the Chacoan as a mysterious race of disappeared people who apparently far surpassed the architectural skills of the contemporary Native Americans of the Southwest. This myth, of a vanished, mysterious race of people, has endured in the 100 years since Holsinger's time and has been very difficult to dispel.

DOCUMENT 12
Prehistoric Ruins of Chaco Canyon
S. J. Holsinger

Mr. Jackson explored eleven of the seventeen ruins but his interesting report, ground plan maps and excellent photographs failed to direct general attention to what he declares to be "preeminantly [sic] the finest examples of extensive remains of the work of unknown builders to be found north of the seat of the Aztec Empire in Old Mexico." Notwithstanding this accessible and reliable report, a quarter of a century has passed and today a true account of what may be seen in Chaco Canyon would be regarded as a fairy tale, not only by the average citizen of New Mexico, but by easterners as well. Even the residents of Colorado, New Mexico and Utah who live within a few hundred miles of the remains of the silent city know little concerning the ruins, where once dwelt a race whose culture possibly equalled if it did not in fact surpass that of all other prehistoric people of the American Continent. Within the crumbling walls of a single building, having twelve hundred rooms, have been found thousands of domestic articles, mute evidence of the existence of a mysterious people whose history will never be told.

How many centuries have passed since the last voice was hushed within these rude temples may now only be conjectured from the progress of decay, discernible in the huge, shattered walls, which year by year have cast their masonry upon the precious relics, as if to bury the secret of these unknown builders beyond the reach of the inquisitive race who view with wonder awe the spectacle of today. . . .

Taking the usual route to the Chaco Canyon Ruins, as heretofore described, the so called Pueblo Bonito is the traveller's destination. His general store of knowledge, concerning pre-historic ruins, will hardly prepare him for what he will find at the end of a hard journey of one or two days. From the highest point of the Continental Divide, which is reached fifteen miles from the ruins, the road follows the course of a draw, which enters the Chaco opposite the pre-historic city. While scanning the outlines of dark mound, perched on the opposite wall of the canyon, which is designated as Pueblo Alto Ruins, a turn in the road brings into full view Bonito, "the beautiful"; and the first impression is a conviction of the appropriateness of the name. From this point of view Pueblo Arroyo, which is also on the floor of Chaco Canyon and not over 150 yards from Bonito to the West, appears to be part of that structure and withall [sic] it impresses the beholder of a city instead of only two buildings. The rich dark browns of the numerous walls and blocks of masonry, appearing as fortresses, bastions, obelisks, spires, and columns contrast sharply with the gray and yellow of the canyon walls in the background.

From this view an accurate idea of the immensity of the structures is gained; but the view, from the opposite or north side of the canyon is more imposing as the walls on that side are in a fair state of preservation. . . .

When further impressed by the fact that from 500 rooms of this ruin, excavated by the Hyde Exploration Expedition, several car loads of relics have been obtained, including 50,000 pieces of turquoise, 10,000 pieces of pottery, 5,000 stone implements, 1,000 wood and bone implements, 14 skeletons, many feather, yucca and cotton fabrics, hair leggings, and numerous other articles; one is willing to admit that Bonito was the treasure house of American antiquity and that Chaco Canyon ruins should properly be the Mecca and paradise of the antiquarian. . . .

It is an astonishing fact that with all the research, and in the excavation of 500 rooms, the Hyde Exploration Expedition has only discovered fourteen bodies or skeletons, of which, they have assurance, were those of the inhabitants of Bonito. Up and down the Canyon, for miles on either side, are small houses consisting of from four to ten rooms, usually built upon a side-hill or on the top of some knoll. Without a single exception, each house has, in the near vicinity, a cemetery or burial mound. Many excavations have been made in these but the burials are so old that the skeletons have returned to dust, and the fairly well preserved pottery, and only a light, limey substance indicates the presence of the dead. It is interesting to note that these small buildings all have a cemetery, while Bonito, where hundreds and possibly even thousands must have succumbed to age and disease, is without a burial field, or anything indicating the manner in which they disposed of their dead. Intermurial burials account for only twelve but somewhere thousands were laid to rest. Whether, somewhere beneath the ruins, or in some hidden cavern in the cliff there is a great catacomb where the army of sleepers are resting in security, is an absorbing question with the archaeologist, interested of the excavations at Bonito. If such a chamber exists, its discovery will doubtless yield a wealth of relics, never heretofore found, for the excavations so far made, show that the Bonitans, from the standpoint of a pre-historic indian, were wealthy.

Of the 50,000 pieces of turquoise discovered, a large percent of them, were lost in the litter by the natives. Following the custom of the Cibola and Tusayan pueblos, these people must have buried with their dead their most valuable ornaments and pottery. No basketry was found at Bonito, but a considerable quantity of coarse grass and yucca matting.

The question occurs to me, whether the Bonitans, divided as they must have been into many families and gens, did not each have an independent burial ground, and whether these are not represented by the many small ruins and burials, to which reference has been made. . . .

As one gazes upon the massive ruins, involuntarily the question comes, whence came and wither have these people gone. Were they beset by enemies, devastated by disease or driven by the sharp whip of famine from their abiding place. The caucasion [sic] conception of the perpetual relinquishment of valuable, proprietary rights, includes only the most extraordinary conditions, such as the fury of war, the terrors of earthquakes and belching volcanoes; not even the scourge pestilential disease being sufficient to drive them from habitations of the most trivial and squalid character.

Desert a city of ten thousand inhabitants, wipe out every vestige of written history, drive through its silent streets; ask in vain for some clue to the people who built it, and let profound silence warp you in awe and wonder. Then, you have a faint parallel of the impression which steals over one as he stands within the walls of these collossal [sic], communal houses, far out on the sand swept desert, where no living thing breaks the stillness during the calm, nor the monotony of the moaning winds, which often wails through the crumbling structures.

S. J. Holsinger, "Report on Prehistoric Ruins of Chaco Canyon, New Mexico." Unpublished manuscript on file, Chaco Culture National Historic Park, 1901, pp. 5–82, passim.

T. Mitchell Prudden's 1903 Discussion of Sites in the San Juan Watershed

> *Just after the turn of the twentieth century, T. Mitchell Prudden, a medical doctor with great interest in archaeology, toured the San Juan drainage in the Four Corners area. He visited the two largest pueblos in the San Juan—Aztec and Salmon—and made some astute observations at both locales. Regarding Salmon Pueblo, Prudden was the first of many to render the name as "Solomon." Given the name of the homesteader (Salmon) and the unusual pronunciation of the word, with the "l" not silent, the attribution of "Solomon" is not surprising. Prudden made note of some damage to the site from "random digging" and the construction of the Salmon irrigation ditch. He believed, however, that the site had great potential if it was speedily excavated. Full excavation of Salmon Pueblo, to realize the potential Prudden observed, finally began in the early 1970s under the direction of Cynthia Irwin-Williams.*
>
> *Prudden's observation on Aztec Ruins are also quite insightful. He noted that while the site had been vandalized, it was nevertheless newly protected by an owner (Mr. Koontz) who wanted to have the site scientifically studied. Such a study began in 1916, when Earl Morris and his crews began work for the American Museum of Natural History.*

DOCUMENT 13
The Prehistoric Ruins of the San Juan Watershed
T. Mitchell Prudden

The only large ruin in the entire San Juan Valley stands upon a low bench at the edge of the alluvial bottom a few miles below Bloomfield.

This is called locally "Solomon's Ruin" after the name of the owner of the land on which it is situated. It is built largely of dressed stone, the walls in some places resting upon a foundation of small boulders. It was several stories in height, and contained many rooms, but is now so fallen and covered with sand and earth that the plan can be only partially made out. This ruin measures about five hundred feet along the back and is of the communal pueblo type like the ruin at Aztec on the Animas and the great pueblos of the Chaco.

Recently considerable random digging has been done in the search for pottery, and water from an irrigating ditch has been turned into the ruin, undermining it in several places. Thus the existence of several rooms has been revealed whose walls beneath the covering of fallen stones and soil appear from without to be largely intact, the well preserved timbers above them being still in place. In spite of the vandalism which had its way with this ruin, there appear to be still promise of interesting results should a proper investigation of what remains be speedily undertaken. . . .

Farther up, near the village of Aztec, on a low gravel bench west of the river, lies the group of large pueblos called the "Aztec Ruin." The largest and best preserved of these was over three hundred and fifty feet long at the back and several stories in height with a court facing eastward. Near by are several large stone and earth heaps, indicating older sites. A large mound near the edge of the low bench bordering the valley bottom gives superficial evidence of many burials. It is said that in early days this ruin was used as a stone quarry by neighboring settlers. It is now on private property, and the owner, Mr. Koontz, wisely appreciative of the importance of systematic study of these relics of the elder folk, has guarded them from the onslaught of the vandals, so that here one of the most promising of the great old pueblos lies waiting for a trained and authorized explorer. A small opening has been made in one corner of the ruin, through which several rooms may be entered in succession. These are practically intact, with the ceiling timbers in place and well preserved. The exact size and form of this ruin are not evident in its present condition. Within sight of this ruin, in valley bottom, several small sites may be located.

T. Mitchell Prudden, *The Prehistoric Ruins of the San Juan Watershed in Utah, Arizona, Colorado, and New Mexico.* Lancaster, PA: The New Era Printing Company, 1903, pp. 1–65, passim. Reprinted from *American Anthropologist*, n.s. 5 (1903): 224–288.

Warren Moorehead's 1906 Discussion of New Mexico Pueblo Ruins

Warren K. Moorehead's account of his expedition to Chaco and the San Juan is illuminating in several ways. First, Moorehead's desire to link his work with that of Pepper and the American Museum of Natural History is obvious. He refers to Pepper's work in several places and even "promotes" Pepper, who did not complete a doctorate, to "Dr." in his written narrative. Interestingly, accounts indicate that both Pepper and Wetherill considered Moorehead's work at Pueblo Bonito intrusive and an infringement on their work. Second, Moorehead's account very clearly places the Phillips Academy's work in the realm of collection, filling the museum's display cases, and not particularly related to research. Lastly, Moorehead's suggestion that the group of Chaco Canyon ruins was the most important in the United States, made in 1906, is prescient. Although knowledge of Chaco Canyon was beginning to be widespread, appreciation of their importance in the scheme of Puebloan and North American history was just beginning.

Moorehead's account of Salmon Pueblo, on the San Juan River, is also very informative. His description of "two small buildings destroyed by fire" certainly does not mesh with our understanding today of the 250-room Salmon Pueblo. As we know it today, Salmon is quite a large building that shows evidence of at least two highly destructive fires. The description of Mr. Salmon's reluctance to have the ruin extensively probed, however, accords well with our understanding that members of the Salmon family were good caretakers of Salmon Pueblo for almost 100 years.

DOCUMENT 14
A Narrative of Exploration in New Mexico
Warren K. Moorehead

In April, 1897, the writer left Farmington, New Mexico, with nine men, a large wagon, and five horses, bound for the Chaco Group ruins, seventy miles south. This had been partly investigated by Dr. George

Pepper in the interest of the American Museum of Natural History, New York, and since the date mentioned Dr. Pepper has conducted more extensive explorations.

It was not the purpose of Mr. Peabody's expedition to attempt a thorough exploration, but simply to make a typical collection in three weeks, and, as a total of about two thousand specimens of various kinds were secured in that time, the object of the visitation was accomplished. For fuller descriptions of the Chaco Group readers are referred to the various articles cited.

For several days the men made careful search of the surface about each ruin and collected a number of large metates, mano stones, arrow points, fragments of pottery, etc. . . .

Archaeologists will rejoice if Dr. Pepper is able to resume the explorations of this remarkable place and carry them to as successful termination. Having begun his work under such auspicious circumstances, it is to be hoped that he will continue. The Chaco Group is the most important in the United States, and there is abundant evidence that the culture of the whole Southwest reached its zenith there.

The party returned from the Chaco Group to Farmington, and the specimens were packed ready for shipment to Mr. Peabody. We visited the Salmon ruins on the San Juan river, about 20 miles from Farmington, finding there two small buildings that had been destroyed by fire. Mr. Salmon did not wish us to carry on explorations for greater length of time than three days, and we were unable to secure more than a few specimens. The site is interesting and merits thorough exploration. Such whole pottery as we obtained from this San Juan pueblo is as finely made as any found in the Southwest. Apparently, the pueblo was attacked, sacked, and burned while it was still occupied. By whom, may be determined after careful exploration.

Warren K. Moorehead, *A Narrative of Exploration in New Mexico, Arizona, Indiana, Etc.*, Phillips Academy Department of Anthropology Bulletin III. Andover, MA: Andover Press, 1906, pp. 33, 53.

Earl Morris's Narrative on Aztec Ruins

In the conclusion to his first report on Aztec Ruins, excerpted below,
Earl Morris attempted to put the West Pueblo at Aztec into a chrono-

logical and cultural context. He identified Aztec as a member of the group of Chaco Canyon sites but commented on differences in layout and ground plan between Pueblo Bonito and Aztec. He quite correctly observed that Aztec more closely resembles Chetro Ketl. The basic E-shape of Chetro Ketl, with an encircling row of rooms closing the open part of the E, forming then a D-shape, is the standard Chacoan ground plan for all sites built between 1000 and 1100 C.E.

Ground plan aside, the comparison Morris makes between Aztec and Pueblo Bonito is apropos. He noted similarities in massive construction, the sheer rise of the back walls, and the open courts or plazas in front, which held great kivas. These characteristics, along with distinctive and specialized construction and use of masonry, set Chacoan-constructed sites apart from all others of contemporary age.

At the time his first report on Aztec was finished in 1919, Morris had spent only a few years professionally excavating sites. His Aztec reports, this first one in particular, reflect this relative inexperience with the broad range of Anasazi-Pueblo culture. In particular, Morris's emphasis on simple description of artifacts belies the insights he would later bring to an understanding of changes in Puebloan culture. By 1939, Morris had completed a large report on excavations in the La Plata Valley (west of Aztec but part of the Middle San Juan area), and he had much greater insight into the regional archaeology.

DOCUMENT 15
The Aztec Ruin
Earl H. Morris

Cultural and Chronological Position of the Aztec Ruin

The study of the numerous specimens which have been briefly described in the foregoing pages is amply justifiable because of the clear ray which it casts backward into the shadows which preceded the dawn of history upon our continent. This ray illuminates for us in fairly true perspective the material accomplishments of a civilization which had passed its zenith and swung into the descending arc of its existence long before the irruption of Europeans into the Southwest.

But our problem is primarily an historical one and it put before us questions that cannot be answered unless we consider the fact of material culture as a means to an end, and not an end in themselves.

Considering the various ruins as symbols of complexes of which they are, it must be admitted, but a partial expression, the main desideratum is to determine the cultural relationship of the Aztec Ruin to those of the neighboring areas, and to establish its relative chronological position in the life cycle of Pueblo civilization as a whole.

Inasmuch as the exploration is only partially completed, ultimate conclusions cannot be drawn at the present time, but a few definite statements may be made without too great risk of error. Architecturally, the Aztec Ruin must be classed with Pueblo Bonito and the other members of the Chaco Canyon group. The similarity is close throughout. To be sure, there is a marked difference between the outline of the groundplan of the Aztec Ruin and that of Pueblo Bonito, but this difference is no greater than that observable between Pueblo Bonito and Pueblo Chettrokettle, a component and integral member of the Chaco group. If the preservation of Pueblo Chettrokettle had been such that it merited exploitation as the outstanding member of the Chaco group, and if it had in consequence become fixed in our minds as such, the similarity between it and Aztec Ruin would have been readily apparent to the most casual observer, for the groundplans of the two are practically identical, except that Chettrokettle covers a somewhat more extended area.

Although the main building of Pueblo Bonito is arc-shaped, while that at Aztec forms three sides of a rectangle, the basic concept of the structures is the same. Each rises with sheer outer walls enclosing an open court which was protected from invasion on the south or sunward side by a low one-storied tier of rooms.

Earl H. Morris, *The Aztec Ruin*. New York: Anthropological Papers of the American Museum of Natural History, vol. 26, pt. 1, 1919, pp. 104–105.

George Pepper's Account of Artifacts from Pueblo Bonito

> In this excerpt from the conclusion to his 1920 monograph on Pueblo Bonito, George Pepper summarizes the major findings of the Hyde Expedition's work. Much of Pepper's energy during the fieldwork and subsequent writing was focused on artifacts of presumed ritual importance, and this emphasis is clear in his conclusion. The ritual importance of macaws has not diminished since Pepper's time, although modern archaeologists are less willing to quickly attribute the presence of these birds

to a macaw clan, ancestral to current macaw or parrot clans at Zuni and Hopi pueblos. The birds may indicate the existence of these clans at Pueblo Bonito and other Chacoan sites, or they may signify other ritual practices that were completely unrelated to the modern-day Pueblo macaw clans.

Pepper highlights the amazing burial goods recovered from Rooms 32 and 33. Even 100 years after the fieldwork, these finds remain unprecedented in the Pueblo Southwest. The meaning of such a cache of turquoise and other significant materials with these burials is, however, subject to much debate. Some archaeologists would agree with Pepper that these individuals were very important men in the Pueblo, probably priests of high status. Others would disagree with this finding and suggest instead that these individuals were unique and special for reasons that are not clear after 1,000 years. Archaeologists who subscribe to this latter view do not believe that any type of status differences existed in the Pueblo Southwest.

Pepper clearly appreciated the quality and beauty of Chacoan architecture and sees clear linkage between people who built beautiful structures and also make amazing ritual artifacts. Without much attention to explanation of the objects, Pepper repeats a summary listing of inferred ritual artifacts from Pueblo Bonito in the excerpt below. His praise for the Chacoans' skill in jewelry and ornament manufacture is certainly appropriate. But from the perspective of a twenty-first century archaeologist, additional discussion beyond aesthetics and art would have been welcome.

DOCUMENT 16
Pueblo Bonito
George Pepper

As in most pueblos of this type the majority of the rooms were angular. Ceremonial rooms, in the form of circular estufas, were represented by many examples and some of the smaller of these showed unusual outlines. Judging by the ceremonial paraphernalia found in the angular living rooms, many of these were employed for ceremonial clan rooms or for clan ceremonies. The most striking examples of this kind was Room 38, where were found the remains of macaws and a platform on which rested encrusted objects and other ceremonial pieces that had no doubt been used by members of a macaw clan, a clan now represented among the Zuni and known as the Mulakwe. The great number of skeletons of macaws beneath the floor are mute evidences of the reverence in which these birds were held. When we consider the distance that separated these birds from their natural habitat, in connection with the fact that very few bones of this bird were found in the other rooms of the pueblo, it is safe to assume that the macaw clan must have been in existence at this early period in the history of the Southwestern pueblos.

The use of certain rooms for burial purposes seems to have been secondary, although intramural burial was not confined to this particular group as other bodies were found beneath the floors of some of the angular rooms at the sides of estufas. The inconsequential number of bodies found in Pueblo Bonito naturally prompts the question as to the general cemetery wherein were buried the hundreds who must have died there. From the character of the deposits in the series of burial rooms, of which Rooms 32 and 33 were a part, and from the accompaniments with the bodies, it is evident that these were members of the priesthood or, at least, people of great importance in the life of the pueblo. Buried with such great stores of treasure, it is but natural to suppose that they were placed in a position secure from the possibility of defilement or of theft.

The artifacts from this pueblo cover the greater part of the activities that one would expect to find among a sedentary people who had reached the high plane of development that is shown by the architecture.

The aesthetic attainment of the old Bonito people is shown most forcibly by the designs in color on the wooden tablets and especially in the elaborately decorated stone mortar. Their mosaic and encrusted ceremonial pieces, as shown by the mosaic basket, the inlaid scrapers, the hematite bird, the lignite frog, and by many other objects, is indicative of the skill of their artisans and the advance of the arts as applied to objects of a ceremonial nature. Nowhere in the Southwest have there been found such masses of turquoise beads, pendants, and inlays as were uncovered in Room 33.

George Pepper, *Pueblo Bonito*. New York: Anthropological Papers of the American Museum of Natural History, vol. 27, 1920, pp. 375–376.

Florence Hawley Ellis's 1934 Discussion of Chetro Ketl

In this excerpt from her conclusion to the study of Chetro Ketl, Ellis offers an opinion on the causes of Chaco's abandonment and discusses environmental factors. In contrast to some recent researchers, Ellis suggests that droughts had little effect on construction activities at Chetro Ketl. She reconstructed a consistence sequence of building activities from the late 900s C.E. until about 1130 C.E. More recent work on Chetro Ketl suggests a more confined period of construction, with several discrete episodes from 1010 to 1115 C.E. Ellis was correct, then, in her assertion that droughts had little effect on Chetro Ketl construction. She apparently was not aware of the long drought that began around 1130 C.E. and had significant impact on Chacoan settlement.

Ellis discusses the possibility of an extensive ponderosa forest in Chaco Canyon in ancient times. More recent research has indicated that only limited stands of ponderosa and Douglas fir trees existed in Chaco. Thus, most of the large ponderosa, fir, and spruce logs that were used in construction of the great houses had to be imported from mountainous areas outside the Canyon. Current studies indicate that the Chuska Mountains to the west, and Mount Taylor, south of Chaco, were used as source areas for high-elevation trees.

DOCUMENT 17
Chetro Ketl
Florence M. Hawley (Ellis)

There is no indication that the abandonment of the Chaco pueblos was the result of a war of extermination or pestilence. We do know that the two long drouths which fell within Chaco history made little impression on Chetro Ketl building activities. If a prehistoric pine forest extended into the Chaco, the ground cover must have been sufficient to conserve all moisture available and hence to protect the constant water supply of the thickly populated area. That such a forest existed is indicated not only by the high consumption of logs in Chaco pueblo building, but also by the preponderance of pinon and pine branch charcoal deposited with refuse from the household fires on the dump. It is sufficient that two modern pines remained a few years ago in the dry and gashed cañon. One factor entering an explanation of the abandon-

ment of Chaco is increasing aridity consequent upon increasing defor-
estation, possibly inaugurated by careless cutting and the impossibility
of reproduction. It is unlikely that the Chaco was ever heavily forested,
and thin forest borders are known to injure easily and may retreat rapidly.

Florence M. Hawley, *The Significance of the Dated Prehistory of Chetro Ketl, Chaco
Cañon, New Mexico*, University of New Mexico Bulletin, vol. 1, no. 1. Albuquerque: University of New Mexico Press, 1934, p. 78.

Edgar Hewett's Vision of Chaco Canyon, 1936

*In the conclusion to his book on Chaco Canyon, excerpted below,
Edgar Hewett addresses many of the pressing concerns of the day and
issues that continue to be of interest for current Chacoan archaeologists:
abandonment, subsistence, and the nature of Chacoan society. In discussing the possibility of warfare as a cause of the Chaco abandonment,
Hewett rules it out on the lack of evidence and by suggesting that Native
Americans never pursued war in the manner that Old World people did.
Few archaeologists or anthropologists would disagree with this statement,
but today there is a greater understanding and appreciation of the role
that warfare and conflict played at certain times in the ancient Pueblo
world.*

*Failing to find evidence of warfare or a scourge of disease, Hewett
suggested that some superstition or omen or the danger of sandstone blocks
splitting from the sides of the canyon caused the Chacoans to abandon
their sites. None of these possibilities would be easy to investigate—in
Hewett's time or now. No single factor is invoked by contemporary Chacoan archaeologists to explain the abandonment of Chaco Canyon. Furthermore, today we understand that not just Chaco Canyon or Mesa
Verde but the entire northern Southwest was abandoned by Pueblo people
in the late 1290s and early 1300s. This regional process of population
dislocation and emigration is the subject of several ongoing studies by
archaeologists, including some associated with the Chaco Synthesis Project
(see Chapter 1).*

*In his final paragraph, Hewett praises the democratic spirit of the
Chacoans, noting that their great houses were monuments, not to kings
or ruling priests but to the people themselves. Hewett is rather obviously
projecting American ideals onto the Chacoans, even going so far as to*

paraphrase the U.S. Constitution: "of the people, by the people, for the people." Nevertheless, this very point is still a matter of debate among contemporary archaeologists: What was the nature of Chacoan political and social society? Few archaeologists today think of Chaco as the center of an empire. But few also believe that Chacoan society was completely democratic or egalitarian. The truth, or the best approximation we can offer, suggests that the answer lies in the middle ground. Chacoan society was not completely hierarchical or egalitarian but some combination of both, which shifted from time to time.

DOCUMENT 18
Chaco Canyon
Edgar L. Hewett

What caused the exodus from Chetro Ketl, from Chaco Canyon? To start with, one naturally inquires into the agencies that have put an end of peoples elsewhere. At the head of the list may be placed the most potent enemy of civilization, war. The traces of war, primitive war, are ineradicable. . . . War means destruction. Chetro Ketl was not destroyed. War may be eliminated in this inquiry. Indians never deliberately sought destruction as has been the fashion among Old World peoples. Epidemics have exterminated peoples both suddenly and through slow degeneration. But the most potent scourges of men leave their record in the bones. Quick-moving scourges that destroy utterly, as on St. Lawrence Island, leave the dead unburied. Epidemics often require collective burial or wholesale burning. Not a sign of this has ever been discovered in Chaco Canyon.

Eliminating then these major causes of destruction and omitting numerous minor possibilities, the field of inquiry is substantially limited. One naturally asks, what were the essential conditions for continued existence in Chaco Canyon? Indispensable are food and water. Food supply becomes precarious from time to time, even under highly civilized conditions, but in one way or another the conditions are usually met. Chaco Canyon could have survived a failing food supply for some years.

However, it must be admitted that there is no way of accounting for an Indian exodus. We know it to have been an old Pueblo custom suddenly to take themselves and all their possessions to some new place, leaving a perfectly good town to fall into ruins. Superstition is a potent force with them. As heretofore suggested, the crashing masses of cliff wall, aside from the actual physical danger, may have been to them a convincing warning from deific power and it would be just about as imperative as a famine. . . .

Summing up the traits and tendencies of the Chaqueños, the following stand out rather distinctly: predominance of domestic, community spirit; dependence upon agriculture, with hunting as a secondary means of subsistence; resourcefulness in meeting environmental conditions; exuberance in the building impulse; mastery in stone masonry; efficiency in ceramic art; intense religious activity.

Of all these traits, as revealed in their monuments, no other impresses me deeply as that of their democratic spirit. . . . The great community houses of Chaco Canyon are an expression of the domestic life of a race at its best. They were built by free men, of their own volition, in their own time and way, as *homes for their families*. They represent the labor "of the people, by the people, for the people," and they are not wanting in the qualities that make for endurance. They memorialize the lives of the people, not of kings. . . . It is significant that only representative government has ever existed among the native American people. [Emphasis in original document]

Edgar L. Hewett, *The Chaco Canyon and Its Monuments*. Albuquerque: University of New Mexico Press and the School of American Research Press, 1936, pp. 138–140.

Neil Judd's 1964 Discussion of Pueblo Bonito's Architecture

In this quotation from his report on Chacoan architecture at Pueblo Bonito, Judd reiterates his hypothesis that the Chacoans migrated in from the San Juan River area. He further discusses the differences he sees between Pueblo II (Old Bonitians) and Pueblo III (New Bonitians) people at Pueblo Bonito. Judd's report was finally finished and published in 1964, more than thirty years after the fieldwork was undertaken.

Judd anticipated the debate over the Chacoan outliers that came decades after his work was finished (see Chapter 6, this volume). He notes that both Lowry and Aztec have been attributed to Chacoan peoples but finds their masonry somewhat inferior and not up to Chacoan standards.

If Judd found Aztec lacking in its Chacoan masonry, one can only imag-
ine his reaction to some of the recently proposed outliers that completely
lack good Chacoan masonry.

Judd also notes the later, so-called Mesa Verde occupation at the
northern outliers. He includes Salmon Ruin (identified as Solomon's Ruin
and incorrectly placed on the south, instead of the north, bank of the San
Juan River) in this discussion, along with Aztec and Lowry. Clearly,
Judd understood the distribution of the primary, large Chacoan outliers
in the Northern San Juan region.

DOCUMENT 19
The Architecture of Pueblo Bonito, 1964
Neil M. Judd

Pueblo Bonito began as a wide-spreading crescent of Pueblo II houses
with storerooms at the rear, several subterranean kivas out in front, and
the village trash pile beyond. After that trash had accumulated to a
depth of 8 feet or more, after 5 feet of sand had settled against the old
P. II houses, another people came to join the original settlers—a Pueblo
III people with a more advanced architecture and a different pottery
complex. Together, the houses these P. III people built and the pottery
they made are now widely accepted as earmarks of distinct social development, "The Chaco Culture." One objective of the Pueblo Bonito
Expeditions was to ascertain, if possible, the origin of this development
and its termination.

We reached part of our goal but not all. After seven summers at
Pueblo Bonito, 1921–1927, I am of the opinion that the P. II and the
P. III peoples who formerly dwelt there had come independently from
beyond the San Juan River, but I can only guess at their destination
after leaving Chaco Canyon. This recognition of the broad area north
of the San Juan as the place of origin—an area in which I have done
no field work for many years—has been substantiated by the published
observations of Kidder, Morris, Martin, Roberts, Brew, and others, and
I have placed great confidence in those observations in what follows.

The so-called Chaco Culture was just short of full bloom when it first
came to Chaco Canyon. At Pueblo Bonito, it introduced veneer-and-
core masonry and architectural precision; it also introduced Corrugated-

coil Culinary ware, Straight-line Hatchure and, among others, a hybrid variety of domestic pottery we designated "the Chaco-San Juan." Seen by various observers and variously described, the Chaco Culture and influence attributed to it have been reported far beyond the borders of Chaco Canyon.

Aztec Ruin, with its predetermined ground plan, its large high-ceilinged rooms, and kiva sunk within the house mass is even closer to Chaco architecture than Lowry. Like the latter, however, Aztec masonry falls shorts of the Chaco ideal because building stone comparable to that of Chaco Canyon is not found in the vicinity. Aztec sandstones, and those generally throughout the northern country, are tough and cross-bedded; they lack the natural cleavage of Chaco's sandstones.

Eventually both Lowry and Aztec were abandoned by their builders and thereafter were appropriated, partially repaired, and reoccupied by Mesa Verde peoples. This was also true of Soloman's Ruin, on the south bank of the San Juan River, and of various lesser structures to the northward. So-called Chaco peoples settled this northern country first and those with a Mesa Verde–like culture moved in later. Where remains of the two occur at the same site "the Mesa Verde is always on top" (Earl Morris, 1939, p. 204)—not Classic Mesa Verde necessarily but its forerunner.

Neil M. Judd, *The Architecture of Pueblo Bonito*, Smithsonian Miscellaneous Collections, vol. 147, no. 1. Washington, DC: Smithsonian Institution, 1964, p. 41.

Cynthia Irwin-Williams's View of the Chaco Phenomenon at Salmon Ruins

> In this excerpt from her 1972 report on Salmon Ruins, Cynthia Irwin-Williams lays out her vision of Chacoan society and her plan for studying it in the San Juan Region. She introduced the term "Chaco Phenomenon" in the early stages of work at Salmon and was one of the first archaeologists to apply a regional approach in Chacoan studies. The focus on Salmon and interest in Aztec mark the first time not only that Chacoan outliers were perceived as legitimate research interests in their own right but that they were seen as avenues for understanding Chacoan culture in its entirety.

Irwin-Williams's brief mention of Mesoamerican or Mexican influence on Chacoan society reflects the currency of this school of thought in the early 1970s. Although a very few scholars still advocate significant intrusion and influence by Toltecs or other Mesoamericans, most see limited Mexican influence on Chacoan society in the presence of imported macaws, copper bells, cloisonné decorated sandstone and pottery, and perhaps some ceremonial-ritual beliefs.

Like Morris at Aztec, Irwin-Williams emphasized the Chacoan qualities of the Salmon outlier. She contrasted Salmon and Aztec with smaller pueblos, built in a less planned and organized fashion. Drawing these contrasts, Irwin-Williams foreshadowed, to some extent, the current debate among Chacoan scholars regarding the nature of the Chaco System and the status of proposed outliers that simply do not meet the standards set by Aztec and Salmon.

DOCUMENT 20
The Structure of Chacoan Society in the Northern Southwest
Cynthia Irwin-Williams

The ancient culture centered in the Chaco Canyon of northwestern New Mexico, which reached a climax in the 11th century A.D., was unquestionably one of the most sophisticated and complex pre-Columbian cultures of Native North America. Evidence accumulated over the past century has suggested the extraordinary levels of development achieved in art, architecture, and town planning; including the construction of the largest community dwellings in the world until the late 19th century, "great houses" such as Pueblo Bonito, Chetro Kettle, Pueblo Alto, Pueblo del Arroyo, etc.

More recent studies have now shown the existence of extensive series of irrigation canals and dams, and of complex networks of roads connecting the principal Chaco towns. In addition, some authorities believe the Chacoan centers were in direct contact with the high civilizations of central Mexico and were focal points for the penetration of Meso-American influence in the Southwest. Other recent and earlier research indicates that in the late 11th century populations from the Chaco Canyon expanded into other areas and created colonial towns duplicating the "great houses" of the Chaco. A principal area for such occupation was the San Juan–Animas River drainage, where at least two of the new towns (Aztec Ruins National Monument and the Salmon Site) rivaled those of the Chaco in size and quality. The current [San Juan Valley Archaeological] Program focuses on one of these as a key to an investigation of the Chaco phenomenon itself.

The Salmon Site, located on the San Juan River about 45 miles northeast of Chaco Canyon, was constructed in the late 11th century, apparently by a group originating in that cultural center. Built in the form of a great C, it stands three or more stories high and extends 450 feet along the back and 200 feet along the arms. It is thus one of the largest of these pre-Columbian "apartment houses." The structure itself is constructed entirely of several grades of carefully worked stone, and the fine-banded masonry and carefully planned architecture reflects a sophisticated knowledge of architecture unknown outside the Chacoan province. A large depression (about 60 feet in diameter) in the plaza almost certainly conceals a great Kiva, the community ceremonial chamber. Preservation at the site is excellent, with roof beams frequently preserved, and entire floors and ceilings intact in some areas. Indications from this and the companion "great house" at Aztec (National Monument) are that these enormous structures were built as massive coordinated efforts in very short periods of time (about a decade). This is in marked contrast to other large Pueblo structures which reached maximum size by eclectic growth through time. A major aim of the research is to understand the character of socio-political control in this apparently egalitarian society which made possible these enormous undertakings.

Cynthia Irwin-Williams, "The San Juan Valley Archaeological Program," in *The Structure of Chacoan Society in the Northern Southwest: Investigations at the Salmon Site—1972*, edited by C. Irwin-Williams. Portales: Eastern New Mexico University Contributions in Anthropology, vol. 4, no. 3, December 1972, p. 4.

Jim Judge's Model of Chacoan Collapse

In this excerpt from his 1989 paper on Chaco, Jim Judge effectively summarizes his view (at that time) of the Chacoan collapse. He integrates environmental conditions, the economic system, and Chaco's role as a ritual center effectively in discussing his model. His use of the term redistribution is perhaps the only dated part of the argument. The 1970s and 1980s work of the Chaco Project introduced this concept of redistribution of goods into the collective Chacoan body of knowledge. In the last two decades, many archaeologists have moved away from this concept, citing the lack of data showing that goods, especially foodstuffs, were truly gathered in Chaco and redistributed across the landscape. In short, the redistribution part of the model has fallen out of favor.

The other change in the last twenty years is a greater emphasis on ritual and the role it probably played in the Chacoan world. Chacoan archaeologists have moved further away from economic-based arguments to explain the rise of Chacoan society and closer to ceremonial-ritual concerns as driving factors.

Judge's strong endorsement of the 1130 c.e. drought as the cause for the Chacoan collapse goes along with the ecological-environmental basis for much recent Chacoan research. Clearly, the environment provided the limits on what the Chacoans could achieve. But the phenomenal growth of the Chacoan system, the "rituality" as we might call it, can perhaps be invoked as the primary cause for the ultimate collapse. Without such growth in the last half of the eleventh century, Chacoan society might have persisted in the face of the declining environmental conditions.

DOCUMENT 21
The Collapse of Chaco
W. James Judge

I suggest, then, that the fundamental cause of the collapse of the Chacoan system was environmental deterioration. The system had operated very effectively in coping with variability in precipitation through formally administered alliance networks that served to redistribute goods among the outlying areas, but this coping took place in a relatively favorable climatic regime. The business of administering and scheduling the network operation was conducted in Chaco Canyon during pilgrimage festivals held as integral components of a ritual system, a system formally shared between the canyon and the outliers. As the system developed, its success attracted even more participants from outside the Basin, and this saturation of population served to make the entire network vulnerable to environmental perturbations. The role of Chaco Canyon as the ritual locus was challenged in the late eleventh century as a brief but severe reduction in summer precipitation. The system was too well integrated, however, and reorganization was the most viable option. Following this reorganization, and the addition of even more groups to the north, an extended period of drought began, which was too severe for the system to handle. Perhaps another reorganization was effected as an initial response, but when this was perceived as ineffective in coping with the unfavorable climate, the three responses noted above were invoked and the Chaco system, effective for some 150 years, came to an end.

W. James Judge, "Chaco Canyon–San Juan Basin," in *Dynamics of Southwest Prehistory*, edited by L. S. Cordell and G. J. Gumerman. Washington, DC: Smithsonian Institution Press, 1989, p. 249.

Gwinn Vivian's Co-Tradition Explanation for Chaco

In this excerpt from his 1990 book on Chaco, Gwinn Vivian discusses part of his model for the explanation of Chacoan society. His work follows that of his father Gordon Vivian and anthropologist Clyde Kluckhohn. The model has been called the Co-Tradition model because it invokes the presence of two distinct cultural traditions (probably two distinct ethnic groups) in Chaco Canyon who were responsible, separately, for the small house and great house constructions. Vivian views these groups as related but distinct.

Like many Chacoan archaeologists, Vivian proposes an egalitarian model for Chaco, rejecting hypotheses that have suggested ranked or hierarchical social units. Nevertheless, Vivian allows for the presence of "rotating sequential hierarchies" among the great house builders at Chaco. In the simplest terms, such hierarchies are temporary and do not lead to permanent, ranked leadership positions. Thus, Vivian explains the organizational challenges that faced the Chacoans (including construction of great houses requiring millions of pieces of masonry and thousands of wooden beams) by suggesting that leaders arose situationally and passed the reigns of leadership on rather quickly.

DOCUMENT 22
Explaining the Chacoan Phenomenon
Gwinn Vivian

It is maintained, therefore, that analysis of internal change is the most fruitful approach to explicating Chacoan culture growth and that such analysis must include consideration of the functional relationships within and between the populations of small and great house settlements. That goal is conditioned by two major premises. The first is that observed settlement and architectural variability in the Chaco Core reflected organization differences of two societies that shared many cultural attributes but that were not organized during most of Chacoan prehistory as a single coherently functioning entity. The second premise is that organizational differences did not represent an egalitarian versus a ranked society, but rather two contrasting egalitarian modes with one utilizing a rotating sequential hierarchy to accommodate larger population units.

R. Gwinn Vivian, *The Chacoan Prehistory of the San Juan Basin*. San Diego: Academic Press, 1990, pp. 420–421.

GLOSSARY

Acomans: The inhabitants of the Western Pueblo village of Acoma.

Acoma Pueblo: A modern Western Pueblo village located on a high mesa in western New Mexico. Acoma is part of the Keresan-language family and is considered a Western Keresan group.

Anasazi: An adaptation of an original Navajo word that means, variously, "ancient enemies," "ancient enemies of ancestors," or "ancient ones or people." Popularized by Richard Wetherill, the term has been used by archaeologists since the late 1800s to refer to the sites of ancient Puebloan people during the Basketmaker and Pueblo periods. In recent years, the term has fallen out of use, mainly because it lacks clear connection to the modern Pueblo people—the descendants of the ancient people identified as Anasazi.

Animas River: A perennial stream that begins in the mountains of southwest Colorado, then flows south-southwest to its confluence with the San Juan River in the current city of Farmington, New Mexico. Important Puebloan sites, such as Aztec Ruins, lie along the course of the Animas River.

Antiquities Act: A law passed by the United States in 1906 that required permits for excavations at archaeological and historic sites on government lands. The law made it illegal to excavate federally owned sites without permission and provided the first protection for historic sites in the United States.

Apache(s): Comprising several groups of Athapaskan language–speaking Native Americans who live in New Mexico and Arizona today.

Archaic period: A time period defined by archaeologists for the American Southwest (and other geographic areas in North America) that dates from 5500–600 B.C.E. Human groups during this time period "made their living" with a mixed pattern of hunting game animals and gathering natural plant foods, along with limited experimentation with horticulture—growing crops such as corn.

Arroyo: From a Spanish word for "gully," a deeply cut wash or intermittent drainage that typically flows only when fed by heavy rain or spring runoff from melting, higher-elevation snow.

Aztec Ruins: Also known as the Aztec Community or the Aztec pueblos. The largest Chacoan outlier (with more than 600 rooms at several sites) outside Chaco Canyon located in northwest New Mexico along the Animas River. The site was occupied from the early C.E. 1100s until almost 1300.

Basketmaker: A period of time identified by archaeologists in the sequence of ancient Puebloan people. This term appears as either the Basketmaker II period (dated from 600 B.C.E. to 500 C.E.), the Basketmaker III period (500–750 C.E.), or more generally as the Basketmaker period (600 B.C.E. to 750 C.E.) or era.

Bluff Great House: A Chaco Era great house located near the contemporary town of Bluff, Utah, on the northwestern periphery of Chacoan influence.

Bonitians: Neil Judd's name for the residents of Pueblo Bonito, separated into Old Bonitians, the original builders and occupants, and New Bonitians, the latecomers who greatly expanded Pueblo Bonito.

Cacique(s): A Spanish word that translates as "chief" or "headman." In the ancient Pueblo world, caciques were the leaders of villages.

Chacoan collapse: A shorthand term for the end of Chacoan society, dated between 1130 and 1150 C.E.

Chaco Canyon: An east-west trending physiographic feature in northwest New Mexico that has a dozen great house pueblos and thousands of Puebloan, Navajo, and other archaeological sites. The name has been rendered as Chaca, as well.

Chaco Culture National Historical Park: The formal name applied to the land set aside in Chaco Canyon as a national park. The name was assigned in 1980 and the park was known before as Chaco Canyon National Monument.

Chaco Era: The time period of greatest Chacoan influence across the northern Southwest. Different dates have been assigned by archaeologists, but the most common interval is 1000 to 1150 C.E.

Chaco Phenomenon: The name given the group of Chacoan sites in Chaco Canyon and including the outliers by Cynthia Irwin-Williams in 1972. Other scholars picked up this term and used it extensively throughout the 1970s, 1980s, and 1990s. Of late, the term is not used by most Chacoan archaeologists. *See also* Chaco System.

Chaco Synthesis: A series of conferences held between 1999 and 2002 and designed to assemble experts on Chacoan archaeology for focused meetings. The goal of the undertaking is a series of synthetic publications representing the current understanding of Chacoan archaeology (planned for completion by the end of 2005).

Chaco System: A term that overlaps with "Chaco Phenomenon" to a great extent. This term is used to identify great houses in Chaco Canyon and outliers around the American Southwest. Use of the term implies the notion of a centrally controlled system based in Chaco Canyon.

Chert: Refers to a wide variety of sedimentary rocks that were used by the ancient Pueblos and other people to make stone tools. The Chacoans preferred a specific type of chert derived from Narbona Pass in the Chuska Mountains.

Chetro Ketl: Also written as Chetro Kettle and Chettrokettle. The second largest great house site in Chaco Canyon. Together with Pueblo Bonito, Pueblo del Arroyo, Pueblo Alto, and Casa Rinconada, it comprises the core of Chaco, also known as "downtown" Chaco. The name was translated by W. H. Jackson as "Rain Pueblo," but this rendering cannot be confirmed in any known language.

Chimney Rock Pueblo: The northeastern-most outpost of the Chacoan world. The great house at Chimney Rock was built by the Chacoans primarily to serve as an observatory of the lunar standstill.

Chuska Mountains: A mountain range that runs along the contemporary New Mexico–Arizona state border. These mountains were a primary source of wood used to build the great houses in Chaco Canyon and elsewhere.

Chuska Valley: The valley east of the Chuska Mountains that was occupied early in the Pueblo sequence. The sites in Chaco Canyon show connection to the Chuska Valley through wood from the Chuska Mountains, Narbona Pass chert, and large quantities of pottery that were made by the inhabitants of sites in the Chuska Valley.

Cobbles: River-derived, oval rocks that were occasionally used for construction of ancient Pueblo dwellings. Cobbles constitute an inferior building material, contrasted with fine tabular sandstone, because of their hardness, oval shape, and difficulty in shaping.

Core-veneer masonry: A specific type of stone architecture in the Chacoan world that consists of two veneers, or outer layers of rock, that enclose a core of unaligned rock rubble, mortar, and dirt.

Dendrochronology: In laymen's terms, tree-ring dating. A technique for dating archaeological and historic sites that matches the growth rings in trees and cut tree timbers to a master chronology. This method allows the age of a tree, and sometimes its death, to be matched to an exact year.

Downtown Chaco: An urban American analogy applied to the central district in Chaco Canyon, consisting of Pueblo Bonito, Chetro Ketl, Pueblo Alto, Pueblo del Arroyo, and the great kiva at Casa Rinconada.

Estuffas (estufas): The word applied first by Spanish explorers (and used by later Anglo-American explorers) to the round, ceremonial rooms of the pueblos that are today called kivas. The word translates as "sweat house"—the Spanish believed the structures were used for sweating connected to ceremonies.

Great Gambler: From a myth in documented Navajo oral history about a chief or leader who was a successful gambler and ruler of Chaco Canyon and who lived at Pueblo Alto. The ultimate origin of this story is unclear—it may have originated with Navajos living in Chaco Canyon in the late seventeenth or early eighteenth century or may have much deeper Pueblo roots.

Great house: A term first used by Earl Morris to describe the large, Chacoan dwellings that are much larger than typical Puebloan small houses. Defining characteristics include massive, core-veneer stone architecture; distinct facing patterns (Chaco masonry) in the stone veneers; multistory construction; and kiva structures built directly into the block of rooms.

Great kiva: A much larger version of the typical Pueblo kiva with capacity for hundreds of people. These structures are usually fourteen to seventeen meters (forty-six to fifty-six feet) in diameter and have a special set of internal features. Archaeologists infer a special, ceremonial function for these structures.

Hayden Survey: Also known as the U.S. Geological and Geographical Survey of the Territories after 1871. One of the great western land and nature surveys commissioned by the U.S. Congress in the late nineteenth century. Led by Ferdinand V. Hayden, M.D., the survey was active in the West from 1871 until 1879.

Hopi: A Western Pueblo people who live in several villages along the Hopi mesas in northeastern Arizona.

Hosta, Francisco: Governor of Jemez Pueblo in the 1840s, who served as guide for Lt. James Simpson on the 1849 expedition through Chaco Canyon. Also guided W. H. Jackson through Chaco in 1877.

Hungo Pavi: Also written as Hungo Pavie. A great house in Chaco Canyon located east of Pueblo Bonito. The derivation of the name is not precisely known. It may represent some variation of the Hopi village of Shungopovi or another Hopi word.

Hyde Exploring Expedition: An expedition sponsored by the American Museum of Natural History that excavated at Pueblo Bonito (and other Chaco Canyon sites) from 1896 through 1900.

Katsina(s): Ceremonial societies or groups that comprise an important part of village life for the Western Pueblo people. Also refers to the mythological figures that represent the society, who are portrayed in public dances by village members (i.e., Katsina dancers).

Keresan: A large language and cultural group among the Pueblo people of the southwest United States. People of Keresan descent are grouped into Western (Acoma and Laguna) and Eastern (Cochiti, San Felipe, Santa Ana, Santo Domingo, and Zia) villages.

Kiva: A ceremonial chamber, typically round in shape but square among the Hopi and other Western Pueblos, of the contemporary Pueblo people. Such structures are found in pre-Hispanic pueblo sites and are usually inferred to be ceremonial in nature.

Lowry Ruin: A Chacoan outlier in southwest Colorado.

Lunar standstill: The northern- and southern-most stopping points of the moon along its apparent path through the sky. The moon has a major standstill (rising at the same point on the landscape) for a period of several years every 18.6 years and a minor standstill every 9.3 years.

Macaw-Parrot clan: One of many kinship-defined groups (clans) among the contemporary Hopi, Zuni (known as the Mulakwe clan), and other Western Pueblo villages. The importance of macaws in Chacoan society suggests that an earlier form of this clan was present among the Chacoans.

Mancos black-on-white: A painted pottery type of the northern San Juan region that dates between 900 and 1150 C.E.

Mano: A handheld grinding stone used by Pueblo people, past and present. Paired with a metate to grind corn and other substances.

Matrilineal: A term related to the study of kinship that specifies the reckoning of descent and inheritance of property or land through the woman's or the mother's side of the family.

Matrilocal: A residence pattern in which a new couple lives with or near the woman's family.

Mayan: A pre-Hispanic people of southern Mexico and Central America who developed a complex society with several large cities and a population numbering in the tens of thousands.

McElmo black-on-white: A highly painted black-on-white pottery of the Mesa Verde region that dates from 1050 to 1250 C.E. This type of pottery was the precursor to and evolved into Mesa Verde black-on-white pottery.

Medicine men: A Euro-American word for traditional Native American healers and spiritual leaders. Most of the contemporary Pueblo villages have medicine men societies, and such societies are inferred for the ancient Puebloans.

Mesa de Chaca: The region identified on the 1776 map of Spanish cartographer Bernado de Miera y Pacheco in the vicinity of Chaco Canyon.

Mesa Verde: A geographic area in southwest Colorado consisting of an elevated plateau (a mesa) that contains thousands of ancient Puebloan and other cultural and historic sites. The name is also applied to a much larger area, described by archaeologists as a branch (a subdivision) of Puebloan culture, that extends south to the San Juan River in New Mexico and west into Utah.

Mesa Verde black-on-white: A distinctive, highly decorated black-on-white pottery of the Mesa Verde region that dates from 1200 to 1300 c.e.

Mesoamerica(n): A term used to describe the region and the archaeology of Middle or Central America, that is, the area south of the current international border all the way to South America.

Metate: A large, flat stone used by Pueblo people, past and present, to grind corn. Metates hold the corn that is ground with a mano into flour.

Moiety system: A system of social organization among the Eastern Pueblos in which a village is divided into two kinship-based groups, moieties, that have exclusive membership.

Montezuma: Emperor of the Aztecs in the early sixteenth century when Spanish conquistador Hernando Cortez arrived.

Narbona Pass chert: Formerly known as Washington Pass chert, a distinctive, high-quality lithic raw material, derived from Narbona Pass in the Chuska Mountains, that was used by the Chacoans and other groups to make fine stone tools such as arrow heads and cutting tools.

Navajo: A group of indigenous American people in the Athabaskanlanguage family. The Navajos are relative newcomers to the American Southwest, arriving, at the earliest, in the c.e. 1400s. Chaco Canyon, abandoned by the Pueblo people by 1300 c.e., was empty, the great houses in ruins when Navajo families first arrived and settled the area.

Obsidian: A black, volcanic rock with a glassy texture that was used by the ancient Chacoans and other groups to make stone tools. The Jemez Mountains, east of Chaco Canyon, provided a ready source of obsidian.

Outliers: A term used to describe outlying great house sites known or assumed to be associated with Chaco Canyon.

Paleoindian period: A distinct time period during the early human occupation of North America that is dated between 10,000 and 5500 b.c.e. Archaeologists have reconstructed a largely hunting-based economy for human groups during this time period.

PDSI: Acronym for Palmer Drought Severity Index. An index used to measure the severity of droughts by including the cumulative effects of prior and subsequent years when calculating the index value for a single year. PDSI values have been calculated for much of the ancient Puebloan chronology using climatic data derived from tree rings.

Penasco Blanco: A Chaco Canyon great house on the west end of the Canyon.

Pre-Hispanic: A term of relatively recent origin that refers generically to the lengthy time period before the Spanish entered the Puebloan Southwest in 1540 c.e.

Pueblo(s): From the Spanish word for "town," an occupied village of the past and present of the northern American Southwest; or an above-ground dwelling built in the pre-Hispanic American Southwest after 700 c.e., or if capitalized, the past or present inhabitants of the northern American Southwest; or a period designation in the history-chronology of Puebloan peoples (for example, Pueblo II, Pueblo III). *See also* Puebloan for comparison.

Pueblo I period: In the Puebloan chronology, the time period from 750 to 900 C.E.

Pueblo II period: The time period from 900 to 1150 C.E. in the Puebloan chronology.

Pueblo III period: In the Puebloan chronology, the time period from 1150 to 1300 C.E.

Puebloan(s): At its simplest, people who built and lived in pueblos; or a member of a contemporary or ancient Pueblo group; or more broadly rendered as a group or groups of ancient people who occupied the northern portion of the American Southwest from 600 B.C.E. until (and after) the Spanish entrada at 1540 C.E. *See also* Pueblo for comparison.

Puebloan Society: The group of people living together in a Pueblo community and their customs, beliefs, and patterns of living.

Pueblo Bonito: The largest great house site in Chaco Canyon. Centrally located in the Canyon and part of "downtown" Chaco.

Pueblo del Arroyo: A large Chacoan great house located close to Pueblo Bonito in "downtown" Chaco Canyon.

Pueblo Pintado: A Chacoan great house located along the Chaco River a few miles east of Chaco Canyon.

Pueblo Revolt: An organized rebellion of Pueblo people, and other Native Americans, against Spanish rule that occurred in 1680. Dozens of Spanish priests, colonists, and officials were killed, and all Spanish presence was removed from New Mexico and Arizona until 1692, when the Spanish returned in force to reconquer the territory.

Pueblo village: A more specific reference for the word *pueblo*, used to more clearly refer to the villages and not the Pueblo people.

Rituality: A term recently applied to Chacoan society. A rituality is a society in which ritual and ceremony are the most important concerns. Further, such societies are governed by leaders from the ritual-ceremonial realm. "Secular" sociopolitical concerns are not critical in such societies.

Ritual structures: Structures used or inferred to have been used for ritual and ceremony. In the Pueblo world, ritual structures include kivas, great kivas, triwall structures, and some great houses.

Salmon Pueblo: Also known as Salmon Ruin(s). The first, largest outlier built in the Middle San Juan region at 1090 C.E. The site had 275 rooms at maximum and was occupied for 200 years.

San Juan: A Spanish word meaning "St. John." The name applied by early Spanish explorers to a river (still known as the San Juan River) running through the area of New Spain. The name is applied more generally to the region drained by the river, covering portions of four modern American states (New Mexico, Arizona, Utah, and Colorado).

San Juan Basin: From the name applied by early Spanish explorers. This term refers specifically to the geologic feature in northwestern New Mexico that is structurally lower than the surrounding mountainous and upland areas.

San Juan River: The name applied by early Spanish explorers to a river that begins in the mountains of southwest Colorado and runs west through the states of New Mexico, Utah, and Arizona before emptying into the Colorado River. Numerous pre-Hispanic and abandoned Puebloan sites lie along the banks of the San Juan River.

Sodality: A restricted non-kin-based society or group within a Pueblo village that performs certain exclusive functions. For example, a medicine sodality, a ceremonial sodality.

Solstice: An event that occurs twice each year, at midsummer and midwinter, when the sun reaches its highest or lowest point in the sky at noon, marked by the longest (in the summer) and shortest (in the winter) days. The solstices are important to the contemporary Pueblo people and, judging by the archaeological evidence, were also important to the ancient Puebloans.

(The) Southwest: A generic reference to the American Southwest, including all of the modern states of New Mexico and Arizona, southwest Colorado, southeast Utah, and (occasionally) west Texas.

Stratigraphy: The study of soil and sediment deposits in archaeological sites (and elsewhere) to determine the sequence of deposition. This method often allows for determination of a relative age of the deposits in an archaeological site.

Sun Dagger: An ancient Pueblo petroglyph consisting of two spirals located on the east face of the highest cliff on Fajada Butte. Using light that passes through three parallel, upright slabs located in front of the petroglyph (but now collapsed), the Sun Dagger tracks the equinoxes and solstices and the minor and major standstills of the moon.

Sword Swallowers: A contemporary Zuni fraternity or society, also known as the Wood society. Zuni oral history identifies this society as occupants of Chaco Canyon, a stopping point during the migrations that ultimately led to the founding of Zuni Pueblo.

Tabular sandstone: A type of sandstone that is thin and of consistent thickness. This material was prized by the Chacoans for use in the construction of great houses.

Tenochitlan: Sixteenth-century capital of the Aztec Empire, located in the valley of Mexico; modern Mexico City overlies this older, ruined city.

Tewa: A language and cultural group within the larger Tanoan family of

Pueblo people of New Mexico, southwest United States, that in-cludes six contemporary villages—Nambe, Pojoaque, San Juan, Santa Clara, San Ildefonso, and Tesuque—and many pre- and post-Hispanic abandoned villages.

Threatening Rock: A massive slab of sandstone that separated from the canyon bluff above Pueblo Bonito over time and ultimately crashed into the site in January 1941, destroying some sixty rooms in the pueblo.

Tiwa: A language and cultural group within the larger Tanoan family of Pueblo people of New Mexico, southwest United States, that in-cludes four contemporary villages: Sandia and Isleta as Southern Tiwa, and Taos and Picuris as Northern Tiwa. Many pre-Hispanic sites are probably Tiwa in origin.

Towa: A language and cultural group within the larger Tanoan family of Pueblo people of New Mexico, southwest United States, that in-cludes one contemporary village at Jemez and one historic village at Pecos Pueblo. Numerous abandoned villages are Towa in origin.

Una Vida: A Chacoan great house located in the western part of Chaco Canyon.

Wheeler Survey: One of the great land and nature surveys of the Amer-ican West in the late nineteenth century. Led by Lt. George Wheeler, this survey was sponsored by the U.S. Army. The survey was ongoing from 1871 through 1879.

White House: A locality or place referred to in the oral history of Acoma and other Keresan villages. White House was a stopping point in a series of migrations by Pueblo people and may be asso-ciated with Pueblo Bonito or another site in Chaco Canyon.

Wijiji: The eastern-most Chacoan great house in the main group of ru-ins in Chaco Canyon.

Wupatki: An archaeological site in Arizona, preserved as a national monument, that represents the western-most example of Chacoan-influenced architecture.

Yucatan: A region in modern Mexico that supported a large population of Mayan and other peoples in the pre-Hispanic past.

Zuni: A group of Western Pueblo people with a distinct language who live in western New Mexico in a single village.

ANNOTATED BIBLIOGRAPHY

Books and Monographs

Cordell, Linda S., W. James Judge, and June-el Piper, eds. *Chaco Society and Polity: Papers from the 1999 Conference*. Special Publication no. 4. Albuquerque: New Mexico Archeological Council, 2001. This volume is a collection of papers from one of the Chaco Synthesis conferences on Chacoan society and polity and provides a good summary of the latest thinking about these issues.

Crown, Patricia L., and W. James Judge, eds. *Chaco & Hohokam: Prehistoric Regional Systems in the American Southwest*. Santa Fe, NM: School of American Research Press, 1991. This volume discusses two regional systems in the ancient American Southwest: the Hohokam System in southern Arizona and the Chaco System in the northern Southwest. In addition to specific, updated information on the two systems (as of about 1990), the volume's contribution lies in the comparison made between Chaco and Hohokam with regard to settlement patterns, exchange and interaction, subsistence, and sociopolitical organization.

Doyel, David E., ed. *Anasazi Regional Organization and the Chaco System*. Anthropological Papers no. 5. Albuquerque: Maxwell Museum of Anthropology, 2001. This volume contains a collection of papers from a Society for American Archaeology symposium held in 1990 and represents a "state-of-the-art" assessment of the Chacoan Regional System, as understood in 1990 (with some updates for the 2001 edition).

Frazier, Kendrick. *People of Chaco*. 1986. Rev. ed., New York: Crown Publishers, 1999. This is a popular book on Chaco Canyon. The author does a good job of conveying archaeologists' perspectives on Chaco, as well as incorporating the perspectives of contemporary Pueblo people regarding Chaco Canyon.

Gabriel, Kathryn. *Roads to Center Place: A Cultural Atlas of Chaco Canyon and the Anasazi*. Boulder, CO: Johnson Books, 1991. With Chacoan roads as the focus, this book explores Chaco Canyon as a central place in the ancient Pueblo Southwest.

Hewett, Edgar L. *The Chaco Canyon and Its Monuments*. Albuquerque: University of New Mexico Press and the School of American Research Press, 1936. This book represents Edgar Hewett's primary contribution to Chacoan archaeology. The volume provides not only a detailed look at Chetro Ketl but also a summary of knowledge about Chaco Canyon as of the early 1930s.

Irwin-Williams, Cynthia, and Philip H. Shelley. *Investigations at the Salmon Site: The Structure of Chacoan Society in the Northern Southwest*. Vols. 1–4. Final Report to Funding Agencies. Portales: Eastern New Mexico University, 1980. This voluminous work comprises the site report for Salmon Ruins. This four-volume set with multiple appendices contains considerable data and many insights into Salmon and Chacoan society, with a focus on 1970s data models.

Judd, Neil M. *The Material Culture of Pueblo Bonito*. Smithsonian Miscellaneous Collections, vol. 124. Washington, DC: Smithsonian Institution, 1954. This book represents the definitive work on the artifacts recovered from the decades-long excavation at Pueblo Bonito, the largest of the Chacoan great houses.

Judd, Neil M. *The Architecture of Pueblo Bonito*. Smithsonian Miscellaneous Collections, vol. 147, no. 1. Washington, DC: Smithsonian Institution, 1964. This volume is the companion publication to Judd's earlier *The Material Culture of Pueblo Bonito* volume. This work provides a comprehensive study of Pueblo Bonito's architecture, incorporating Pepper and the American Museum's earlier work.

Kanter, John, and Nancy M. Mahoney, eds. *Great House Communities across the Chacoan Landscape*. Anthropological Papers of the University of Arizona no. 64. Tucson: University of Arizona Press, 2000. This publication is part of the "new wave" of Chacoan research in the late twentieth century. The essays in this edited volume summarize and assess Chacoan communities across the San Juan Basin.

Lekson, Stephen H. *Great Pueblo Architecture of Chaco Canyon, New Mexico*.

Albuquerque: University of New Mexico Press, 1986. This monograph is the single best source of information about the architecture of the Chaco Canyon great houses.

Lekson, Stephen H. *The Chaco Meridian: Centers of Political Power in the Ancient Southwest*. Walnut Creek, CA: Alta Mira Press, 1999. Drawing upon a much larger geographic area than most southwestern archaeologists use, Lekson postulates the existence of a meridian that structured massive communities across a large part of the prehistoric Southwest. Lekson proposes movement of the Chacoans from Chaco Canyon to Aztec to Casas Grandes, Mexico, over a period of several hundred years.

Lister, Florence C., and Robert H. Lister. *Earl Morris and Southwestern Archaeology*. Albuquerque: University of New Mexico Press, 1968. The Listers' biography of Earl Morris is an important source of information, not only about Morris and his life, but also about the course of southwestern American archaeology in the first half of the twentieth century.

Lister, Robert H., and Florence C. Lister. *Chaco Canyon: Archaeology and Archaeologists*. Albuquerque: University of New Mexico Press, 1981. This book provides an excellent summary of Chaco Canyon, through almost a century of research from the 1890s until the late 1970s.

Lister, Robert H., and Florence C. Lister. *Aztec Ruins on the Animas*. Albuquerque: University of New Mexico Press, 1987. This book is easy to read and very informative about Aztec Ruins and its history.

Lister, Robert H., and Florence C. Lister. *Aztec Ruins National Monument: Administrative History of an Archaeological Preserve*. Southwest Cultural Resources Center Professional Paper no. 24. Santa Fe: National Park Service, 1990. Despite its official-sounding title, this publication provides an excellent and highly readable history of Aztec Ruins.

Malville, J. McKim, and Gary Matlock. *The Chimney Rock Archaeological Symposium*. USDA Forest Service General Technical Report RM-227. Fort Collins, CO: Forest Service, Rocky Mountain Forest and Range Experiment Station, 1993. This publication reports the findings of researchers who attended the 1990 Chimney Rock Symposium and represents a good summary, although a little dated in 2004, of archaeology and astronomy at the Chimney Rock site.

Malville, J. McKim, and Claudia Putnam. *Prehistoric Astronomy in the Southwest*. Boulder, CO: Johnson Books, 1993. This book discusses evidence for pre-Hispanic astronomy in the Southwest, with most of the emphasis on ancient Pueblo sites. A good discussion of the observatory at Chimney Rock is included in the book.

McNitt, Frank. *Richard Wetherill Anasazi: Pioneer Explorer of Southwestern Ruins.* Albuquerque: University of New Mexico Press, 1957. This work is the definitive biography of Richard Wetherill. Author McNitt also provides a good summary of the detailed history surrounding Wetherill, particularly his time at Chaco Canyon.

Morris, Earl H. *The Aztec Ruin.* New York: Anthropological Papers of the American Museum of Natural History vol. 26, pt. 1, 1919. This monograph represents the main report prepared on Morris's work at Aztec Ruins. It contains primary data that is not duplicated in any other report.

Morris, Earl H. *Archaeological Studies in the La Plata District.* Washington, DC: Carnegie Institution of Washington Publication no. 519, 1939. This monograph represents Earl Morris's most comprehensive and synthetic statement on early Pueblo archaeology. Although the focus was on the La Plata Valley of New Mexico, Morris drew upon his work at Aztec and throughout the northern Southwest to offer a reconstruction of early Pueblo history.

Neitzel, Jill E., ed. *Pueblo Bonito: Center of the Chacoan World.* Washington, DC: Smithsonian Books, 2003. This volume represents one of the most recent new publications on Chaco Canyon. Authors in the volume address architecture, human burials, artifact distributions, labor, and population and advance our understanding of Pueblo Bonito, arguably the most important Chacoan site.

Noble, David Grant. *New Light on Chaco Canyon.* 1984. Rev. ed., Santa Fe: School of American Research Press, 2001. This book provides a popular perspective on Chaco Canyon informed by the contributions of professional archaeologists and scholars.

Peck, Mary (photographer), John R. Stein, Simon J. Ortiz, and Stephen H. Lekson. *Chaco Canyon: A Center and Its World.* Albuquerque: University of New Mexico Press, 1994. This popular "coffee-table" book contains many beautiful photographs of Chaco Canyon. But the essays by archaeologists Stein and Lekson and Acoma Pueblo poet Ortiz go well beyond the surface and offer interesting and unique insights into Chacoan life and society.

Pepper, George. *Pueblo Bonito.* New York: Anthropological Papers of the American Museum of Natural History, vol. 27, 1920. Reprint, Albuquerque:

University of New Mexico Press, 1996. This recently reprinted monograph is the first comprehensive report that was published on excavations
in Chaco Canyon. Pepper's detailed descriptions of the amazing rooms in
Pueblo Bonito and their artifact contents are unparalleled in Chacoan
literature.

Power, Robert B., William B. Gillespie, and Stephen H. Lekson. *The Outlier
Survey: A Regional View of Settlement in the San Juan Basin*. Reports of the
Chaco Center no. 3. Albuquerque: Division of Cultural Research, National Park Service, 1983. This 1983 report represents a great source of
data and interpretation on Chacoan outliers, particularly in the northern
portion of the San Juan Basin.

Roberts, Frank H. H. *Shabik'eshchee Village: A Late Basketmaker Site in the Chaco
Canyon, New Mexico*. Smithsonian Institution Bureau of American Ethnology Bulletin no. 92. Washington, DC: Government Printing Office,
1929. In this monograph, Frank Roberts reports on the excavation of
Shabik'eshchee Village, one of the first known Basketmaker III sites in
Chaco Canyon. The work was significant, particularly because it showed
the time depth of sedentary Pueblo occupation of Chaco.

Schelberg, John. D., and W. James Judge. *Recent Research on Chaco Prehistory*.
Reports of the Chaco Center no. 8. Albuquerque: Division of Cultural
Research, National Park Service, 1984. In this report, the contributions
of many authors, working on the National Park Service's Chaco Project,
are brought to light. It represents another "state-of-the-art" publication
on Chaco, dated to the early 1980s.

Sebastian, Lynne. *The Chaco Anasazi: Sociopolitical Evolution in the Prehistoric
Southwest*. Cambridge: Cambridge University Press, 1992. In this work,
the author offers an alternative hypothesis for the rise of Chacoan society,
based on competition and development of a political hierarchy.

Simpson, James H. *Navaho Expedition: Journal of a Military Reconnaissance from
Santa Fe, New Mexico to the Navajo Country*. 1850. Edited and annotated
by Frank McNitt. Norman: University of Oklahoma Press, 1964. This
work contains Simpson's famous journal with his observations of Chaco
Canyon in 1849. This book is essential for people with a serious interest
in Chaco Canyon and its history.

Stuart, David E. *Anasazi America: 17 Centuries on the Road from Center Place*.
Albuquerque: University of New Mexico Press, 2000. In this work, Stuart
tracks the development of ancient Pueblo (Anasazi) culture and society

over more than a millennium and a half. Despite the title, a good portion of the book is focused on exploring Chaco Canyon, making the book required reading for serious students.

Vivian, R. Gordon, and Tom W. Mathews. *Kin Kletso, a Pueblo III Community in Chaco Canyon, New Mexico*. Globe, AZ: Southwestern Monuments Association Technical Series no. 6, 1965. This monograph reports excavation at a Pueblo III community in Chaco Canyon. In this work, Gordon Vivian discusses his idea of a Co-Tradition, involving two distinct ethnic groups in Chaco Canyon.

Vivian, R. Gwinn. *The Chacoan Prehistory of the San Juan Basin*. San Diego: Academic Press, 1990. This book represents the single best summary and synthesis of Chacoan prehistory available.

Vivian, R. Gwinn, and Bruce Hilpert. *The Chaco Handbook: An Encyclopedic Guide*. Salt Lake City: University of Utah Press, 2002. As the title indicates, this book serves as an encyclopedia for Chaco Canyon. Almost every Chacoan topic imaginable is covered in this excellent guide.

Select Journal/Periodical and Book Articles

Altschul, Jeffrey H. "The Development of the Chacoan Interaction Sphere." *Journal of Anthropological Research* 34 (1978): 109–146. In this article, the author formalized a model of a Chacoan interaction sphere modeled after a similar phenomenon described for the prehistoric southeastern United States.

Grebinger, Paul. "Prehistoric Social Organization in Chaco Canyon, New Mexico: An Alternative Reconstruction." *The Kiva* 39, no. 1 (1973): 3–23. Grebinger's work represents one of the first examinations and interpretations of Chaco as a complex, hierarchical society.

Judd, Neil M. "Archaeological Investigations in Chaco Canyon, New Mexico." Washington, DC: Smithsonian Miscellaneous Collections vol. 78, no. 7, 1927, pp. 83–91. This short paper represents one of the first—if not the first synthesis-syntheses of Chaco Canyon archaeology completed in the early 1900s.

Kantner, John. "Political Competition among the Chaco Anasazi of the American Southwest." *Journal of Anthropological Archaeology* 15, no. 1 (1996): 41–105. In this article, the author proposes a new model based on competition for understanding the rise of Chacoan society.

Lekson, Stephen H., ed. *Archaeology Southwest* 14, no. 1 (2000). In this dedicated issue of the Center for Desert Archaeology's quarterly publication, Chaco Canyon is explored in depth. The various articles summarize new research into Chaco's history, economic organization, ecology, architecture, and society.

Lekson, Stephen H., Thomas C. Windes, John R. Stein, and W. James Judge. "The Chaco Canyon Community." *Scientific American* 256, no. 7 (1988): 100–109. This article, written for a popular scientific journal, introduced the public for the first time to the idea that the ruins in Chaco Canyon society were the result of an integrated, planned society.

Mills, Barbara J. "Recent Research on Chaco: Changing Views on Economy, Ritual, and Society." *Journal of Archaeological Research* 10, no. 1 (2002): 65–117. In this article, Mills provides a comprehensive assessment of Chacoan research—a "state-of-the-art" summary as of 2002.

Reed, Paul F., ed. *Archaeology Southwest* 16, no. 2 (2002). This dedicated issue of *Archaeology Southwest* focused on Salmon Pueblo and the surrounding San Juan area. It provides a good summary of Salmon and new research in the area.

Saitta, Dean J. "Power, Labor, and the Dynamics of Change in Chacoan Political Economy." *American Antiquity* 62, no. 1 (1997): 7–26. This journal article articulates a leading Marxist archaeologist's interpretation of politics and change in Chaco Canyon.

Sofaer, Anna, Michael C. Marshall, and Rolf M. Sinclair. "The Great North Road: The Cosmographic Expression of the Chaco Culture of New Mexico." In *World Archaeoastronomy*, edited by A. Aveni. Cambridge: Cambridge University Press, 1989, pp. 365–376. This article advances the hypothesis that Chaco's great north road is mostly a cosmographic expression and not primarily a transportation route. Many Chacoan archaeologists see support for this view in recent work on Chaco Canyon and the outliers.

Wills, W. H. "Political Leadership and the Construction of the Chacoan Great Houses A.D. 1010–1140." In *Alternative Leadership Strategies in the Prehispanic Southwest*, edited by Barbara J. Mills. Tucson: University of Arizona Press, 2000, pp. 19–44. In this article, the author proposes that Chacoan great houses were not ritual structures, in contrast to the view espoused by most Chacoan archaeologists. Wills suggests that the great houses were largely residential architecture, built for secular, political reasons.

Films/Videotapes

Ancient America—The Southwest. Camera One Production, 1994. This one-hour video, narrated by actor Wes Studi, provides a tour of ancient Pueblo sites in the American Southwest. Chaco Canyon, Mesa Verde, and other Puebloan sites are featured.

The Chaco Legacy. PBS videotape vol. 209, 1980. This film is older but provides an excellent summary of Chaco Canyon and its archaeology and interpretations of Chacoan society in the late 1970s.

Hisatsinom—The Ancient Ones. National Park Service video, 1995. This film is a general summary of the Puebloan peoples across the northern Southwest and from the Basketmaker period through the end of the Chaco System.

The Mystery of Chaco Canyon. The Solstice Project, 1999. This film specifically addresses research completed mostly by Anna Sofaer on astronomy and cosmology in Chaco. The film, narrated by Robert Redford, incorporates the views of several archaeologists and Pueblo people and provides a nice framework for interpreting the sites in Chaco Canyon.

The Sun Dagger. Bullfrog Video, 1983. This film provides a summary of the Pueblo presence in Chaco Canyon, with particular emphasis on the Sun Dagger and ancient astronomy.

Web Sites

Web sites change frequently and servers go down. Although all of the following locations provided good information as of March 2004, some may not be accessible in the future.

salmonruins.com. This is the official Web site for Salmon Ruins, New Mexico. Information is presented on the site's history and archaeology, collections, research, and regarding public outreach.

www.colorado.edu/Conferences/chaco. This Web site is titled "Evaluating Models of Chaco: A Virtual Conference." It provides basic information on Chaco Canyon and then offers an evaluation of several models of the development of Chacoan society by leading archaeologists and scholars in the field. It dates to 1997 and is not the most updated Web site available but provides data not found anywhere else online.

www.jqjacobs.net/southwest/chaco.html. This Web site contains an excellent photographic gallery of the sites in Chaco Canyon.

www.nps.gov/azru/index.htm. This is the official National Park Service Web site for Aztec Ruins National Monument. It contains a myriad of useful data on Aztec, including sections on history, nature and science, maps, and other information.

www.nps.gov/chcu. This is the official National Park Service Web site for Chaco Culture National Historic Park. It has lots of useful information on the sites in Chaco, as well as travel data, maps, and links to other sites.

INDEX

About the Author

PAUL F. REED is Preservation Archaeologist with the Center for Desert Archaeology, Tucson, Arizona, and currently works as the Chaco Scholar at Salmon Ruins, New Mexico.